Charlie is an artist. He has used his paintb... the beauty, mystery and deep invitation in ... message of the Song of Songs.

He helps uncover the sacred and the s...al, the spiritual and physical, with lightness of touch and richness of imagery, drawing one into the most beautiful and tender embrace of God. To read this will be to feed your soul . . .

KAREN BAILEY, New Wine UK

Powerful and provoking.

Charlie Cleverly leads us through one of the most passionate stories of the Bible, pulling significant insights from each verse. Married couples may deepen their love relationship and their bond of union as they meditate on the teachings in this glorious book. This book will stir up your hearts to fall more in love with Jesus, give everything to the only One who is worthy, and to know who you are in him. I pray for many to take the invitation to step up as the mature Bride who gladly runs to the harvest fields with her Beloved, giving her life for the broken and lost of the earth.

HEIDI G. BAKER, Iris Global

This is a brave and large-hearted book, meditating on humankind's 'holy longing' for our passionate God; its subject is the unabashedly erotic love-poetry of the Song of Songs, celebrating the love that is at the heart of the mystery of humanity, but which we too timidly resist. Charlie Cleverly offers some very sharp challenges to the Church today, helping us to touch people where they hurt, and so give them the loving help that they need as they walk in darkness and pain. This book is touching and tender and deeply moving.

NICK KING SJ, Visiting Professor at Boston College BC,
formerly lecturer in New Testament
and Greek at Oxford University

Sometimes you chance upon a book that impacts upon your life in a totally disproportionate way. *Epiphanies of the Ordinary* was that book to me. Charlie Cleverly is one of those writers who weaves poetry and theology, doxology and spirituality into an exquisite tapestry. It was like oil being poured over my soul. Working with the persecuted Church is of the greatest and most transformative privileges of my life. Yet at times it's possible to get lost in the struggle. That book literally lifted my eyes to heaven and continues to do so.

With the same grasp of language and passion for Christ, Charlie has now turned his attention to the Song of Songs. I believe that this human author has had great help from the Author who is above all authors. It will inspire you to worship, to an encounter with the lover of your soul. It's time we evangelicals wakened up to the fact that we are deeply loved by our heavenly Father. Charlie has opened the door to that awareness. I dare you to enter in.

EDDIE LYLE, President of Open Doors UK & Ireland

The Song of Songs: is about romance and about the divine. On one side, the book explores the common pursuit of humanity for the amorous, for that exaltation of body, mind and spirit in finding another person with whom one shares one's self. On another side the book addresses that common human experience of the fragility of the amorous, and points to the divine as the ultimate fulfilment for the most emphatic of all human longings.

Charlie Cleverly's gift is his ability to present this dual message of the Song of Songs, skilfully knitting the rich heritage of its interpretation, from the early Church Fathers to the modern interpreters, and infuse the content of the book with his own experience of church planting, mission, preaching, and all that pastoral care encompasses.

Most of all, the book is an invitation to the believer to 'dare' to respond to the divine romance, and discover in it the fullness of all human longing, the ascent of the soul to be united with God.

KOSTA MILKOV, Senior Associate RZIM Europe
and Balkan Institute for Faith and Culture President

'They have sent me here to feast with my king.' So wrote Samuel Rutherford, seventeenth-century Scottish Covenanter, while imprisoned for his faith. Charlie Cleverly has long feasted with King Jesus, and in his beautiful and profound meditation on the Song of Songs, he leads us to the banquet hall where the banner over us is love.

SIMON PONSONBY, St Aldates, Oxford

My love was awakened afresh in reading this book: for the power of the Scriptures, for the wealth of commentary on the Song of Songs, for the friend and pastor who writes with such integrity and passion, for the human love I enjoy, and most of all for the Love that sings from its pages. This is a book that will refresh your soul.

PHIL POTTER, Archbishops'
Missioner and Team Leader of Fresh Expressions

This exploration of divine love will appeal to earnest Christians. It may also bring enlightenment and meaning to those denizens who occupy our 'existential' age – those men and women who are alienated from God, from themselves, and from the puzzling world in which they are wandering.

Charlie's prose is poetic and peppered with exquisite references from the great mystics of the Church as well as many classical and secular thinkers. *The Song of Songs* is a book which reveals why inquisitive dreamers bathed in mere starlight are mesmerised by the 'divine graffiti' and then, in a place deeper than their will, long to be kissed by the God of Light.

ELLIOTT TEPPER, Betel Madrid

I cannot think of higher praise for a book than to say that every chapter I read made my soul soar and my heart beat faster. More often than not tears formed in my eyes as Charlie's words drew me closer to the heart of God and stirred within me such awe at his unbelievable love and his never ceasing invitation to draw deeper and closer to the one who loves me best. Charlie's writing brought me back to the heart of worship, and to me that is the mark of a great book indeed. His words are so timely for our generation and for our Church in the UK, and in his weaving together of Scripture, historic interpretation, story, application and an abundance of beautiful quotations I found an inestimable treasure trove of riches.

JO VITALE, RZIM itinerant speaker

The Song of Songs

Exploring the Divine Romance

CHARLIE CLEVERLY

HODDER &
STOUGHTON

First published in Great Britain in 2015 by Hodder & Stoughton
An Hachette UK company

1

A CIP catalogue record for this title is available from the British Library

ISBN 978 1 444 70204 0
eBook ISBN 978 1 444 70351 1

Typeset in Adobe Garamond by Hewer Text UK Ltd, Edinburgh
Printed and bound by CPI Group (UK) Ltd, Croydon, CR0 4YY

Hodder & Stoughton policy is to use papers that are natural, renewable and recyclable products and made from wood grown in sustainable forests. The logging and manufacturing processes are expected to conform to the environmental regulations of the country of origin.

Hodder & Stoughton Ltd
Carmelite House
50 Victoria Embankment
London
EC4Y 0DZ

www.hodderfaith.com

CONTENTS

Foreword

Pete Greig

It was embarrassing, to say the least. I was a busy young pastor planting innovative new churches, I had more invitations to speak than I could possibly accept, but I was a hypocrite. I was a fraud. My guilty secret? The prayerlessness of my inner world. The way I traded off other people's experiences, revelations and even their sacrifices to bolster and conceal my own unbelief. The fact that I preferred to outsource my prayer needs to godly old ladies than to intercede for myself.

'Thou hast put salt on our lips', observed Augustine in prayer, 'that we might thirst for Thee.' God loves us too much to leave us staring in the mirror. He will do anything, and I mean anything, to attract us away from life's distractions – even Christian distractions – so that we will at last focus ourselves solely on the source of all joy. This cycle of desperation and desire, leading eventually to refreshment and encounter, is the story of the entire Bible. *'All night long on my bed I looked for the one my heart loves; I looked for him but did not find him'*, says the Bride in the Song of Songs (3:1). The psalmist describes such yearning in even starker terms, depicting a dehydrated deer dying in the desert, its tongue sticking to the cleft of its mouth, its legs unsteady as it pants, half-delirious for water: 'so', he says, 'so my soul pants for you, my God.'[1]

I was waking in the night, pacing the house, trying to pray, sometimes even with tears of frustration, repeating a mantra again and again: 'I want to know you, Lord. I want you, Lord.' God was '*arousing desire*', to quote the Song of Songs. Or as Augustine put it, he was rubbing salt on my lips, to make me spiritually thirsty. But it didn't feel very spiritual at the time. It felt merely frustrating. I was sick and tired of my own compromises. I was also weary of all the stories of God's power breaking out in other people and in other parts of the world and at other times in history. Something in me was awakening with an uncomfortable desperation: 'Do it here, Lord. Do it now,' I prayed, and more vulnerably, 'Please do it with me,' and most vulnerably of all, 'Please don't just do it here with me and through me; please, Lord, do it *in* me.'

It was thirst that first provoked me to prayer. Where else could I find a drink? And so I persuaded my friends that my problem was theirs too, and together we launched a simple night-and-day prayer room. We sought God in that room tucked away in an unglamorous warehouse on an uninspiring industrial estate in a semi-rural backwater on the south coast of England, and as we sought him we found him there. Prayers were answered. We learned to recognise the still small whisper. We began to find our own unique language of intimacy with God. We learned to drink deep.

And then that little prayer room went viral. The last time we counted, it had somehow self-seeded itself into more than half the nations on earth. It turned out that a whole generation was as thirsty as us for a deeper intimacy with God and a greater impact in the world. We were desperate to know Him truly and to be truly known. We desired, I suppose, to be swept off our feet in 'the divine romance'.

* * *

I am so grateful to Charlie Cleverly, whose own 'divine romance' has provoked the creation of this beautiful love-song of a book. I suspect that it may well be his life-message. He and his wife, Anita, have spent many years calling the Church to prioritise the presence of God in prayer and adoration. In fact, when they moved from an inner-city congregation in Paris to lead the famous St Aldates in Oxford, they immediately declared the church a house of prayer for all nations. They are prayerful and passionate people. In person Charlie Cleverly is gentle, thoughtful and kind. In the pulpit he is winsome and passionate. In the city of Oxford he is a catalyst for Christian unity.

This deeply personal book unlocks the secret of one of the most misunderstood and overlooked books in the Bible, drawing on the Church Fathers and other heroes of the faith, from Origen (who wrote a ten-volume commentary on the Song of Songs) to that great apostle to China, Hudson Taylor, for whom it was a source of unspeakable delight. I particularly appreciate the balanced way in which Charlie celebrates both the sacred allegory and the earthy, erotic actuality of the text. As such this book will be an enormous blessing to anyone longing for deeper intimacy with God, to worship leaders looking for fresh inspiration, to pastors who've never yet dared preach on the Song of Songs and even to evangelists seeking to convey the passion of Christ to a culture so salted with desire.

As I write, I am reminded of a particularly touching story recounted in one of Charlie's previous books (the excellent *Epiphanies of the Ordinary*) which perhaps explains not only the passion he expounds in this latest book, but also the underlying paradigm of love which has defined so many years of fruitful ministry. One day Charlie asked his father who was 'not a particularly theological person and not really a churchgoer' about the meaning of life. In response, his father made a beautiful piece of calligraphy as a gift for his son. It was Augustine's summary of the meaning of life: *Ama et Fac Quod Vis*, 'Love and do as you please'. It is in loving God – putting the first commandment first – that we are liberated to do as we please in life, because we begin to want what God wants, our choices therefore become his, we love because he first loved us and our wills are gently harnessed to the will of God. As we understand the love of God and reciprocate, everything else makes sense. The Song of Songs becomes the song of our hearts. We abandon ourselves to the divine romance.

As you prepare to immerse yourself in this ancient love song, may Christ's extravagant desire for you awaken a reciprocal passion, exciting you afresh to abandon yourself completely to that divine romance for which we have all been designed.

Pete Greig
Guildford, November 2014
24-7prayer.com
EmmausRd.com

For Anita
(who else?)

'You are altogether beautiful, my love' (Song of Songs 4:7)

'In speaking of this desire for our own far off country, which we find in ourselves even now, I feel a certain shyness. I am almost committing an indecency. I am trying to rip open the inconsolable secret in each one of you . . . the secret which hurts so much . . . the secret we cannot hide and cannot tell, though we desire to do both . . . the scent of a flower we have not found, the echo of a tune we have not heard, news from a country we have never yet visited.'

C. S. Lewis, 'The weight of glory'[2]

CHAPTER ONE

Alienation, Our Sexuality and the Holy Longing

At the heart of the Book of Books lies the Song of Songs. Sandwiched between Ecclesiastes and Isaiah lies this jewel. Between the sadness of Solomon and the comfort of the coming Christ, this song shines like a mysterious pearl in the sea. If you blink you might miss it, so short are its four pages, its 117 verses. And many do miss it, or miss its meaning. And yet for those who know it, it is 'The greatest of all the songs', 'The best of all songs', or simply: 'The Song of Songs'. Why is it that through the centuries, this little poem has held people enthralled? Why is it that as the twenty-first century comes of age, many are meditating on this love song?

I believe the Song is the greatest song because it treats of the subject of greatest importance in life. This is the one thing needful, the one priority that matters in this transitory life: our love relationship, we might even say love affair, with the God of love. It explores an end to alienation and offers an answer to the existential ache and the yearning for connection in the heart of humankind.

For within humankind there is a longing, an aching, a dreaming – for home: for both a physical connection and spiritual connection. We were born into a world, into a condition, of disconnection. Almost the first thing new-born babies do is cry.

Human beings are mere scraps of life, here only for an

instant. We appear briefly and are gone in a moment. According to Gregory of Nyssa, we live a 'dead life' in a world where death is all around us. This marks our lives, for unlike all the animals, we know we are going to die.[3] But within this dread are the seeds of grace, for there exists in the human soul a longing, a yearning – intimations of immortality.

This book is about that holy longing[4] – a longing for human connection, including sexual connection; and ultimately for connection with God: a longing for the divine romance.

Most people, deep down, know this sense of loss or restless homesickness. In his great exploration of love written for his grandchildren, *The Sunrise of Wonder*, Michael Mayne notes: 'There are times when we ache for that which will fulfil and complete us. This longing may be for the lost state of innocence, the Eden of our childhood, or for a future when all questions are answered and we are home at last. The sense of lost freedom, as George Steiner says "hammers at our human psyche".'[5]

In fact in the account of the loss of Eden, in the book of Genesis, we read of a triple alienation: Man and Woman are separated from God and cut off from the garden from which they were expelled. They are also alienated from one another. That which was merciful provision of companionship becomes fallen and broken. Ever since then the story of human history can reasonably be said to be a constant yearning for connection.

Our attempts to overcome this chaos are expressed in literature everywhere – the Old and New Testaments follow the story of this longing and nostalgia and call a people to this. Then it is seen through the early Church Fathers, medieval, metaphysical and modern writers. Saint Augustine succinctly captures the essential idea with the famous phrase in the opening of his *Confessions*, 'Our hearts are restless until they find their rest in Thee.'

This is arguably what lies behind restless writings of medieval courtly love. It is expressed in some of the Enlightenment writings, such as Voltaire's *Candide*, candidly describing how he feels cut off from the culture he is living in. It is seen in the great German Romantic writer Goethe, who in a poem coined the term 'The Holy Longing' (*Selige Sehnsucht*), saying: 'so long as you haven't experienced this . . . you are only a troubled guest on this dark earth'.[6] Such restlessness continues right down to the Alienation literature of the twentieth-century existentialists. This movement, still so influential today, charts the longing and the frustration of not finding any answer.[7]

Camus's 1942 classic *L'Étranger* – 'the stranger' or 'the outsider' – has the hero cope with aloneness by rejecting God. He 'comes to his senses' and speaks as follows: 'gazing up at the dark sky spangled with its signs and stars, for the first time, the first, I laid my heart open to the benign indifference of the universe'. Nevertheless there is an ache and a tender regret within the decision to reject the comforts of faith. This is expressed in novelist Julian Barnes' remark: 'I don't believe in God . . . but I miss him.'[8]

In a previous century, Dostoyevsky, writer of arguably the first existentialist novel,[9] put the same thing rather differently: the hero of his novel *The Idiot* describes his longing for meaning: 'he remembered now how he had stretched out his arms to that bright, infinite blue and wept. What had tormented him was that he was a total stranger to it all. What was this great everlasting feast, to which he had long been drawn, always, ever since childhood, and which he could never join?' Compared to nature, which seems to know its place, the 'Idiot' reflects that it is only he who 'knows nothing, understands nothing, neither people nor sounds, a stranger to everything and a castaway'.[10]

The existentialists essentially reject God, but they still cannot escape a longing for him – a 'holy longing'. Postmodern authors such as Douglas Coupland speak of this sense of yearning too: 'Time, Baby – so much, so much time left until the end of my life . . . I have to remind myself that time only frightens me when I think of having to spend it alone. Sometimes I scare myself with how many of my thoughts revolve around making me feel better about sleeping alone in a room.'[11] Coupland ends his novel *Life after God* (a telling title in itself) by confessing what he calls his 'secret', which he wants to 'tell with an openness of heart that I doubt I shall ever achieve again'. What is his secret at the end of it all, 'requiring us to be a quiet room' as we hear these words? 'My secret is that I need God – that I am sick and can no longer make it alone. I need God to help me to give as I no longer seem capable of giving; to help me to be kind as I no longer seem capable of kindness; to help me to love, as I seem beyond being able to love.'[12]

Pop musicians echo this – you don't have to look far to find songs with a longing for 'Home' and a desire to be 'Homeward bound'. Made all the more poignant by the fact that he later died from a drug overdose, Michael Jackson expressed this yearning: 'We have to heal our wounded world. The chaos, despair, and senseless destruction we see today are a result of the alienation that people feel from each other and their environment.'

This longing for home is found in artists such as the Russian Jawlensky, who went as far as to say, 'Great art can only be created with religious feeling. Art is longing for God.'[13] He is expressing a kind of nostalgia (from Greek *algos* – 'pain, grief, distress' – + *nostos* – 'homecoming'), which also can equally be described as holy longing.

This longing for an end to alienation is expressed in all kinds of ways, including through our sexuality. This, too, goes all the way back to the beginning. The mythic story[14] of the expulsion from the Garden of Eden has to do with a severing of humanity: man from woman and humankind from God. Our sexuality is about how we reconnect to another person but also with God. And our struggles with it show how profoundly we may feel severed and cut off.

It is posited that the origin of the word 'sex' lies in the Latin *seco*, from *secare* ('to divide or cut'), and thus intrinsically involves the concept of division, indicating for each sex a 'half' of the race. The link can be seen in the word 'section' and 'dissect'. So it seems fair to say that the act of sex and the way we think of our sexuality speak of a longing in the heart of humanity for the opposite of division, namely connection. As a result of our original disconnection there is in humankind a desire, which we can legitimately call a 'Holy Longing', a nostalgia, for the Garden of Eden, and connection with God and with people.

This holy longing in humankind is for connection. It includes a longing for the act of sex, but is not confined to it. Sexual union is certainly one way people re-connect, but there are many others.

Not long ago I spent a weekend with family members in a house next to the sea, where an estuary ran past the front of the house, bringing sea birds, crabs – a whole variety of stunning wildlife – nearly up to our front door with the ebb and flow of the tides. One after the other in our group spoke of how they 'felt connected', of how they felt 'remade' or just 'rested'. Is it that the closeness of nature can do this if you are not used to it? There is a connection to the land and sea that brings re-creation of the soul, and with this comes rest. This happens when we get close to creation, perhaps because behind it we are aware of the Creator. We sense deep down that 'the sea is his, for he made it, and his hands formed the dry land'.[15]

Connection can also be found when we are involved in God's works of justice. The psalmist speaks in passages like Psalm 85 of the idea of 'kissing' to express a deep truth about justice: 'Love and faithfulness meet together; righteousness and peace kiss each other. Faithfulness springs forth from the earth, and righteousness looks down from heaven' (Psalm 85:10–11). Perhaps this connection is so strongly felt because those working for justice, at the moment they are engaging in righteous actions for the poor, are in fact pouring themselves out like the woman who wiped the feet of Christ with her tears – and thus connecting with God. 'The King will reply, "Truly I tell you, whatever you did for one of the least of these brothers and sisters of mine, you did for me"' (Matthew 25:40). As Mother Teresa famously said when accepting her Nobel Prize: 'we may be doing social work in the eyes of the people, but we are really contemplatives in the heart of the world. For we are touching the Body of Christ twenty-four hours . . . Love begins at home, and it is not how much we do, but how much love we put in the action that we do . . . how much we do to Him in the person we are serving.'[16]

Rob Bell's book *Sex God* sets out to explore 'the endless connections between sexuality and spirituality'. He writes of this aspect of connection among the poor: 'A friend of mine has given his life to standing with those that have been oppressed the most. He's in his early thirties, he's single, and he talks openly about his celibacy. What makes his life so powerful is that he's a very sexual person, but he has focused his sexuality, his "energies for connection" on a specific group of people.' Then he adds: 'Some of the most sexual people I know are celibate. They sleep alone. They have chosen to give themselves to lots of people, to serve and connect their lives with beautiful worthy causes.'[17] If the origin of the word 'sex' is to do with disconnection and reconnection, then 'sexual people' may be those who are most deeply connected to God.

This may explain why, in the Bible, love for God is frequently described in sexual or marital language. The latter we may find easy to relate to, but the former can be challenging. This language, in speaking of the sexual act and its powerful imagery, is used because perhaps nothing else will carry the weight of what is being described.

In literature we see this connection clearly in the poems of John Donne,[18] who became Dean of St Paul's Cathedral in 1621 due to his brilliant preaching and humble spirituality, and whose 'Holy Sonnets' compared themes of unfaithfulness to God with unfaithfulness to a spouse. He does not hesitate to invite God's love to conquer him:

> Batter my heart, three-person'd God; for you
> As yet but knock, breathe, shine, and seek to mend
> I, like an usurpt town, to another due,
> Labour to admit you, but Oh, to no end,
> Yet dearly I love you, and would be loved fain,
> But I am betroth'd unto your enemy:

Divorce me, untie, or break that knot again,
Take me to you, imprison me, for I
Except you enthral me, never shall be free,
Nor ever chaste, except you ravish me.

As the poem ends Donne calls on the language of marriage to emphasise his need for God to break in radically – 'Divorce me' from my love of the world and my selfishness; 'enthral me' – 'ravish me'.

It is because of this link between sexuality and the holy longing for connection that I want in this book to explore the divine romance through the Song of Songs – one of the shortest books in the Bible, but one of those with the weightiest meaning. It is worth travelling through Solomon's wisest song with care and wonder. As we do, we will explain and expound nearly every verse. With the Song, we will be using sexual language to describe an intimate connection to God. Because of a conviction that connection matters, we will dare to go on a journey of seeking to be ravished by God, to use John Donne's phrase.

We may ask: how can this be? Is such a voyage an appropriate thing for the life of the mainstream Church? Or should this kind of language be confined to the domain of remote mystics?

The answer, I believe, is that precisely because of the obsession of society with sexual matters, with sexualisation creeping into all areas of life, this kind of language will be truly helpful for the Church to express a holy – as opposed to unholy – longing.

The Bible contains several passages where the love of God is described as being like that of a Bridegroom. Look beneath the surface, indeed, and it is hard to avoid the metaphor; so the aim of this book is to make a virtue out of necessity, and dig more deeply than usual into it.

The prophet Hosea likens Israel's position in relationship to God to that of a bride. Despite extreme relationship difficulties, described in graphic – even sexual – detail in the book of Hosea, the Lord 'will allure her' and 'will lead her into the wilderness' where she will respond in love. '"In that day," declares the Lord, "you will call me 'my husband'; you will no longer call me 'my master' . . . I will betroth you to me forever . . . I will show my love to the one I called 'Not my loved one'."'[19]

The prophet Isaiah reassures the barren and desolate woman that she can 'Sing . . . for your Maker is your husband' (Isaiah 54:5). He writes of God's people: 'No longer will they call you Deserted, or name your land Desolate . . . for the Lord will take delight in you, and your land will be married. As a young man marries a young woman, so will your Builder marry you; as a bridegroom rejoices over his bride, so will your God rejoice over you' (Isaiah 62:4–5).

Seven hundred years later, Jesus himself compares the kingdom of God to friends waiting for a Bridegroom who is delayed in appearing for his wedding.

Later still, the Apostle Paul makes marriage – the male and female union found in the book of Genesis – a metaphor for the union between Christ and his Church: he loves her, he washes her, he gives himself up for her, and mysteriously, he becomes one with her: 'For this reason a man will leave his father and mother and be united to his wife, and the two will become one flesh . . . This is a profound mystery – but I am talking about Christ and the church' (Ephesians 5:31–32).

Then, at the end of time, John sees 'the new Jerusalem, coming down out of heaven from God, prepared as a bride beautifully dressed for her husband'. The consummation of intimacy described by John at the end of time is the same completion in each other seen in the prophetic story of the Song of Songs: 'And I heard a loud voice from the throne saying, "Look! God's dwelling place is now among the people, and he will dwell with them. They will be his people, and God himself will be with them and be their God. He will wipe every tear from their eyes. There will be no more death or mourning or crying or pain . . ."' (Revelation 21:2–4).

The Song of Songs is part of a group of books at the heart of the Bible called 'Wisdom Literature'. They include the Psalms, Job, and the three books of Solomon: Proverbs, Ecclesiastes and the Song of Songs.[20] So we will journey into the landscape of Wisdom, praying that the insights of this book will make us wise.

The earliest Christian interpreters certainly felt they would, devoting much time to expounding and explaining the Song. The Church Fathers, as the earliest Christian commentators are called, can teach us and stretch us today, often writing with tenderness and genius. This book will bring many direct quotations from them into the text in the hope of recovering and hearing afresh their voice for the Church of today. Bernard of Clairvaux (sometimes called the last of the Fathers), in introducing one of his eighty-six sermons, reflects their nostalgia for heavenly affections: 'But there is that other song which, by its unique dignity and sweetness, excels all those I have mentioned and any others there might be; hence by every right do I acclaim it as the Song of Songs. It stands at a point where all the others culminate. Only the touch of the Spirit can inspire a song like this, and only personal experience can unfold its meaning . . . It is a tune you will not hear in the streets, these notes do not sound where crowds assemble; only the singer hears it and the one to whom he sings – the lover and the beloved. It is preeminently a marriage song telling of the mutual exchange of the heart's affections.'[21]

A thousand years later, Karl Barth puts his seal also on the value of the Song:

> The Song of Songs is one long description of the Rapture, the unquenchable yearning and the restless willingness and readiness with which both partners in this covenant hasten towards an encounter.[22]

In his book on pastoral care, *Five Smooth Stones for Pastoral Work*, the inspired Bible translator Eugene Peterson chooses the Song as his point of departure for helping pastors understand that the ache in so many hearts is in fact a desire for intimacy. In the Song, he says, 'sex becomes a parable for prayer, prayer being the inner quest for intimacy with God of which sex is the bodily expression with persons'.[23] Peterson singles out the Song of Songs and Revelation as the most misunderstood books in the Bible.

Spiritual exercises

In order to deepen and apply the exploration of the divine romance, I will end each chapter from Chapter 3 onwards, once we are unpacking the text of the song, with 'Spiritual Exercises'. The term comes from Ignatius of Loyola, who first published his *Spiritual Exercises* in 1548 – tens of thousands of people still benefit from them today. He writes: 'The term spiritual exercises denotes every way of examining one's conscience, of meditating, of contemplating, of praying vocally and mentally . . . as will be explained later. For just as strolling, walking and running are exercises for the body, so "spiritual exercises" is the name given to every way of preparing and making ourselves ready to get rid of all disordered affections so that, once rid of them, one might seek and find the divine will in regard to the disposition of one's life for the salvation of the soul.'[24]

The exercises in this book will draw sometimes on Ignatian ideas and sometimes on other practices such as *Lectio Divina*[25] and other disciplines of intimacy. If you want to skip these or leave them for a better time, then move straight to the next chapter.

But how are we to understand the Song? Is it about sex or is it about God? Is it about Discipleship and Wisdom or about Marriage and Intimacy? In our next chapter we will provide a unifying answer to these questions.

'People have erected a middle wall of partition between two forms of love: the love of God (the New Testament word *agape)* and passionate human yearning (*eros* – a word never found in the New Testament). I want to argue that these divorced partners need reuniting.'
Philip Seddon[26]

'The ancients did not read the Song of Songs devotionally because they were embarrassed by its sexuality but because they understood sexuality in sacramental ways . . . If we read the sexual language of the Song of Songs in different terms from the glossy magazines . . . this may not be evidence that we are afraid of sex, but that we are bold with God.'
Eugene Peterson[27]

'Spiritual literature tends to be naïve in its denial of the power of sexuality, as if it could be dismissed as some insignificant factor in the spiritual journey, and as if it could be dismissed at all! It cannot be. It will always make itself felt, consciously or unconsciously.'
Ronald Rolheiser[28]

CHAPTER TWO

Understanding the Song

The Song of Songs, which is Solomon's.
Songs of Songs 1:1 (ESV)

C. H. Spurgeon, prince of nineteenth-century preachers, who gathered thousands in what was then the largest church in London, in one of his fifty-two sermons on the Song gives this judgement: 'The Song occupies a sacred enclosure into which none may enter unprepared. "Put off thy shoes from off thy feet, for the place whereon you stand is holy ground," is the warning voice from its secret tabernacles.

'The historical books I may compare to the outer courts of the Temple; the Gospels, the Epistles, and the Psalms, bring us into the holy place or the Court of the priests; but the Song of Solomon is the most holy place: the holy of holies, before which the veil still hangs to many an untaught believer . . . The Song is a golden casket, of which love is the key rather than learning.'[29]

At first reading it seems erotic and earthy, but for those who have eyes to see it is also mysterious and heavenly.

Accepting mystery – even mysticism – when it comes to describing encounters with God should not be too hard for us if we can accept that he is 'other'. Rather like a tiny Tardis opening up into a vast spaceship, or a wardrobe leading to a hidden world, so the Song can be seen as a doorway to another world – a 'Narnia' for nostalgia and new birth. In a way all Scripture is like this, multi-levelled, so packed with allegory and metaphor that we never get near the end of it – and yet the Song stands out like a jewel in Scripture's crown. 'Good art compresses the coal of Truth into a diamond', said Auerbach.[30] That is a great description of the compression of weighty spiritual themes and the rich explorations of sexuality to be found compressed in this 'jewel'.

The Song is a mixture of the sensual and the spiritual. There is allegorical interpretation and there is ardent intimacy. In the past, broadly speaking, commentators have divided into two schools: the allegorical school and the literal. In this book, I will endeavour to get these two rival interpretations to leave their isolation, cleave to each other and become one.

We will take the book chapter by chapter so that no stone is left unturned in the belief that, as Paul put it to Timothy, all Scripture is God breathed and useful. As we feed on this manna, or *browse among these lilies* (Songs 2:16), we expect to be nourished with wisdom for the journey onward.

There are riches in the book for those exploring sexuality and the journey of a love affair between a man and a woman – from the abrupt beginning of the demand: *Let him kiss me*, through the hurt of someone who has been badly *burned* in the past. There is a woman coaxed out of hiding away, into finding her voice and not being ashamed of her appearance. There is a realistic balance to the whole: on the one hand, it has an erotic, sensual aroma; the Bride like a flower, unfolding and opening into fullness and fragrance. But there is winter and desert and night as well – pain in relationship followed by healing, growing, trusting, completion and consummation. Then there is partnership, maturity and delighted freedom as the book comes to an end.

But there is another way of reading the Song, a parallel universe: to read it allegorically is to explore a different but related set of challenges, ones that have been instructive and vital to Christians throughout the ages. For those daring to tread this path, a rich and sometimes seemingly chaotic abundance overflows the borders of the book. Here the '*kiss*' of the Bridegroom means transforming intimacy with God. The 'dark beauty' of the Bride can mean the Bride beautiful despite flaws; the aroma of myrrh or mysterious martyrdom can mean courage in the Bride. There is the famous 'banqueting table' that the Bride can feast at. How we come to this table and how we get under the 'banner of love' to experience unbroken communion with God is the theme of a future chapter. Then there is *sitting down*, which will give us an invitation to rest or abide in Christ; and there is the *not awakening* – not forcing love before it is ready. A later theme is the ending of winter and the arrival of springtime in the Church. There is a description of the experience of revival or reformation.

Far from being chaotic, though, we will argue rather that this book teems with the energy of life itself. All these themes are found in the first two chapters out of the eight and there is more to come: how to view and travel through spiritual darkness and depression is explored in Chapters 3 and 5. These chapters became the primary source for St John of the Cross's great writings on the Dark Night of the Soul. The skill of navigating trouble is so needed today in the demanding atmosphere of spiritual climate change worldwide, where sections of the Church experience darkness and intense persecution and others come into springtime and revival:

extreme weather is interestingly part of the landscape of the Song of Songs.

Beside these weighty and intriguing subjects, though, as I have said, there is also kissing and contemplation of breasts and thighs and neck and cheeks. There is the secret garden which is 'locked' but into which in the end the Bridegroom is invited to come into and *feast on all its delights*. In each chapter, we will deal with this 'plain meaning' of the Song: passionate love and consummation of relationship between a man and a woman. We will at several points consider what the book has to say to us about love, sex and intimacy.

We will also consider the particular privileges and challenges of singleness, and the insights the Song offers in this regard also. In this greatest of all songs, there is something for everyone. In different seasons, of course, the Church has elevated singleness and celibacy as the highest calling for spiritual people. More recently in Protestantism, the Church, aware of the longing for connection and seeking to direct it in healthy paths, has often appeared to be obsessed by marriage and focused on getting people into relationship, taking an interest in matchmaking and giving a subliminal message that to be single is to be unsatisfied or second class in some way.

Recently, in our church community in Oxford, we discussed and taught about this longing for 'Connection' in humankind over the course of several weeks. Those on the teaching team who are married found on different occasions that we wanted to apologise publicly to single people, who make up the majority in our community. We realised there was a contrast between our assumed values and what the Bible actually says, namely that if you are single you can be just as connected with God as if you are married – if not more so. The Apostle Paul says: 'An unmarried man is concerned about the Lord's affairs, how he can please the Lord. But a married man is concerned about the affairs of this world, how he can please his wife' (1 Corinthians 7:32–33). In fact the Bible is clear that people who aren't married are not therefore missing out on God's plans for them. A correct understanding of the Song will help us in this area of being single and satisfied in a marriage-obsessed Church, and single and holy in a sex-obsessed culture. It will also help those who are married to live holy lives that are sacrificial and sacramental. Paul's goal in these passages is our goal in this book: 'not to restrict you, but that you may live in a right way in undivided devotion to the Lord' (1 Corinthians 7:35).

The interpretation of the book as an allegory came first from the Jewish fathers. They saw in the Song of Songs a depiction of the relationship of Yahweh to his chosen people, Israel. This is found from the earliest known Jewish interpreters in the Midrash,[31] via the great medieval commentators, through to present-day orthodox scholarship. The Jewish commentator Akiva's love for the Song of Songs is famous:

> The entire history of the world from its beginning to this very day does not outshine that day on which this book was given to Israel. All the Scriptures, indeed, are holy . . . but the Song of Songs is the Holy of Holies.

Akiva had not believed in Christ, but nevertheless it was for him God's choice of Israel to be his Bride more than the goodness of faithful married love that made this book holy.

The earliest Christian interpreters on record took a similar tack. Hippolytus, who lived around AD 200, gives us our first known example of allegorical interpretation. He was soon followed by Origen, who wrote a ten-volume commentary and a series of homilies on the Song, then by Gregory of Nyssa, Ambrose of Milan, Jerome, and a host of other giants of the faith, including some in our own century. All these have seen the Song primarily as a foreshadowing of the love of Christ and his Church.

Picking up on the Song's beginning, *Let him kiss me with the kisses of his mouth – for your love is more delightful than wine* (1:2), Gregory the Great wrote as follows:

> Words are set down that pertain to bodily love so that the soul, wakened out of its listless state by language to which it is accustomed, may heat up by the language of a lesser love aroused by a higher.
>
> 'For in this book kisses are mentioned, breasts are mentioned, cheeks are mentioned and the holy picture these words make is not meant for mockery . . . rather we should notice how marvellously and mercifully he reaches down to the vocabulary of our sensual love in order to set our heart on fire, aiming to incite in us a holy loving . . . He also elevates our understanding for from the words associated with this sensual love we learn how fiercely we are to burn with love for the divine.[32]

It is fair to say that all these writers pass over the literal interpretation of the earthy sexuality of the book in silence. It is as if no comment is desirable or needed on the more obvious meaning of a phrase like *Let him kiss me . . .*, for to comment would be to lower the tone. Denys Turner reaches exactly this conclusion in his masterly *Eros and Allegory*: 'Medieval Song commentaries provide no evidence for a generalized moral disapproval of sex. What on the other hand they do wholeheartedly disapprove of is an interpretation of the Song as being *about* a human sexual relationship. That, they say, is *hermeneutical* adultery.'[33] The only focus is on 'Presence, absence; now and not yet; possession, elusiveness, separation, longing, fulfilment' in the divine romance.[34]

Throughout the period of the Church Fathers and the medieval commentators, the idea of drawing from the Song any theology of relationship or marriage is similarly never taken up, and for the same reasons.

As if by reaction, and in complete contrast, more recent commentators have done the exact opposite: they have abandoned allegorical readings in favour of a literal down-to-earth interpretation that the Song is only to do with marriage and sexuality and has nothing to say about these great themes treated by the Church Fathers. These in their turn are passed over in silence. It is as if it is seen as too dangerous, now, to go even a step in that direction. Some, following Freud, speak of a 'hermeneutic of suspicion'[35] concerning anything approaching a spiritualising of the themes. Some see a danger in over-spiritualising plain meanings. Some commentators even fear that heresy might arise from over-allegorising. Gledhill mentions the heresy of Docetism (Christ only *seemed* to have a body); or Arianism (Christ was only semi-human and semi-divine), or again Monophysitism (Christ had only one nature, which was spiritual). All these can lead to withdrawal from the world in recommending monasticism as the highest call or even, paradoxically, to teaching of total sexual abstinence as the higher spiritual value – the celibate life as being the best option.

What are we to make of this divide?

My conviction is that, as so often, it is not a question of

'either/or'; rather we need 'both/and' if we are to discern the shining, prophetic message God has for our times.

Catholic writer Christopher West has devoted the recent years of his life to interpreting the important ideas contained in Pope John Paul II's *Theology of the Body* (of which more later) and urges: 'Let us again look to the Song of Songs in search of the right balance between the physical and the spiritual. As with all of Scripture, we must hold the human and the divine elements of the Song together in a potent fruitfulness. For the content of the Song is at one and the same time sexual *and* sacred, physical *and* spiritual.' West concludes: 'If we ignore the sacred, the Song appears merely as a secular erotic love poem. But if we ignore the sexual, we see the Song merely as an allegory of "spiritual" love and fall into allegorism. It is only by putting these two aspects together that one can read the book in the right way. That's the essential . . . "both-and".'[36]

In C. S. Lewis's *The Voyage of the Dawn Treader*, Lucy and Eustace have landed on a remote island in Narnia. They ask Ramandu, a dazzlingly wise person, about himself:

> 'I am a star at rest, my daughter,' answered Ramandu.
>
> 'In our world,' said Eustace, 'a star is a huge ball of flaming gas.'
>
> 'Even in your world, my son, that is not what a star is but only what it is made of.'[37]

The Song may be made up – as some say it is – of merely a collection of wedding songs and fragments of poems recounting a rustic romance between a young man and a peasant girl. But there is a difference between what the Song is made of and what it truly is.

Eugene Peterson quotes the conversation above from C. S. Lewis before giving his own judgement on what the book is:

> No book of the Bible has been served so badly by its modern interpreters (unless it is Revelation). They have made their way through it like flat-footed philistines. They have taken it apart and flattened it out in explanations that are about as interesting as a sex education chart in an eighth grade hygiene class. They have assumed that the long centuries of the book's allegorical, typological and devotional expositions have been misguided – pious attempts to cover up explicit sexuality by a veneer of devotion. These assumptions – and they recur throughout scholarly literature – are breezy arrogance. *The ancients may not have known what the book was made of, but they knew what it was*: an exposition of love in a creation in which all love in one way or another is an aspect of salvation.[38]

Following a lengthy discussion of provenance, authorship dates and different readings, in his scholarly 2003 New International Commentary, Tremper Longman concludes similarly: 'In summary then, the Song of Songs has a large, but often neglected contribution to make. In the first place, it affirms love and sex . . . Human sexuality is part of the story of the creation, fall and redemption of human relationships. God created marriage, but that relationship was harmed by sin. Yet the Song holds out the promise of healing . . .

'Second, throughout the Bible, the relationship with God is described by the metaphor of marriage . . . From the Song, we learn about the emotional intensity, intimacy, and the exclusivity of our relationship with the God of the universe.'[39]

I conclude that the book is both sacred and sexual.

Because of this reconciliation of sexual and sacred, I am convinced that the Song is contemporary and prophetic. I believe it is a timely, instructive 'now' book for the Body of Christ worldwide.

In his excellent introduction to this theme, Philip Seddon rightly observes: 'People have erected a middle wall of partition between two forms of love: the love of God (the New Testament word *agape*) and passionate human yearning (*eros* – a word never found in the New Testament).

'I want to argue that these divorced partners need reuniting. Hebrew has only one word for love: "*ahabh*" and conversely the verb for *know* – "*yadha*" – also regularly means "have intercourse with", "make love to".

'In order to marry what has been often put asunder . . . I will suggest that the theme of the Song is "yearning for union".'[40]

Summing up these introductory remarks: some ask 'Is not the Song better seen as an earthy affirmation of sex, intimacy and marriage rather than as allegory?' We can concede that some may have abused the book by an excessive spiritualising. And yet the answer to abuse is not dis-use but right use. If some have over-allegorised, let us not throw out all allegorising, but rather respect the plain meaning as well as any allegorical meaning. Allegorical interpretations should not be plucked from thin air, but should illustrate truths that are solidly revealed in Scripture. We should refuse to make our primary interpretation of Scripture allegorical, which was perhaps an error of the Church Fathers at times. Thus, if the book is about marriage and intimacy, let us explore all it teaches on married love. But let us also follow Paul for whom marriage itself is a picture, a snapshot of the real thing. To paraphrase Paul, the Song may be a mystery, like marriage, but it is speaking of Christ and his Church.

C. S. Lewis writes of this in *The Four Loves* when he says: 'We were made for God. Only by being a manifestation of His beauty, lovingkindness, wisdom or goodness, has any earthly Beloved excited our love. It is not that we have loved them too much, but that we did not quite understand what we were loving . . . (we shall turn) from the portrait to the Original.'[41]

Much of the Bible, as well as being literally true, can be taken allegorically or typologically. For example, the great story of the escape from slavery in Egypt is a type of the escape to salvation of the believer. The story of Joseph sold into prison is a type of Christ sold and betrayed but finally the gatherer of his brothers. I don't take it for granted that the Song of Songs is open to an allegorical interpretation, so here are some of the arguments for reading it thus.

Following Paul, the Church Fathers felt that what Origen calls the 'plain reading' of some Bible books limited the whole revelation contained in them and missed out themes of great importance in the Bible – for example, the theme of Christ hidden in the pages of the Old Testament. One could say the idea of allegory with regard to the Bible is first introduced by Paul himself in Galatians 4:22–24: 'For it is written that Abraham had two sons, one by a slave woman and one by a free woman. But the son of the slave was born according to the flesh, while the son of the free woman was born through promise. Now this may be interpreted allegorically' (ESV). The KJV also has 'which things are an allegory'. In this light Origen says Paul has provided a 'rule of interpretation for the Old Testament': 'Take note how much Paul's teaching differs from the plain meaning; what the Jews thought was a crossing of the sea, for Paul is baptism. What they supposed was a cloud, he said was the Holy Spirit. What

Exodus calls a rock, for Paul is Christ.'[42] Such reconfigurings are not uncommon in the way the Bible interprets itself.

For James Durham (Geneva Series, 1840) it was the appearance of titles like *'The King'*; *'O thou whom my soul loves'*; the *'chief among ten thousand'*; *'the Rose of Sharon'*; *'a seal upon my heart'* that led him to read the Song as a description of the divine romance.

Furthermore, the king's garden (5:1) can be viewed in the light of the Garden of Eden, bringing to mind the Messiah who was expected to restore Israel to an Edenic state. In our day, some of those involved in a call for careful stewardship of the planet appropriate the Song of Songs and its glorious gardens as treating the theme of creation – and they may not be wrong. Finally, at the end of the Song, the lovers are portrayed as having overcome the alienation produced by the Fall and as being at last reconciled.

We should be wary of over-allegorising, as it may diminish the attention and weight given to the glory of sexual love, so clear and earthy and strong in the book: the Bible is truly remarkable in its passionate engagement with this – in authorising it, making it sacred. But in my view, the book is meant to be taken on both levels.

Hopefully, this introductory survey has whetted our appetite for *le vif du sujet*: 'the life of the matter', or more colloquially, 'the heart of the matter'. We are about to enter upon a prophetic journey into wisdom through the Song of Songs, and we will not shy away from treating it as an allegory of the Love of Christ for his Bride and her love for him, even as we will explore also its immediate and literal meanings.

It is my contention that both levels of understanding are of great importance. The elevation of romantic passionate monogamy between man and woman is vital in a day where sex is worshipped as a god but, in fact, only a counterfeit, addictive sexuality is on offer. But also, for the Church to deepen in passionate love for Christ is a theme for now. It is vital to the Church today for three reasons.

First, we live in an age of martyrs. We live in a time of crisis for the Church. Increasingly, business-as-usual Christianity will not be enough for her to survive. In a world groaning with the constant threat of terror, a world where in the West a more or less marginalised Church struggles in a society governed by political correctness, the Church further afield is often demonstrating vividly to us the need to recover a passionate love for Christ. This passion was seen in the days of martyrs like Latimer and Ridley. Ridley greeted his last day on earth before being burnt at the stake in Oxford joyfully as the day of his 'marriage supper'. We may need to recover the affections of Latimer who spoke in his letters of the fairness of the 'dear darling Son of God in whom was all his Father's delectation'. In a day when Christians may again be perse-cuted, beheaded or crucified, one could argue that only this passionate intimacy will get through the waters of persecu-tion about to break on the Church.

We live in a world full of fears: extreme weather, economic upheaval and the threat of terror. As Christ said: 'Nations will be in anguish because of the roaring and tossing of the sea. People will faint from terror, apprehen-sive of what is coming on the world' (Luke 21:25–26). Mike Bickle in his plea for a reawakening of what he calls 'the pleasures of loving God' writes: 'Something is on the horizon for Planet Earth for which the Church is completely unprepared. An unprepared Church cannot possibly prepare an unprepared world. God's mercy to the world is a prepared Church, a prepared Bride. She will be prepared because she will be prepared by a holy romance with her Bridegroom God.'[43]

I believe that as she discovers the divine romance, the Church will be able to view everything differently. When the Bride is lost in the pleasure of spiritual lovesickness she will be able to interpret the events of the last days through a lens of love. Currently the Church in the West is focused on the things of this world and not on the Bridegroom. Because of this we are often not grounded in love and so are frequently completely unprepared to be of much use in society as agents of grace. But I believe it is as if God is beckoning the human race. He is calling us to live the divine romance. Many have said 'yes' to this, but few have truly meditated on it and been fed and sustained deeply by the word of God so as to live in the light of this daily. Hopefully this exploration will be nourishing in the pursuit of this end.

Second, we live in an age of Mission. I have in my hand, as I write, a little jewel of a book written by J. Hudson Taylor, which is one of the best commentaries on the Song, entitled *Union and Communion*. It seems at first glance mystical, passionate and impractical, talking as it does of the unsatisfied life and its remedy; the joy of unbroken communion. And yet Hudson Taylor was responsible for one of the most powerful missionary movements of the nineteenth and twentieth centuries, which turned China around for Christ. He wrote: '

All scripture is given by the inspiration of God and is profitable. Few portions of the word will help the devout student more in the pursuit of this all-important knowledge of God than the too-much neglected Song of Solomon. But what

28

shall be the dignity and blessedness of the risen and exalted Bride? Can a study of the book which helps us to understand these mysteries of grace and love be anything other than most profitable?[44]

The book was first published in serial form in Hudson Taylor's magazine entitled *China's Millions*. His disciple, Watchman Nee, also a key agent for change in China, who was jailed and died young for Christ, likewise wrote a commentary on the Song of Songs. Thinking of these men and their example, I ask: who will give up their small comforts and go and serve those living under Islamic skies? Who will live a life of poured-out love for those in European, secular, liberal, hard and post-Christian countries under such darkness? Who will bring some fire to change the climate of the spiritual ice age that Europe is living through? It will be those passionately in love with Christ as Hudson Taylor was before them.

The third and last reason for, in the words of Eugene Peterson, 'eating this book'[45] is for pastoral accompaniment of people searching for intimacy. The rich themes covered here can be healing balm to many and provide a response to different kinds of questions asked by people searching today. For example, for those travelling through trouble, there are signs of hope here: warmth in the winter and light in the darkness. For those craving intimacy (arguably at the root of so much addictive behaviour today) there are signposts to connection with the One who is the lover of our souls. Of course there is the description of a human love relationship that is instructive and inspiring to human relationships too. This is why Eugene Peterson singles out the Song as supremely useful for the work of 'prayer directing'. Its ancient wisdom can be future healing for people and can minister to our quest for intimacy and connection.

I believe it is the song above all songs. Marvin Pope translates it 'the sublime song'.[46] *The Most Holy Place* is the name chosen by Spurgeon for his 500-page commentary. I conclude that there are many reasons to believe with Bernard of Clairvaux that: 'This work was composed, not by any human skill but by the artistry of the Spirit, difficult to understand indeed but yet enticing one to investigate.'[47]

We now move on to the enticing prospect of investigating the first great themes of the Song, the human kiss and the 'kisses of God'.

'At that first kiss I felt
Something melt inside me
That hurt in an exquisite way
All my longings, all my dreams, and sweet anguish,
All the secrets that slept within me came awake,
Everything was transformed and enchanted
And made sense.'
Herman Hesse[48]

'Then I did the simplest thing in the world. I leaned
down . . . and kissed him. And the world cracked open.'
Agnes de Mille[49]

CHAPTER THREE

The Kisses of God

She

> *Let him kiss me with the kisses of his mouth – for your love
> is more delightful than wine.*
> *Pleasing is the fragrance of your perfumes; your name is like
> perfume poured out. No wonder the young women love you!*
> *Take me away with you – let us hurry! Let the king bring
> me into his chambers.*

Friends

> *We rejoice and delight in you; we will praise your love more
> than wine.*

She

> *How right they are to adore you!*
> *Dark am I, yet lovely, daughters of Jerusalem, dark like the
> tents of Kedar, like the tent curtains of Solomon.*
> *Do not stare at me because I am dark, because I am dark-
> ened by the sun. My mother's sons were angry with me
> and made me take care of the vineyards; my own vine-
> yard I had to neglect.*

Song of Songs 1:2–6

The much-celebrated start of the Song rushes headstrong
into the plea: *Let him kiss me with the kisses of his mouth!* This
is immediately demanding, intimate, intense. 'How shall I
explain so abrupt a beginning, this sudden irruption as from

a speech in mid-course? For the words spring upon us as if indicating one speaker to whom another is replying as she demands a kiss—whoever she may be' (Bernard of Clairvaux). The Bride has got to the point of pleading for this intimate next stage of relationship. And so it is that the person who has become a follower of Christ, who has started to read his word, who is enjoying friendship and community, when in prayer or when reflecting on the story of the New Testament will often find themselves looking and longing for – *more!*

On a human level, the kiss requires vulnerability and trust, it is 'not to be undertaken lightly'. It is a point of no return. Kissing opens the beloved to the lover: it is a sign of saying, 'Come in through the gate – see who I really am.' It is a bold, risky thing but can be a relational breakthrough, bringing life and joy.

This is expressed evocatively by Agnes de Mille as she describes the world-changing nature of a kiss: 'Then I did the simplest thing in the world. I leaned down . . . and kissed him. And the world cracked open.' Tennyson puts this thought poetically: 'Once he drew with one long kiss my whole soul thro' my lips, as sunlight drinketh dew.'[50] Rodin's massive sculpture *The Kiss* explores and celebrates an understanding of the iconic power of the kiss.

For me one of the best descriptions of the effects of the kiss is from Herman Hesse:

> At that first kiss I felt
> Something melt inside me
> That hurt in an exquisite way
> All my longings, all my dreams, and sweet anguish,
> All the secrets that slept within me came awake,
> Everything was transformed and enchanted
> And made sense.[51]

In a way, this thing we call a kiss is a symbol for an epiphany in which the meaning of life is discovered.

'The Glory of God is the human person fully alive,' said Irenaeus. There is a sense in which one is never more alive than when in a relationship of love. Dianne Bergant, referring to this famous saying, compares the characteristics of the spiritual life with the physical act of kissing: 'Attitudes called forth from us by . . . a relationship . . . include courage, vulnerability, defencelessness, mutual respect, unselfishness, fidelity, to name a few.'[52] The kiss breaks open these virtues, which will unfold throughout the book. The imagery is extravagant: the woman tastes his kisses, she smells his fragrance, she feels deeply drawn to him and wants at first to run and then be brought into his chambers. Biography writer Emil Ludwig describes exactly this progression: 'The decision to kiss for the first time is the most crucial in any love story. It changes the relationship of two people much more strongly than even the final surrender; because this kiss already has within it that surrender.'[53]

In a spiritual interpretation, one could say that all eight chapters of the Song unfold the implications related to the divine kiss. Her lover's kisses are the theme of the Bride's life; it is also the theme of everyone who seeks God, to know him deeply and to be known.

In our desire for restraint we may not use the language *Let him kiss me* . . . but the Pauline longing to be 'filled with all the fullness of God' (Ephesians 3:19) is the same. The kiss of God is a metaphor: a picture painting a thousand words. We should not think of kissing Jesus in a sexual way; this is entirely outside the boundaries of God's will. Rather, think of Christ as the kiss of God to the world. Or think of God's hand on our heart expanding our capacity to give ourselves to him and receive his love.

'On occasion a man will come up to me and say: "I can't picture Jesus kissing me on the mouth,"' says veteran Song of Songs commentator, Mike Bickle. 'I say, "Good, you're not supposed to!" It is only a metaphor speaking of the deepest things God gives the human spirit.' He concludes: 'The divine kiss is God's invitation to casual Christianity to go deeper.'[54]

What then does it truly mean to be kissed by God? The truth is that this tiny phrase has multiple nourishing interpretations.

Some Church Fathers said that being kissed by God means welcoming the incarnation as the kissing of humanity and coming into flesh of God. For Origen it meant this but also the teachings of Christ – 'For the kisses of Christ are those that he bestowed on the Church when in his advent he himself present in the flesh spoke to it words of faith and love and peace.'[55]

During the Welsh revival the hymn 'Here is love vast as the ocean' became known as the 'love song of the revival':

On the mount of crucifixion fountains opened deep and wide
Through the floodgates of God's mercy flowed the vast and
gracious tide,
Grace and love like mighty rivers poured incessant from above
Heaven's peace and perfect justice kissed a guilty world in love.[56]

Kisses, then, may mean also the death of Christ with all that it meant for our salvation.

For others, this 'kiss' has meant the touch of the Holy Spirit. Lovers have many ways to tell each other of their love: the word, the touch, a letter or a kiss. In the same way, the Father gave the gift of his Son. Christ is the Word of God, the

Bible His love letter, but the Spirit is God's kiss. In this sense of being filled with the Holy Spirit we can be 'kissed by God' and receive *more*.

Certainly this is how the Fathers read it. Then, in the medieval period, Bernard of Clairvaux writes of 'the sacrament of endless union with God'. He contrasts the poor state of the Church of his generation with this potent kiss of God:

> 'I can scarcely restrain my tears, so filled with shame am I by the lukewarmness, the frigid unconcern of these miserable times.' He interprets the kiss as follows: 'The mouth that kisses signifies the Word who assumes human nature; the nature assumed receives the kiss; the kiss is none other than the one mediator between God and mankind, himself a man, Jesus Christ . . . A fertile kiss then, a marvel of self-abasement that is not a mere pressing of mouth upon mouth; it is the uniting of God with man.'[57]

Five hundred years later, Scottish preacher James Durham explores this generous response to our unworthiness, suggesting: 'By kisses we understand most lovely friendly sensible manifestations of his love. Let Him who is the most excellent and singular person in the world kiss ME a contemptible creature redeemed!'[58] Another five hundred years and another commentator, James Pennington, continues: 'What is the kiss of your mouth? It is where the human and divine become completely one. How much we struggle with the belief that you divine lover really love this poor little human so plagued with sin and infidelity: O give me the kisses of your mouth!'[59] Jumping back to medieval times, Bernard in another sermon extends his interpretation: 'True it may be I am fulfilling the commandments in one way or another, but "my soul is like earth without water" (Psalm 142:6). Therefore if my whole burnt offering is to become worthy, Let him I pray and beseech "kiss me with the kisses of his mouth"[60] – thus he felt this image related to refreshment for the one who is fulfilling the commandments, trying to obey the devout life, but utterly dry.

This is challenging for many Christians, bordering as it does on mysticism. I have sometimes wondered whether a reluctance to embrace theologically the manifest experience of sealing or filling by the Holy Spirit, or – to put it more poetically – the Divine Kiss of the Holy Spirit, is responsible for the reluctance of some to dare to read the Song of Songs allegorically. It is just too challenging in terms of emotional vulnerability.

C. H. Spurgeon came across similar reticence in his day. In his sermon on Songs 1:7, 'Love to Jesus':

> 'Let Him kiss me with the kisses of His lips, for His love is better than wine.' 'No,' you say, 'that is too familiar for me.' Then I fear you do not love Him, for love is always familiar. Faith may stand at a distance, for her look is saving. But love comes near, for she must kiss, she must embrace. Why, Beloved, sometimes the Christian so loves his Lord that his language becomes unmeaning to the ears of others who have never been in his state. Love has a celestial tongue of her own and I have sometimes heard her speak so that men have said, 'That man rants and raves – he knows not what he says." Hence it is that love often becomes a Mystic and speaks in mystic language, into which the stranger intrudes not.[61]

We are at the border here between the doctrines of evangelical assurance and union with Christ and the more heart-driven experience of charismatic mysticism – and risk becoming 'charismystics', to coin a phrase. But we shall find this to be in fact a rich vein of tradition, from the Fathers through the medieval commentators to the Puritans; from the language of affection in the eighteenth-century Love Feasts of Whitefield's and Wesley's day, on to Moody, Finney and Spurgeon, preachers of the nineteenth century and into modern-day Pentecostalism as well as Catholic contemplatives who are hungry for, and indeed have experienced, the *more* of God. Presbyterian pastor Tim Keller uses the helpful phrase 'intelligent mysticism' to describe the same thing in his book on prayer which is subtitled: 'Experiencing Awe and Intimacy with God'. He quotes John Owen: 'It is necessary for us to recognize that there is an *intelligent mysticism* in the life of faith . . . of living union and communion with the exalted and ever present Redeemer.'[62]

Henri Nouwen is another who saw the need for this:

> To live a life that is not dominated by the desire to be relevant but is instead safely anchored in the knowledge of God's first love, we have to be mystics. A mystic is a person whose identity is deeply rooted in God's first love. If there is any focus that the Christian leader of the future will need it is the discipline of dwelling in the presence of the One who keeps asking: 'Do you love me?'[63]

By the time of the Westminster Assembly in the mid-seventeenth century, 'desire' had become the heart-blood of Puritan spirituality. John Cotton of First Church in Boston proclaimed that the best assurance of truly having acquired Christ is a continued longing for more of his love. 'It will inflame our hearts to kisse him again, if kisses be from God', Cotton said in his exposition of the Song of Songs.[64] Thomas

Hooker, the Puritan founder of Connecticut and for some the father of American Democracy,[65] used the intimacy of marriage to describe the saint's love for God: 'The man whose heart is endeared to the woman he loves, he dreams of her in the night . . . the heart of the lover keeps company with the beloved.'[66]

At the end of this we may well ask: but how? We do not ask this of the physical act of kissing – it comes naturally. Few are the seminars on the art of kissing, thankfully. And so may it be with the kiss of God: it will come spiritually – in worship, in meditating, in prayer, as we revel in the glory of creation, we become aware of being folded into God's presence. We can just love him and 'taste and see that the Lord is good'. We can remember that the Greek word for worship, *proskuneo*, literally means 'to come towards to kiss'. We can, to use the words of Psalm 2, 'bow down and kiss the Son'. This may mean standing before him and asking for his intimate kiss: often I will in fact do just this when standing in worship in our church community. I will ask God that we receive a manifest experience of this even in the whole assembly. And it happens. Here is the testimony of a student, not yet a Christian when she first came in to church:

I became a Christian on the evening of 2 October in Berlin, after an amazingly intricate process, through indifference, hostility, curiosity and longing which brought me to the knowledge that there is a real, unique God, who knows who I am, and just wants me to know Him. It all started when my boyfriend became interested in the claims of Christianity and began exploring it . . . In second year, I ended up going with him to church the day after I had confronted him about this. I had only gone to prove a point, and to refuse being excluded, yet from the moment I walked in I was astounded that it was absolutely nothing like I had expected church to be. There was so much light, so many people, so many students, and they seemed to be so happy to be there. I felt something so tangible in the worship, something I had never encountered and could not explain, but that was so powerful, speaking right into me, and drawing tears I didn't understand.

This young girl experienced right at the start of her journey the 'Welcome Home' kiss of the father to the prodigal.

Here is another young woman's experience of the tender embrace of God:

I first came across the church when looking for an Alpha course. I will always remember that day as the turning point of my life, when a ray of light shone into the darkness. The truth is that my life was very twisted and deluded back then. I was living in the aftermath of being a wild party-er and co-habiting with my boyfriend. I worked in a restaurant and lived from pay-cheque to pay-cheque, not planning for the future at all. I will always remember walking through the entrance of St Aldates feeling intimidated by the grand church building, but being wrapped up in a feeling of peace. It's this feeling of peace that kept me coming back – I was addicted to this effortless 'high' that I got from being in Church.

This woman exchanges wild partying for the Kiss of God and discovers that indeed *your love is better than wine*. She speaks of being 'wrapped up in a feeling of peace' which is reminiscent of the wrapping up we experience as the embrace of the divine lover of our souls.

It is good to make a point of making room for these 'kisses of God', this union and communion, whether alone with God in the 'daily-ness' of our encounters with him or in our corporate gatherings.

The theme of the 'kisses of God' could be said to answer three deep cries of humankind. First, an existential cry to see God's Presence made manifest, something we are seeing throughout the worldwide Church at the start of the twenty-first century. Second, it is the great philosophical cry. It answers the question of the purpose of life: if we get this, if – no matter what else happens – we come home to being lovers of God, we 'succeed'. This is our inheritance and destiny and, yes, our joy, even in a collapsing culture. Ignatian spirituality, which I have observed becoming more and more popular, speaks of the fact that, as a person is given over to love, praise and serving God, they will experience 'Indifference' to other things by comparison. This brings freedom from being reliant on them for ultimate happiness.[67] Third, this metaphor and the reality behind it answers the great psychological cry of the human heart: it shows how the human heart is healed of alienation and finds happiness.

The aroma of Christ

The kiss leads to becoming aware of the other's fragrance. *Your name is like perfume poured out.* The fragrance of this perfume suggests the aroma of Christ, and looks forward to Paul's insight in writing to the Corinthians: 'But thanks be to God, who . . . through us spreads everywhere the fragrance of the knowledge of him. For we are to God the aroma of Christ.'[68] We will return to this in the next chapter.

To smell the fragrance we may need to get physically closer, and now we read that: *Let the king bring me into his chambers.*

Not into a meeting room, not into a public place but into the inner chambers – into his heart: to be alone with her lover to explore their affection is all that the Bride longs for and wants to be drawn in to. *We rejoice and delight in you; we will praise your love more than wine. How right they are to adore you!* (v. 4). Although they are meeting in a private room, others are aware: their love is no secret, and here for the first time the 'others' present in the book, the friends of the Bridegroom, rejoice over this passionate expression of love. When someone starts going out with someone, leading in due course to engagement and marriage, the beginning itself is often a great source of joy among friends who have prayed and perhaps longed for this! Passionate love for the Bridegroom is something to rejoice over, because it is set to last long and be strong, even as strong as death.

The dark beauty of the Bride

We will close this chapter with a meditation on the evocative phrases of verses 5–6 (ESV):

> *I am very dark, but lovely, O daughters of Jerusalem, like the tents of Kedar, like the curtains of Solomon. Do not gaze at me because I am dark, because the sun has looked upon me. My mother's sons were angry with me; they made me keeper of the vineyards, but my own vineyard I have not kept.*

Origen interprets this thus: 'I am that Ethiopian woman. I am the one who, because of her low status at birth, is *dark*. But is *beautiful* because of her faith and penitence. For I have appropriated the Son of God within myself, I have received the word made flesh. I have come to Him who is the image of God . . . and I have become beautiful.'

43

Bernard, meanwhile, speaks of the black curtains of the night sky – 'He (the One greater than Solomon) spreads out the heavens like a curtain (Ps 103). Nevertheless the heavens cannot be compared with the glorious beauty of the Bride. Her beauty is justice . . . patience . . . voluntary poverty, holy fear of the Lord . . . prudence, for temperance, for courage . . .'[69]

We have here, introduced for the first time, the idea that Christ finds his Bride beautiful. Some say that it is the lover who is interjecting the phrase *but lovely* in response to the Bride's picture of herself that she is *dark, very dark, darkened by the sun – do not gaze on me* . . . He responds: *No, but you are lovely.* But his admiration of her loveliness is rejected by the Bride as she says: *Don't look at me!* Perhaps there is a feeling of unworthiness here, which she will set aside as time goes by and which shows the Bride is on a journey. Her skin is darkened by her hard work out in the elements, and she struggles with this – yet knows she is beautiful regardless.

In fact, so it is with many on the journey of love: it is being loved that beautifies us – anyone and everyone – if we will but allow that love through our defences.

The Bride gives another reason for feelings of inadequacy: the treatment she has received at the hands of her mother's sons; having to keep the family vineyards and feeling that she has neglected her own vineyard. The theme of the vineyard is rich in meaning and here the woman speaks of literal vineyards and then of her own, more personal vineyard, speaking of her own inner life and outer beauty. Many feel this sense of disappointment over relationships with siblings or within a community: either we have disappointed them, or they have disappointed us, or indeed both. In the family or the Church (remembering that 'the vineyard of the Lord of hosts is the house of Israel'[70]), we may be distracted and burdened by many duties and cares and just plain hard work so that we lose our confidence or sense of purpose.

This has a message for marriage. Although the main thread here concerns the beginnings of love, there is a challenging message for the long term: a bride (or husband) may neglect themselves, and get fat or thin or become unkempt and badly dressed, feel unlovely or seem unavailable. It happens as the stress of life or perceived rejection in a relationship forms habits of neglect, which bring risk to intimacy. A loving 'conversation that matters' between partners can heal and restore a relationship. That is the level of intimacy we see in the Song. Time out together to talk and reaffirm a relationship can change everything, even for the most threatened couple. The decision and the time then given to 'tend your vineyard' and take care of yourself can change everything.

I remember a couple coming up to me after a marriage seminar and miserably confiding that they had not made love for seven years. The wife had taken to talking in the bedroom at length with their teenage daughter each night. The husband approved of the communication – which had been a lifesaver for the daughter – but felt rejected each night in the marriage and would fall asleep on the couch in the living room, coming up to bed at 2 a.m., by which time his wife quite reasonably said: 'I'm just too tired.' I asked if she wanted this to change and she replied with an unhesitating: 'Yes!'

Sometimes healing is simple, all too simple. It requires conversation and confession and the hope that springs up from that.

In this case, the husband shot an incredulous, hopeful look at his wife which meant: 'Really?' I asked if they had ever talked with anyone about this. They replied no, not even each other. As they spoke I felt the relief that speaking the truth at last brought to them. It was as if some secret, hidden in a black corner, was being coaxed out into the light and looked at. As they looked at it, it lost its power. I told them that this was what was happening. By the end of the week, they told me that as a result of this conversation they had made a change in lifestyle, and intimacy had been restored.

Far more often, it will take much more than one conversation. To repair intimacy will take careful, active listening without interrupting, and forgiveness and openness and honesty about our brokenness. But communication, forgiveness and the intention to make a new start can change everything.

In the 'song of the soul', the vineyard the Bride speaks of can refer to her own heart; taking it in the spiritual sense, her own walk with God. In the same way, a Christian may all too easily neglect their own intimacy, their love affair, the quiet times of contemplation with Jesus – the 'better part' of which he spoke to Martha, sitting at his feet. So in the end all becomes slavery instead of sonship, and joy and refreshment and adventure depart, to be replaced by religion – a neglected vineyard where there is no fertilising affection. The 'Kiss of God', the drenching with the Holy Spirit, does not happen, because of sin.

This is the rebuke of Christ to the Church in Ephesus: despite her 'hard work and your perseverance . . . you have forsaken the love you had at first'.[71]

Neglecting our own vineyard

How can we take care of our own vineyard? I remember once asking a wizened old viticulturist in a vineyard in the South of France what the secret of a good vineyard was. His reply after reflection was: '*Il faut l'aimer*' ('You have to love it') – love the soil, the vines, the grapes; prune and prevent disease; and train the vines, replacing them when they get old, watering and protecting them against bugs and disease. ('It is much easier to prevent disease than to cure it when it comes in a vineyard,' he said.)

Jesus says to us: 'Love your neighbour as you love yourself.' One might say that the secret of beauty is to love yourself by taking care of yourself as much as you take care of others. Health, diet, reading, friendships, internet use – all need to be healthy. Similarly, daily love times with Christ, daily listening through his word, meditation, contemplating, exercising spiritually in the same way as we might exercise physically to take care of the body are what it means to take care of our own vineyard. At the risk of mixing metaphors, perhaps before experiencing the 'Kiss of God' there is a need to clear out the overgrown weeds in the vineyard.

So we may need to dig up the weeds of bad habits, discipline ourselves and prepare our personal soil, coming back to a 'discipline of intimacy'. Jesus disciplined himself and got up early each morning to pray, even though 'everyone was looking for him'. Paul 'beat his body and made it his slave' to reach spiritual fitness. And so can we.

Revival, whether personal or for a whole community, has, it seems, always been preceded by pruning and preparing the vineyard. Often it has been a prayer awakening that precedes a general awakening. But are we ready and available for this?

Spiritual exercises for taking care of your vineyard
Give some time to taking stock of the state of your inner landscape: is it a beautiful garden, or overgrown with thorns, neglected, uncared for or unfruitful? Buy a journal (you could even buy a 'garden record') and use it to record your progress. Ask these questions, today and daily:

Where did I miss God yesterday?

Where did I meet God yesterday?

Meditate imaginatively on the sights, smells, sounds of Song of Songs 1:6 and a parallel passage, Isaiah 5:1–7: 'I will sing for the one I love, a song about his vineyard: My loved one had a vineyard on a fertile hillside . . .' What is your vineyard like? Note down what you see in assessment of your life. In what way, if any, is it 'dark – darkened by the sun'? Has life taken its toll? Listen to what God says to you and write it down in your journal.

'Every branch that does bear fruit, he prunes, that it may bear more fruit' (John 15:2).

Do you dare ask God to prune you, so that you bear more fruit? This is a big question, but an important one to answer at the start of the journey through the Song of Songs. If your response is 'yes', then ask him to do so. Listen to God and then write down any area for pruning in your life. Ask his help to work through this with him.

Yet lovely.

Try to hear this as the voice of the divine lover and sense his affection for his Bride, namely you. End your time with grateful thanks and spoken or sung worship: *Let him kiss me with the kisses of his lips.*

'All I have is a voice . . .'
W. H. Auden[72]

'Sometimes strident, often tender, never afraid and seldom without humour, [his] voice will always be the voice of the voiceless.'
Nelson Mandela, speaking of Desmond Tutu[73]

CHAPTER FOUR

Passion, Perfume and Finding Your Voice

Tell me, you whom I love, where you graze your flock and where you rest your sheep at midday. Why should I be like a veiled woman beside the flocks of your friends?

Friends

If you do not know, most beautiful of women, follow the tracks of the sheep and graze your young goats by the tents of the shepherds.

He

I liken you, my darling, to a mare among Pharaoh's chariot horses. Your cheeks are beautiful with earrings, your neck with strings of jewels.

We will make you earrings of gold, studded with silver.

She

While the king was at his table, my perfume spread its fragrance. My beloved is to me a sachet of myrrh resting between my breasts. My beloved is to me a cluster of henna blossoms from the vineyards of En Gedi.

He

How beautiful you are, my darling! Oh, how beautiful! Your eyes are doves.

She

How handsome you are, my beloved! Oh, how charming! And our bed is verdant.

He

The beams of our house are cedars; our rafters are firs.

Song of Songs 1:7–17

Loving conversation

The second half of the first chapter of the Song is given over to loving conversation. For the first time the Bride and beloved each find their voice to speak of the other's beauty.

When a new pastor joins our staff, I ask myself the question: 'Has he/she found their voice?' It is not to be taken for granted. Some people put on the voice of someone else whom they have admired, others use a voice that they think will please or persuade, others again are simply quiet. It is a breakthrough moment when someone finds their own true voice, whatever that may be.

A plant may be choked and stifled by weeds and thorns. Some children are almost completely silent even at home. Of course, some people may just be quiet by nature, but also trauma or intimidation may take away someone's voice.

Conversely, healing and flourishing will result in a person finding their voice. As Christians, we need to find it in the place of prayer, of friendship, of simple conversations about Christ. For some, it will come forth in preaching. John was 'the voice of one crying in the wilderness', and so – however public or private our calling – are we.

But it is the voice of love that is perhaps the deepest, most vulnerable, most authentic and most needed. This is the voice we hear here.

> *you whom my soul loves . . .*
> *O most beautiful among women . . .*
> *my love . . .*
> *your cheeks are lovely . . .*
> *you are beautiful, my love . . .*
> *you are beautiful, my beloved . . .*
> (ESV)

These are the simple greetings used by these lovers – and they are telling, because many today have so little capacity to express or hear love. It pleases and moves a lover to hear words of love from the beloved. In the next chapter we read: *O my dove in the cleft of the rocks: let me hear your voice . . . for your voice is sweet* (2:14).

The same is true of the divine lover of our souls, apparently, who wants to hear our voice; the psalmist talks of his pleasure at discovering this secret when he says: 'I love the LORD, for he heard my voice; he heard my cry for mercy. Because he turned his ear to me, I will call on him as long as I live' (Psalm 116:1–2).

Nietzsche said, 'The voice of beauty speaks softly; it creeps only into the most fully awakened souls.'[74]

'All I have is a voice . . .' says W. H. Auden. 'We must love one another or die.'[75]

Here we see the awakened souls of the two lovers saying: *Behold, you are beautiful* to one another. This love language is a mark of any great awakening, whether of romance or revival.

At the end of the chapter we read: *Behold, you are beautiful, my love; behold, you are beautiful; your eyes are doves. [She] Behold, you are beautiful, my beloved, truly delightful* (1:15–16; ESV). In a relationship between a man and a woman, a man daring to express the thought 'You are beautiful' and a woman returning the compliment can be a world-changing breakthrough, if sincerely meant. Words like these can act as a powerful aphrodisiac. To speak of the beauty of the other directly, saying 'You are beautiful' – not just admiring some aspect – is to make oneself vulnerable and is a kind of declaration of love. In a marriage relationship, it is certainly to be recommended, because love deepens when it is expressed. Yet many people have difficulty finding their voice in this way. Or if they have found it once, such as on their wedding day, they may have lost it in the sickness or stress or sorrows of normal life.

There is an old story of a couple in difficulties. Finally the husband confronts his wife and asks her why she is so miserable and resentful. She candidly replies, 'I just wish that occasionally you would tell me you love me.' The husband then replies, 'Listen, on our wedding day I said I love you. If the position changes, I'll let you know.' Though a banal story, the truth is that love deepens, strengthens, enriches when it is spoken out. If not spoken, it can shrivel.

In the same way, love from God is to be heard and appreciated (like a draught to be drunk deeply), and love for God is to be poured out in praise.

The conversation begins, *Tell me, you whom my soul loves, where you pasture your flock* (ESV) – the Bride is unguarded, her tone personal and intimate: her lover is *you whom my soul loves*. She asks where she can find him, where he rests at noon – wanting proximity to her beloved, somewhere she can be unveiled and close with him. He responds immediately, addressing her as *most beautiful among women*, and asking her to follow the tracks of the flock in order to find him at noon as she wishes.

To find the good shepherd, find his flock. To find Jesus, follow in his Church's tracks – follow in prayer, in gathering together, in teaching, in getting to know the ways of God. Catch up with his Church and you will catch up with him.

I liken you, my darling, to a mare among Pharaoh's chariot horses. Your cheeks are beautiful with earrings, your neck with strings of jewels (1:9) Caught up together again, he calls her a mare among Pharaoh's chariots: in Pharaoh's stable were to be found the most expensive, powerful, free-running war horses, the most impressive in the world.

He goes on to admire her cheeks, then her neck with its 'ornaments of gold studded with silver'. Reading this allegorically, some see the cheeks as meaning our emotions and the neck as to do with the will. In this case, the emotions and the will of the Bride are found beautiful and are adorned now with gold – that is to say royal – attributes, making her character beautiful and delightful to God. This apparently is how the Bridegroom sees all who are part of the Bride of Christ.

Passion and perfume

My beloved is to me a sachet of myrrh resting . . . (1:13)

This perfumed ointment can mean the virtues of the Holy Spirit, fragrance coming from the character of the Holy Spirit spilling out of believers. Here there is an echo of verse 3: *Your name is like perfume poured out.* There is an old song: 'His name is as ointment poured forth: Jesus'.[76] To rehearse the names of Christ is like healing ointment. This echoes Gregory the Great, who wrote: 'Your name is an unguent poured out of its divine immensity for the sake of our nature; from being invisible it renders itself visible . . .' He then remembers that Christ 'emptied himself, taking the form of a servant' and says: 'What Paul calls "emptied" Solomon calls "emptied out". Since then the Lord was made known to the human race by the humility of the incarnation, it is said to him: "Your name is like ointment poured out."'[77] Those who are kissed by the kindness and presence of Christ will find his fragrance imparted to them: they will themselves become fragrant.

This is picture language expressing internal beauty. The

perfumes of the ancient world came from the inside of a plant, crushed so that the fragrance came out. The crushing of Christ for us and our being pressed into his likeness, even through suffering, yields the aroma of Christ.

Coming back to a more earthy view of perfume, Fernand Dumont speaks of 'a woman not yet seen, but whose perfume accumulates on the horizon like a storm cloud'.[78] The Bible seems to suggest the idea of perfume as a kind of aphrodisiac – as the book of Ruth attests[79] – and so, I guess, we should not shy away from its power.

It is a rich theme; as has been said: 'Perfume is the key to our memories'[80] – when one partner is bereaved it is often the sense of smell that recalls the loved one most vividly, and evokes tears and deep emotions.

Looking in the other direction, Coco Chanel is reputed to have said: 'A woman who doesn't wear perfume has no future.' To cultivate love, perfume will help – both for a man and for a woman. Chanel may have had a vested interest but she was right to say: 'Perfume is the unseen, unforgettable, ultimate accessory of fashion . . . that heralds your arrival and prolongs your departure.'

Speaking spiritually, we can say that a Church that is not imbued with the aroma of Christ has no future. We need his character, his love, his patience, his sacrificial acts, his wise words, his sweet-smelling presence to envelop us as we go out from his chamber before the watching world.

In verse 13, the perfume is specifically identified as myrrh: the substance associated with burial, and hence with suffering in the face of death. One Church Father, Nilus of Ancyra, movingly comments, 'She calls him "sachet of myrrh" on account of his suffering and his death and the apparent disgrace that derives from the cross when he compressed the power of the Godhead, inactive, into his body as into a tiny bag.'[81]

Jesus Christ, then, is like myrrh to us. Myrrh is precious, powerful, pleasant, perfumed and has preservative powers. It is not only a disinfectant but also a cure: it can be healing balm. Let us have it, have Christ close to us at all times.

In his sermon 'A bundle of myrrh' preached in London in February 1864, C. H. Spurgeon concludes: '"My Beloved is to me a bundle of myrrh." He, or rather, it, "shall lie all night between my breasts." The Church does not say, "I will put this bundle of myrrh on my shoulders" – Christ is no burden to a Christian. She does not say, "I will put this bundle of myrrh on my back" – the Church does not want to have Christ concealed from her face. She desires to have him where she can see him, and near to her heart . . . He shall always be upon our heart.'

Mysteriously, the same aroma of Christ comes to perfume the Bride of Christ. Spurgeon's passion for God yielded a book of sermons on the Song which helped build a church of 'over 10,000' people at the heart of London. He concludes on the subject of the bundle of myrrh: 'It is an expression of desire – her desire that she may have the consciousness of Christ's love continually . . . My desire is that Jesus may abide with me from morn till even, in the world and in the Church, when I awake, when I sleep, when I go abroad, and when I come home into the bosom of my family. Is not that your desire that he may be always with you?

'But then, it is not only her desire, but it is also her confidence. She seems to say, "He will be with me thus." . . . Christ never will go away from people really. He will be all night betwixt your breasts . . . his heart never can depart from you. He has set you as a seal upon his heart, and increasingly will make you sensible of it . . .

'To conclude, this is also a resolve. She desires, she believes, and she resolves it. Lord, thou shalt be with me, thou shalt be with me always.'[82]

Love from God

The Bride hears the words: *You are beautiful, my love . . . you are beautiful; your eyes are doves* (1:15; ESV). She is well aware of her imperfections – she was concerned she was *darkened by the sun*, she relates that people have been angry with her, and she said, *Do not gaze at me.* Her self-image, the sense that she is flawed, is no doubt true in one sense. Yet she hears the Bridegroom say: 'No, to me you are beautiful; you are my love, your eyes are doves.' Doves are seen as peaceful and steadfast. For us the dove stands for the Holy Spirit at the baptism of Jesus and at the baptism of the Church in the Spirit on the day of Pentecost.

Following the miraculous catch of fish, as told in Chapter 5 of Luke's Gospel, Jesus looked at Peter and knew him. Simon thought of himself as a sinful man as he knelt before Christ on the shore. But Jesus pronounced him a man with a destiny, a Fisher of Men. Later he says Peter will be the Rock on whom he will build his Church. Mind you, Peter is still subject to trial and being tripped up as a 'Satan' who is told to get behind Christ. But he has begun a journey to see himself as Jesus sees him. Later, after Peter's betrayal, he is restored to rocklike-ness through a conversation whose whole subject is Love, with the thrice-repeated question: 'Do you love me?' Peter finds his voice to say loud and clear: 'You know that I love you.' As this encounter unfolds, shame drops off him and he steps back into closeness to Christ – which in turn unlocks in Peter world-changing effectiveness.

Similarly, the Bride here is at the start of a journey to

wholeness. For her and for us, the key to our own wholeness and deliverance from dark thoughts in our perception of ourselves as those with whom people are angry, and who have been battered by the heat of the battle of life, is to hear (in the words of Horatius Bonar's famous hymn) 'the voice of Jesus say: come unto me and rest', to receive his cleansing forgiveness, and to hear his assessment of us as 'beautiful and with steadfast eyes'. He speaks the future into our present and sees us as we really are.

Arguably, there are four reasons for this loving, positive assessment: first, the finished work of Christ; second, the gift of the Holy Spirit, who moves our heart to be born from above and to become children of God – we cannot overestimate how beautiful this is to God; third, the nature of God's personality, which is the *hesed* covenant love of God for his people;[83] and fourth, our destiny as his future Bride.

The fact is that God sees the end from the beginning. He foresees from the start that there will be a glorious betrothal. It is real and true and for this reason also he says: 'You are beautiful' – and knows it to be true. In Hosea, the details of the divine romance have to do with a voice, speaking tenderly, saying, 'Therefore I am now going to allure her; I will lead her into the wilderness and speak tenderly to her. There I will give her back her vineyards, and will make the Valley of Achor a door of hope . . . "In that day," declares the LORD, "you will call me 'my husband' . . . I will betroth you to me forever . . . and you will acknowledge the LORD"' (Hosea 2:14–16, 19–20).

There is indeed for us a door of hope. There is transforming, beautifying mercy: 'In that day you will call me "my husband",' says Hosea. In fact the Bride calls him *beautiful, my beloved, truly delightful.*

So then – the Bride has overcome shyness and is caught up in daring to speak. This can be a breakthrough moment for Christians as they are released into articulating love. As renewal movements flow through the continents, it certainly seems the Bride is finding her voice across the world. In the spiritual ice age that Europe finds herself in, though, we may find ourselves frozen and thus unable to speak. C. S. Lewis identified a particularly 'British' reserve or 'cultural shyness'. In his famous sermon at Oxford, 'The weight of glory', he evokes the dilemma in which many find themselves: 'In speaking of this desire for our own far off country, which we find in ourselves even now, I feel a certain shyness . . . I am trying to rip open the inconsolable secret in each one of you . . . the secret we cannot hide and cannot tell, though we desire to do both. We cannot tell it because it is a desire for something that has never actually appeared in our experience. We cannot hide it because our experience is constantly suggesting it, and we betray ourselves like lovers at the mention of a name.'

Lewis then begins to comment on categories that we escape into out of shyness. It may be that people feel freer to express themselves now, but his argument still stands: 'Our commonest expedient is to call it beauty and behave as if that had settled the matter. But these things – the beauty, the memory of our own past . . . are not the thing itself; they are only the scent of a flower we have not found, the echo of a tune we have not heard, news from a country we have never yet visited.'[84]

It is as if here, at the end of Chapter 1, the Bride breaks into this unvisited country, its beauty an echo of the longed-for Garden of Eden. Soon she will enjoy its scents and sing its new songs. For the moment, his loveliness fills her horizon, his beauty enlarges her heart and heals her: she has already found her voice.

She speaks out words of love – and instantly grows up.

Spiritual exercises for loving Christ and finding your voice

My beloved is to me a sachet of myrrh resting between my breasts. My beloved is to me a cluster of henna blossoms from the vine-yards of En Gedi.

He
How beautiful you are, my darling! Oh, how beautiful! Your eyes are doves.

She
How handsome you are, my beloved! Oh, how charming!

Song of Songs 1:13–16

Reflect on the allegory of the love of God for his Bride. In the light of this, consider the sights, sounds, smells and noise of this scene. Read the passage through four times, viewing it each time from a different angle and pondering (weighing) it all. Listen to his voice of love for you.

Focusing on the phrase *my beloved is to me a sachet of myrrh resting*, Ignatius gives the following exercise:

> Imagining Christ our Lord present before me and nailed to the cross, speak and ask how it came about that the Creator became a human being and from eternal life came to temporal death and thus to die for my sins. Then turning to myself will I ask,
> What have done for Christ?

What am I doing for Christ?

What ought I to do for Christ?

Finally, seeing him in that state hanging on the cross, go over whatever comes to mind.[85]

It would be good to use a spiritual journal to record your thoughts. Note that the question: 'What am I doing for Christ?' can of course include simply being present for people and should not provoke frenetic activism, but, rather, Christlike service.

One of the things we may be led to consider is that to be a person of loving praise and expression of affection is something that we can be doing for Christ. 'The human person is called to praise reverence and serve God our Lord' (Ignatius).[86] Spend time in silent contemplation of his beauty and listening to him. Now spend time doing this in words – 'find your voice'.

'I sit. I renounce my restless running about, my striving to be creative on my own – to possess, to capture as my own something of his fruitfulness. Rather, I sit in his shadow, I acknowledge that all is of him. I delight in this.'
Basil Pennington[87]

'Holy love is the only subject treated in this song. We must remember that love reveals itself, not by words or phrases, but by actions and experience. It is love that speaks here. If anyone wishes to understand it, let him first love. Otherwise it would be folly to read this song of love, because it is absolutely impossible for a cold heart to grasp the meaning of language so inflamed.'
Bernard of Clairvaux (Sermon 70:1)

CHAPTER FIVE

Entering into His Rest

She

I am a rose of Sharon, a lily of the valleys.

He

Like a lily among thorns is my darling among the young women.

She

Like an apple tree among the trees of the forest is my beloved among the young men. I delight to sit in his shade, and his fruit is sweet to my taste.

Let him lead me to the banquet hall, and let his banner over me be love.

Strengthen me with raisins, refresh me with apples, for I am faint with love.

His left arm is under my head, and his right arm embraces me.

Daughters of Jerusalem, I charge you by the gazelles and by the does of the field: Do not arouse or awaken love until it so desires.

Song of Songs 2:1–7

We are exploring the Song of Songs and all it has to say about divine romance. At the same time, on the surface, the Song of Songs is a description of passionate love between a young man and a shepherd girl. These two continue to enjoy speaking to each other in this second chapter of the Song. He calls her a lily among thorns; she says he is different to all the others, like an apple tree in a forest, with sweet-tasting fruit. She is unabashed in her desire to taste his fruit – 'apples' and 'raisins', verse 5 – and feel his touch. Again, the challenge to speak out her enjoyment in their relationship, both metaphorical and physical, is clear.

She is longing for lovemaking; she is alive to her beloved, initiating contact. She is the opposite of a frigid bride, and those aspiring to grow in married love can learn from her example. Faint with love, the woman is enjoying his touch, as they eat together and as they embrace. Importantly, his banner over her is not lust, but love: 'his look is love'. Bergant writes: 'like nothing else in life, erotic love in its straining for union reveals . . . the woman's fundamental need for the other as well as her craving to give herself without reserve'.[88] No lesser commitment is true of the man. It is good to reflect: what is this and why is this?

From a biblical point of view, I believe the key to understanding this intense longing built into our design – and its counterpoint, our sense of alienation – lies in the Genesis account of creation where the woman is taken from the man and brought to him so that 'the two shall become one flesh'. Divine surgery is undertaken, under a divine anaesthetic. Out of undifferentiated humanity, two new beings emerge, male and female. Having made Woman, God brings her to Man. Adam breaks into the first love song: 'This is now bone of my bones and flesh of my flesh' (Genesis 2:23).

John Stott writes, 'The Bible teaches that heterosexual intercourse in marriage is more than a union; it is a kind of reunion. It is not a union of alien persons who do not belong to one another and cannot appropriately become one flesh. On the contrary, it is the union of two persons who originally were one, were then separated from each other, and now in the sexual encounter of marriage come together again.' Stott concludes: 'It is surely this which explains the profound mystery of heterosexual intimacy, which poets and philosophers have celebrated in every culture. Heterosexual intercourse is much more than a union of bodies; it is a blending of complementary personalities through which, in the midst of prevailing alienation, the rich created oneness of human being is experienced again. And the complementarity of male and female sexual organs is only a symbol at the physical level of a much deeper spiritual complementarity.'[89]

If the Bride longs for her Bridegroom, for union, for the experience of resting in his arms (and thus an end to alienation), so humankind, we can say, longs for union with the divine lover of our souls. The love relationship, the successive betrothal and completed union between man and woman, is in fact a snapshot of the real thing: our longing for an end to alienation from God and full union with him from whose image we originally came.

Chinese church leader Watchman Nee wrote: 'This marks the starting point of real spiritual progress. It is an inward spiritual longing for the Lord Himself: the ultimate realization that His love and this quest of the heart with its fervent desires are eternally inseparable.' From a Chinese prison he writes not of a desire for himself to be released from prison, but of the Bride and her desire for kisses: 'If a believer does not have this reality of a questing spirit created within him by the Holy Spirit – the dissatisfaction with the ordinary and this ardent pursuit of Love's full end – then it is utterly impossible to attain to any intimate relationship with the Lord.' He goes on, 'How is it that one is able to have such an intense spiritual longing for the Lord Jesus Christ? The answer lies in spiritual vision. To some, revelation is given of the glorious person of the Lord Jesus by which they perceive that "his love is better than wine" . . . and long for "the kisses of thy mouth".'[90]

This second chapter begins where Chapter 1 left off with a continuation of the dialogue between the lovers. She describes herself as a *rose of Sharon*. Maybe we can pause to think of the uniqueness of the rose as a flower: beautifully scented, majestic, a fitting adornment for a bride. In Tudor times this comparison was picked up in the traditional Christmas carol about Mary:

> There is no rose of such virtue
> As is the rose that bare Jesu;
> Alleluia.
> For in this rose contained was
> Heaven and earth in little space;
> By that rose we may well see
> That he is God in persons three.

In this carol's wonderful imagery, Mary is seen as holding God inside her: a symbol for the Bride of God, the Church. Mary is the rose of Sharon: unique, scented, rare.

The Bride goes on to say she is like a lily of the valley, and the Bridegroom builds on this; she is not just a lily, but a lily among thorns, its beauty heightened further by contrast.

Spurgeon speaks of this passage: 'We take it for granted that the Song of Solomon is a sacred marriage song between Christ and His Church and that it is the Lord Jesus who is here speaking to His Church and indeed of each individual member saying: As the lily among thorns, so is my love among the daughters . . .' He then quotes a certain Dr Thompson writing of a real Middle Eastern lily, 'It grows among thorns, and I have sadly lacerated my hands in extricating it from them. Nothing can be in higher contrast than the luxuriant, velvety softness of this lily, and the withered, tangled hedge of thorns about it.' Spurgeon then applies the message: 'Ah, beloved, you know who it was that in gathering your soul and mine, lacerated not his hand only, but his feet, and his head, and his side, and his heart, yes, and his inmost soul. He spied us out, and said, "That lily is mine, and I will have it"; but the thorns were a terrible barrier; our sins had gathered round about us, and the wrath of God most sharply stopped the way. Jesus pressed through all, that we might be his; and now when he takes us to himself he does not forget the thorns which girded his brow, and tore his flesh, for our sakes.

'This then is a part of our relationship to Christ, that we cost him very dear. He saw us where we were, and he came to our deliverance . . . Never will he forget Calvary and its thorns, nor should his saints allow the memory thereof to fade.'[91]

The promise of entering his rest still stands

The next section (v. 3) speaks of the extraordinary and precious privilege of learning to rest in Christ – to 'abide in him'. *Like an apple tree among the trees of the forest is my lover among the young men. I delight to sit in his shade, and his fruit is sweet to my taste.*

Like the Bride with her lover, here before the Lord Jesus, we can say: I sit. I renounce my usual relentless running about. We can give up our need to be activists, forever running on the treadmill of modern life – and instead take a Sabbath rest. We can sit down, and be still, saying:

> All honour and glory is my loved one's.
> I can sit in total delight.
> I no longer need to be concerned about what others think of me.
> I sit in the delight of perfect contemplation.[92]

I am determined not to be like Peter, agitating for activity on the Mount of Transfiguration, asking to build three booths so as to be a builder of something useful. Instead, I sit down and rest . . .

Finding an apple tree in the midst of a forest is a rare gift to a dehydrated traveller. It provides an image of a delicious, refreshing, satisfying and sustaining nourishment: *Let him lead me to the banquet hall, and let his banner over me be love.* Matthew Henry comments on this with tenderness: 'See . . . How she was introduced: He brought me, wrought in me an inclination to draw nigh to God, helped me over my discouragements, took me by the hand, guided and led me, and gave me an access with boldness to God as a Father. We should never have come into the banqueting-house, never have been acquainted with spiritual pleasures, if Christ had not brought us, by opening for us a new and living way and opening in us a new and living fountain.'

The banqueting house, or 'house of wine' (Septuagint) or 'wine cellar' (Vulgate), is a place to sit and eat and drink with him. Wine has a rich symbolism through the Bible from Noah to Jacob to the prophets and through to Christ who multiplies wine at Cana. Wine stands for his blood poured out for all in abundance.

'Behold I stand at the door and knock,' says the risen Christ to the lukewarm Laodiceans. 'He who hears my voice and opens the door I will come in and eat with him and he will eat with me.' The Church has an ancient symbol of the future supper of the Lamb in the Eucharist or Communion: we will sit down truly then and eat and drink with him. In the meantime, may he be known to us in the breaking of the bread.

But as at Pentecost, which was the birth-day of the

Church, when renewal movements break over the Church sometimes there can be a new experience of apparent 'drunkenness' in God's love that is healing joy for some and offence for others. These movements often appropriate this idea of 'New Wine'.[93]

It is interesting that modern renewal movements find themselves (often unconsciously) using the same language as ancient mystics and monastics. Thus the Cistercian Alan of Lille, one of the best known twelfth-century teachers in Paris and Montpellier, comments on this 'wine cellar': 'The word cells or cellars is just the right word for it signifies what belongs to the "celestial" . . . The wines which fill and inebriate and release the mind from the cares of the world are stored in cellars; in the same way celestial happiness inebriates the mind and thereby detaches it from company with and altogether removes it from the love of earthly things.'[94] Picking up the line *His banner over me be love*, Basil Pennington goes on in this way: 'Love, let your very hand press me close to your own heart. In this I want to abide.'[95]

As I have said, in times of revival many are the stories of the experience of God's 'banner of love'. Here is Sarah Edwards, wife of Jonathan who led the eighteenth-century American Great Awakening, describing her experience of 'the banqueting house': 'I continued in a sweet and lively sense of Divine things, until I retired to rest. That night, which was Thursday night, Jan. 28, 1742 was the sweetest night I ever had in my life . . . all night I continued in a constant, clear and lively sense of the heavenly sweetness of Christ's excellent and transcendent love, of his nearness to me, and of my dearness to him; with an inexpressibly sweet calmness of soul in an entire rest in him.'

This resting and calmness is a mark of being under the

banner of God's love, it seems. Sarah Edwards continues in what is really a Song of Songs experience:

> I seemed to myself to perceive a glow of divine love come down from the heart of Christ in heaven, into my heart, in a constant stream, like a stream or pencil of sweet light. At the same time, my heart and soul all flowed out in love to Christ, so that there seemed to be a constant flowing and reflowing of heavenly and divine love, from Christ's heart to mine . . . So far as I am capable of making a comparison, I think that what I felt each minute was worth more than all the outward comfort and pleasure which I had enjoyed in my whole life put together. It was a pure delight, which fed and satisfied the soul . . . It seemed to be all that my feeble frame could sustain, of that fulness of joy, which is felt by those who behold the face of Christ, and share his love in the heavenly world.[96]

Two hundred years later, on a different continent, during the 1949 revival in the Hebrides in Scotland, Margaret Macdonald tells a similar story of the intensity of being under the 'banner of love' that was experienced: 'Revival began in Lemreway. Through the fullness of the revelation they received, their faces were radiant as they reflected the heavenly visions which they beheld. I have seen this on a number of occasions. No one understands these experiences except those who were thus moved. People will not believe if you tell them. The people would weep. The spirit of prayer would come on people.

'That was how it was in revival. Some people were so overcome with the presence of God they fell to the ground . . . The presence of God was everywhere. At family worship one night the atmosphere was so charged with the presence of God that one felt one could reach out and grasp that which surrounded us. Along with this came a sense of unspeakable joy . . .

'People who have never been in revival do not understand the intensity of it all. God is real, eternity is real, people come to Christ in the atmosphere of God. There is no flippancy or lightheartedness. You are dealing with eternal things. I thank the Lord I was privileged to be there.'[97]

Let his banner over me be love (v. 4)
This evocative phrase has been the inspiration for a veritable wealth of well-loved songs through the ages. One of the best known is that of Palestrina. This sixteenth-century Italian composer, in the preface to his great work, says: 'There exists a vast mass of love songs of the poets . . . the songs of men ruled by passion . . . I blush and grieve to think that once I was of their number. But . . . I have mended my ways and now have produced a work which treats of the divine love of Christ and His spouse the soul, the Canticle of Solomon.'[98]

Palestrina, the musician of the Church of St John in the Lateran in Rome, perhaps speaks for many in expressing a kind of conversion or 'ordering' in his sexuality, helped by a reading of the Song of Songs. The Latin Vulgate translation of this 'banner' verse says 'He has set love in order' in me. We know he intends us to love him with heart, soul, mind and strength; and to love our neighbour as our self. This is 'setting love in order'. It begins in the love of God the Father for his child and the love of the Bridegroom for his Bride: all the healing we need flows from this. The result is this: that we can contemplate; we can be satisfied in him; we can be seated in the heavenly places.

It is in this sense that the Song of Songs brings comfort, strength and satisfaction for single people as much as for those in couple relationships. The fact is that finding joy and delight and intimacy in Christ is our very highest, and hence most fulfilling, our most beautifying calling. If we are single and we understand his banner of love to be over us, if we delight in God's presence and his healing love, if we are sitting down resting, as when Mary sat at the feet of Jesus, this will help us. We may find we can be single, holy and truly happy in a sex-obsessed culture – and single, strong and satisfied in a marriage-obsessed Church.

This is what the Bible says: 'I would like you to be free from concern. An unmarried man [or woman] is concerned about the Lord's affairs . . . I am saying this for your own good, not to restrict you, but that you may live in a right way in undivided devotion to the Lord' (1 Corinthians 7:32, 35).

In the Song of Songs, both single and married people can discover intimacy. We may be brought to the point where we are able truly to say: 'His banner over me is love; he refreshes me with apples; I am faint with love.' Then this fascination with God will keep us from being led into other fascinations. But if we are not captivated by and drawn into his beauty we can easily get caught by other beauty, and that can become unhealthy.

This is not to say that all this is one simple step. Ronald Rolheiser's *The Holy Longing* has helpful reflections on what healthy celibacy might mean, including the deep insight that 'sexual incompleteness is solidarity with the poor'. He quotes Henri Nouwen, who offers 'four steps to turning our restful incompleteness into a restful solitude' – or, to subvert this for our purposes:

Four Steps to Resting under the Divine Lover's Banner of
Love –

1. Own your own pain or incompleteness.
2. Give up false messianic expectations ('Our life is a short
   time in expectation in which sadness and joy kiss each
   other at every moment . . . In every embrace, there is
   loneliness. In every friendship, distance . . . But this intimate experience in which every bit of life is touched by a
   bit of death can point us to beyond the limits of our exist-
   ence. It can do so by making us look forward to the day
   when our hearts will be filled with perfect joy.')
3. Go Inward (I would rather say: 'Go under the banner of
   His love').
4. Understand it is a movement that is never made once for
   all.[99]

How do we enter this rest?

The idea of 'rest' finds fulfilment in Jesus, who gives this
invitation to his disciples: 'Come to me, all you who are
weary or burdened, and I will give you rest. Take my yoke
upon you and learn from me, for I am gentle and humble of
heart, and you will find rest for your souls' (Matthew 11:28–
29). This loving invitation comes after bereavement with
John the Baptist's death, a time when there is contestation
and vulnerability among the disciples. Rest is often most
needed when the battle is fiercest. 'Sitting down in his
shadow', and letting him protect us from the heat of the
battle, is a skill to be learned.

Taking it a step further, Hebrews calls a whole people to
enter this rest:

Therefore since it still remains for some to enter that rest, and since those who formerly had the good news proclaimed to them did not go in because of their disobedience . . .

'Today, if you hear his voice, do not harden your hearts.'

There remains, then, a Sabbath-rest for the people of God . . . Let us, therefore, make every effort to enter that rest . . .

(Hebrews 4:6–7, 9, 11).

In the contemplative tradition of the Church, people from Teresa of Avila onwards have talked of a three-fold process to take us toward what I call 'soul-resting'. They recommend:

1. *The Prayer of Recollection*[100]: a time to re-assemble yourself from the fractured times in which we live and 'call all our thoughts home', sitting quietly and peacefully *in his shadow* (2:3). We live lives which are often pressed and stressed, scattered and disintegrated. We are interrupted many times in an hour by messages and emails and texts. The economic and social pressure to perform is such that we may live fractured lives. If you are not used to this 'Recollection', it will be a significant victory to be still just for ten minutes, and yet there is a sense in which we *must* be still to know that he is God; we must recollect that he is our refuge.[101]

2. *The Prayer of Quiet*: this is a listening stillness. Our hearts are softened and attentive. We are alert and awake, as if on tiptoes, ready in our spirits to listen. We respond to God's instruction about his Son whom he loves: listen to him. François Fénelon says, 'Be silent, and listen to God. Let your heart be in such a state of preparation that his Spirit may impress upon you such virtues as will please

him. The silence of all outward and earthly affections and thoughts is essential if we are to hear his voice.'[102]

3. *Union and Communion*: this was Hudson Taylor's phrase to describe the journey of the Song of Songs.[103] Other mystics call this stage that of Ecstasy. It describes 'Divine Connection'. Julian of Norwich says: 'The whole reason we pray is to be united into the vision and contemplation of him to whom we pray.' Madame Guyon writes: 'We now come to the ultimate stage of Christian experience: Divine Union. This cannot be brought about merely by your own experience . . . Eventually it will take an *act of God* to make union a reality.' Richard Foster has a helpful definition: 'Put simply, we receive his love for us and love him back in return . . . contemplation is love on fire with devotion.'[104]

This is what Sarah Edwards, as quoted above, is describing when she speaks of 'the heavenly sweetness of Christ's excellent and transcendent love, of his nearness to me, and of my dearness to him; with an inexpressibly sweet calmness of soul in an entire rest in him'.

From another tradition, Smith Wigglesworth, the Pentecostal preacher, speaks of this moment of 'Union and Communion': 'my body became full of light and Holy Presence, and in the revelation I saw an empty Cross and at the same time the Jesus I loved and adored crowned in the Glory in a Reigning Position'. He goes on: 'The glorious remembrance of these moments is beyond my expression. When I could not find words to express, then an irresistible Power filled me and moved my being till I found to my glorious astonishment I was speaking in other tongues clearly. After this a burning love for everybody filled my soul. I am overjoyed in giving my testimony, praying for those that fight this truth, but I am clearly given to understand that I must come out of every unbelieving element. I am already witness of signs following.'[105]

To revert to the Song, we can draw near to God and be strengthened by the 'raisins' (wine) of grace and the 'apples' (soul food) of mercy.

These three steps – Recollection; Quiet; Union and Communion – are necessary to this important achievement of entering into his rest. Many, many witnesses testify to this experience of knowing the banner of his love over them.

This is also referred to as the *wound* of love (2:5, Septuagint). The King James Version and English Standard Version translate it *for I am sick with love*, and Gregory of Nyssa comments: 'The Bride says: I am wounded by love. By these words she designates the arrow that sinks deep into her heart. Love is the archer. Now love is God . . . God shoots his chosen arrow, his only begotten Son . . . Thus the soul sees in itself the sweet arrow of love with which it has been wounded and glories in its wounding in the words: "I am wounded by love."'[106]

Daughters of Jerusalem, I charge you by the gazelles and by the does of the field: Do not arouse or awaken love until it so desires (v. 7)
This is the first of three refrains repeating this closing phrase: *Do not arouse or awaken love until it so desires* (the others may be found at 3:5 and 8:4). There are two main possible interpretations of this verse. The first has to do with not awakening a love relationship until a person is ready for it, or old enough for it. This could be like not unwrapping the gift before the

birthday – in this case, not entering a sexual relationship until marriage. I believe that in Chapter 8 this is the primary interpretation, when we are speaking of a 'little sister', and we will return to this interpretation then.

The second interpretation is that when a person is in this state of soul-resting in their love – of Union and Communion – they don't want to be lifted out of it or have it interrupted. This seems to fit the context here, where it has to do with enjoying the presence of God and not giving away the presence of the lover, whether by changing the subject or rushing off to the next thing. Often we need to 'learn to linger' rather than get up and get on. James Durham expresses this well: 'The charge itself is that "they stir not up nor awake the beloved"; as a wife would say (when her husband is come home and resting in her arm) be quiet all, and let no din be in the house to awake him: and this charge reaches herself, as well as others . . . Hence, observe. 1. If a sensible presence be not tenderly entertained, it will not last. 2. Believers should be most careful then, when they are admitted to near and sensible fellowship with Christ, that nothing may fall out which may provoke him to depart. 3. The least sinful motions and stirrings of corruption should be suppressed, as having a great tendency to provoke and stir up the beloved to be gone.'[107]

In hundreds of thousands of gatherings of Christians each week around the world, we spend time praying for the presence of God, singing songs of pleading to God for visitation. The invocation is the same – whether it is an ancient song like Rabanus Maurus's ninth-century *Veni Creator Spiritus* with its inspiring lines, 'Come, Holy Ghost, our souls inspire / and lighten with celestial fire', or a more contemporary song like Martin Smith's 'Waiting here for you / with our hands lifted high'[108] – or something halfway between like this by Bianco da Siena from the fifteenth century:

> Come down, O love divine,
> seek thou this soul of mine,
> and visit it with thine own ardour glowing;
> O Comforter, draw near,
> within my heart appear,
> and kindle it, thy holy flame bestowing.

We are longing for the presence of the comforter upon the Church, for the banner over the Church to truly be that of Love. Usually the liturgy (whether formal or informal, traditional or free-flowing) moves on swiftly – so that if ever the presence did come, rare are the communities that would recognise it and change their programme accordingly. Instead, we have already moved swiftly on to something else . . . the announcements, perhaps.

In times of true revival all this changes. Until such time, may our waiting be genuine, expectant – and may we learn to lean.

For the time being, I suggest the use of this passage for more private, personal communion, where there is no agenda other than him! Durham continues: 'Lastly, this charge is qualified in these words, "till he please." The meaning is, see that by your fault he be not awaked, till his own time come . . . Often believers are guilty in marring Christ's fellowship with them before he please, and they might enjoy Christ's company much longer oftentimes, if they did not sin him out of house and doors.'[109]

Spiritual exercises for soul-resting

Two exercises are to be recommended in this quest for a lifestyle of soul-resting: biblical meditation and contemplative prayer. Christian meditation can be used as a daily discipline, if only we will give time for it. Meditation means 'to consider or contemplate'. It leads us to explore contemplation.

Find a quiet place for a quiet hour. Meditate on the verses below:

> *I delight to sit in his shade, and his fruit is sweet to my taste. Let him lead me to the banquet hall, and let his banner over me be love. Strengthen me with raisins, refresh me with apples, for I am faint with love.*

Enter this biblical scene and use your imagination to see, hear, smell and encounter the living Word. Teresa of Avila defined meditation as follows: 'By meditation I mean prolonged reasoning with the understanding.'

For this exercise, use the three steps described in the paragraphs below to consider or contemplate the mystery of the incarnation:

1. *Recollection*: Allow Christ to say to the storms of your heart: 'Be still.' You may feel anxiety rising at all the things need to get on with. But lean on and look towards the One who is our peace.
2. *The Prayer of Quiet*: Stillness, but a listening stillness. St John of the Cross uses the phrase 'my house now all being stilled' for the moment to go out into the night to meet the Beloved.
3. *Union and Communion*: 'The whole reason we pray is to

be united into the vision and contemplation of him to whom we pray.' 'We now come to the ultimate stage of Christian experience: Divine Union. This cannot be brought about merely by your own experience. Eventually it will take an *act of God* to make union a reality.' 'We receive his love for us and love him back in return . . . contemplation is love on fire with devotion.'[110]

'Are the days of winter sunshine just as sad for you, too? When it is misty, in the evenings, and I am out walking by myself, it seems to me that the rain is falling through my heart and causing it to crumble into ruins.'
Gustave Flaubert

'The Song of Songs describes the joy and mutuality, beauty and power, agony and ecstasy of human sexual love. It speaks of marriage as it ought to be – the beautiful intimacy of marital love between man and woman.

'Yet marriage is, in a sense, a metaphor to describe something even more beautiful – the relationship of God to his people. Supremely, it is used to describe the relationship between Christ and his church (Ephesians 5:21–33). It is a picture of God's deep and passionate love for us and our intimate relationship with Jesus. For this reason, throughout church history, people have used this book as a metaphor to express the intimacy between God and the church.'
Nicky Gumbel[111]

CHAPTER SIX

The Winter is Over

She

> Listen! My beloved! Look! Here he comes, leaping across the mountains, bounding over the hills.
>
> My beloved is like a gazelle or a young stag. Look! There he stands behind our wall, gazing through the windows, peering through the lattice.
>
> My beloved spoke and said to me, 'Arise, my darling, my beautiful one, come with me.
>
> See! The winter is past; the rains are over and gone. Flowers appear on the earth; the season of singing has come, the cooing of doves is heard in our land.
>
> The fig tree forms its early fruit; the blossoming vines spread their fragrance. Arise, come, my darling; my beautiful one, come with me.'

He

> My dove in the clefts of the rock, in the hiding places on the mountainside, show me your face, let me hear your voice; for your voice is sweet, and your face is lovely.
>
> Catch for us the foxes, the little foxes that ruin the vine-yards, our vineyards that are in bloom.

She

> My beloved is mine and I am his; he browses among the lilies.
>
> Until the day breaks and the shadows flee, turn, my beloved, and be like a gazelle or like a young stag on the rugged hills.
>
> Song of Songs 2:8–17

In this well-loved passage, we see a change in tempo and a dramatic lift of energy. The time comes for activity, for running, for singing, for delight in nature. Apparently the long, shut-in winter is coming to an end and the Bridegroom is looking to the great outdoors. The Bride compares him to a young stag leaping across the mountains and hills. This passage will speak powerfully both of the human love affair and of the divine romance.

In this famous section, often used as a wedding reading, the Bridegroom is seen calling to his Bride to come out, to come and see the world transformed. She is his 'beloved', he calls her his 'darling', his 'beautiful one'. There is mutual respect and reciprocity; there is no male domination in this relationship. He is insistent that she joins him, but invites her out; he does not force her. She in turn is enthusiastic and proactive, without reserve, inviting him to 'browse among the lilies' – an enigmatic phrase redolent with sensuality and the enjoyment of his attention.

Perhaps, rather than a next step in the relationship, this passage is a general summary of what has happened between these two: the winter is indeed over. The sleeping winter state of being shut in, unawakened, has come to an end. Love has become ready and has woken up. Perhaps before this there was a fear that there would be no love in this life. But now there is: everything is changed into springtime – spring with her buds and birdsong and scents and blossoms.

Christopher Marlowe put it thus in his poem 'The Passionate Shepherd to His Love':

> Come live with me and be my love,
> And we will all the pleasures prove
> That valleys, groves, hills, and fields,
> Woods, or sleepy mountain yields . . .

By shallow rivers to whose falls
Melodious birds sing madrigals.
And I will make thee beds of roses
And a thousand fragrant posies . . .
The shepherds' swains shall dance and sing
For thy delight each May morning . . .[112]

The young stag

For the song of the soul, this next phase of the Song speaks of
the dynamic, adventurous, daring, vibrant being that is Jesus
Christ. I hope I can capture him for you. He is named as a
'young stag' and a gazelle. What can we say? Red deer are the
largest of all wild animals in Europe. A mature stag stands
about four feet high at the shoulder, and weighs up to three
hundred pounds. The stag is famous for its proud bearing and
magnificent antlers. White-tailed deer run very fast, up to thir-
ty-six miles per hour. They are great swimmers and can leap far
as well. Deer can leap over eight feet high and thirty feet along
the ground. We are invited to catch the energy behind the
image. Often our image of Christ is one of a somewhat effem-
inate figure holding a hand weakly in the air and looking
longingly to heaven. Few images of Christ give any sense of
movement or energy – take Doré's Bible illustration engrav-
ings, influential for generations of Christians. This contrasts
with illustrations of other heroes. But here there is life, energy,
joy, youthfulness: for *My beloved is . . . a young stag*.

Christ is said to be leaping and skipping on the mountains. For the Fathers this had to do with his overcoming
Principalities and Powers. James Durham builds on this: 'this
imports an agility in him, and a facility to overcome whatever
is in the way; a cheerfulness and heartiness in doing of it; he
comes with delight over the highest hill that is in his way,

when he returns to his people. It holds forth speediness: Christ comes quickly, and he is never behind his time, he cannot mistryst a believer; it imports a beauty, majesty and stateliness in his coming, as one in triumph; and so he comes triumphantly and in great state; and what is more stately than Christ's triumphing over principalities and powers, and making a show of them openly, by over-coming the difficulties in his way to his Bride.'[113]

The winter is over

The image of the time when the 'winter is over' is one of the best-loved images in the Song. C. S. Lewis uses this image of the end of winter to great effect in his book *The Lion, the Witch and the Wardrobe* as the power of the witch, under whose dominion it was always winter but never Christmas, is broken.

> Now they were steadily racing on again. And soon Edmund noticed that the snow which splashed against them as they rushed through it was much wetter than it had been last night . . . All around them, though out of sight, there were streams chattering, bubbling, splashing and even (in the distance) roaring. And his heart gave a great leap (though he hardly knew why) when he realised that the frost was over.[114]

This is a simple but powerful metaphor: winter cold suggests the deathblow wrought by evil in human lives; and springtime suggests personal transformation and the redemption of the whole human race.

What might the end of winter stand for? In terms of marriage, it may mean the end of singleness and the springtime of fruitfulness. Clearly not all single people would say they are frozen – many feel completely fulfilled. Some single people, however, may feel they are frozen – until the spring-time of relationship comes. Within marriage too, though, there can be seasons where feelings of intimacy and also of affection can seem completely frosted up. It is a many-levelled metaphor. The Disney film *Frozen* is the highest-grossing animated feature film of all time, and uses exactly this metaphor to treat the subject of the great danger issuing from frozen relationships and emotions. Its songs contain immediately memorable lines like 'Please don't shut me out again, please don't slam the door. You don't have to keep your distance any more' – words now memorised and sung by a whole generation of children.

From the arguably banal to the truly sublime, in an allegorical reading of the Song, the most popular meaning is that the end of winter comes with the incarnation: the birth, death and resurrection of Christ. Christina Rossetti's 1872 hymn 'In the Bleak Midwinter' pictures the earth as 'hard as iron, long ago'. It is in the context of this frozen earth that 'in the bleak midwinter / a stable place sufficed / the Lord God Almighty / Jesus Christ'. The carol is sometimes criticised as being an 'anatopism'; certainly it seldom snows in Bethlehem. But Rossetti's true achievement lies in describing the symbolism of this Song of Songs image as she imagines the earth where 'snow had fallen, snow on snow' now receiving the thawing love of Christ, whose love longs to warm up our world.

For Origen, writing beautifully in the third century, winter being over speaks of the Resurrection of Christ and the defeat of death and this invitation to the Christian to arise: '"Arise my beloved . . ." Why does He say "Arise"? Why does He say "Hasten"? For you I have endured the raging storms, I have borne with the waves that would have assailed you; on your account my soul became sorrowful even unto death. I rose from the dead after drawing the sting of death and loosing the bonds of hell. Therefore I say to you "Arise my fair one and come away, my dove for lo the winter is past; the rain is over and gone. The flowers appear on the earth." I have risen from the dead, I have rebuked the storm, I have offered peace. And because, according to the flesh I was born of a virgin and of the will of my father, and because I have increased in wisdom and stature, "the flowers appear on the earth".'[115]

These verses have spoken to the Church in different centuries: at the time of the Reformation, the winter of formal Latin religion was thawed by evangelical truth. At times of revival, there has been an end to winter in a different way. When, at a Love Feast in Fetter Lane, the Wesleys and George Whitefield felt their cold hearts 'strangely warmed', the result was that instead of the cruel winter of a revolution, as in France, England enjoyed the springtime of revival. Pentecostal or renewal movements are beautiful times when the coldness of people's lives is invaded by springtime and they are transformed forever.

These are major scenes of history, but on a pastoral level I have sometimes spoken these words over a dying person as a blessing. It can speak tenderly of rest coming at the end of a life when the winter of death is, we trust, changed to spring. The dying person will hear the voice of God himself saying, *Arise, my darling, my beautiful one, come with me . . .*

The question may be asked: how can a text possibly 'mean' so much? We may become suspicious that almost anything can be read into the Song of Songs. And yet all the above interpretations are at root the same. They all speak of Christ's invasion of individual lives – and the whole of history – with his saving presence.

For what is winter? I believe that in any life there will be affliction; cold winter, dark night, dry desert or overwhelming waters. This may come as a result of bereavement, depression, sickness or a breakdown in relationships. There may be circumstances of debt or disaster; or simply, in the midst of apparent normality, the absence of God or gladness.

One of the greatest skills in life is to learn how to travel through such troubled times; how to survive them and proceed on our journey. How do we get warm when we have no awareness of the warming love of God and we fear we might die of exposure in discontented winter?

How do we see when we are in the middle of the dark night and the absence of hope is almost crushing us to death?

What direction can we take when all we can see is desert?

Who will throw us a lifeline when we feel we are drowning in the floodwaters?

These four experiences – the winter of death or bereavement; the night of doubt or atheism; the desert of depression or despair; and the waters of disaster – take us into terrain that is tough indeed, but a terrain that is seemingly an unavoidable part of humankind's journey on earth. These four environments are all found in the Song. The Song of Songs is eloquent concerning how we deal with suffering.

Winter and the 'Great Sadness'

Over thirty years ago, our first son died unexpectedly, suddenly, in his cot. It was Sudden Infant Death Syndrome (SIDS). I have written elsewhere about the shock of this and its effect on everything since, and the long winter that followed.

When I was writing a former book, *Epiphanies of the Ordinary*, another winter began for us. A policeman knocked at our door and told us that our personal assistant and dear friend had been suddenly killed – crushed by a cement lorry as she cycled to work. The same day, we agreed with the police that it fell to me to telephone her parents in France to let them know that their beautiful, yet-to-be-married, only daughter was dead. There was a loud cry and deep wailing in the family in those days, like 'Rachel mourning for her children and refusing to be comforted'. Joanna's parents were the most extraordinary example to me of courage and Christ-likeness, forgiving the driver of the lorry when the case finally came to court and speaking to all, including the media, without bitterness and with tenderness. But if we her friends were in a winter, then they her parents were in the beginning of an ice age.

In the popular novel *The Shack*, the death of a child is referred to as the 'Great Sadness'.[116] I used to think such a 'Great Sadness' was pretty rare. But I have come to realise that most people, if not all, walk through a winter of bereavement. This may be the death of a colleague, a parent, a spouse, a sibling, a child, a dear friend. But it may be the death of a relationship: divorce or estrangement from a child or colleagues. Or it may be the death of a dream – afflicting us for stretches of our life. At the time of writing, several parts of the world are plunged into war or terror, with the ensuing loss, sometimes, of literally everything. Of course each pain is relative in its severity. But all are real and all are, in a way, 'winters'.

We may feel such times should be an exception and are to be snapped out of. Christians particularly may feel that they should be the happiest people on earth and that if they don't have an upbeat attitude and optimistic faith, then they are a failure at life. But to pretend to have such a positive attitude when the world is cold around us only feels wrong and is not true either to ourselves or to the circumstances.

On that bleak day of the death of our child, our world lost all its colour at a stroke, turning to sunless grey. I remember hunching my shoulders and bracing myself at death's icy blast. I prayed for resurrection from the dead. But no answer came; not of the kind I wanted. And so a cold and constrained time began.

It did not end for three years.

This is the experience of winter. In Europe we know that winter should only last three months before spring comes. But there can be parts of our lives, and there are parts of the world, where it never ends. In Lewis's Narnia, the effect of the White Witch's occupation is exactly that: 'always winter but never Christmas'.

However, the Song of Songs is often most eloquent in what it leaves unsaid and this is true of its description of the winter's end. The Song simply says that it is over. In one of the best-loved passages of the Bible, often quoted at weddings, the beloved 'darling' Church is told: *Arise, my darling, my beautiful one, come with me. See! The winter is past; the rains are over and gone. Flowers appear on the earth; the season of singing has come . . .* (2:10–12).

How does winter end? Well, it just ends: one day we are 'surprised by joy'. We feel it wrong to laugh, but laughter comes. It is the end of winter.

The Song speaks here of flowers, singing, blossom, fragrance and fruit. It is a change of climate, a season change. With time, it will happen. Time and tears are great healers. The word of God will gently warm us each day, if we will let it. Now, we may feel this spring will not happen till heaven – and we may even be right. Someone wrote to me this week speaking of something so complex he opined that it may be in the category of what he called P.W.B.R.T.S.O.H. ('Probably

Won't Be Resolved This Side Of Heaven'). But if this is the case, even then we can take heart, as heaven will come sooner than we think. 'Behold, you have made my days a few hand-breadths' (Psalm 39:5; ESV). But one day we will join him in an eternal springtime: 'He will wipe every tear from their eyes. There will be no more death or mourning or crying or pain' (Revelation 21:4). When heaven comes down to earth, springtime will be here and all will be well. As the saying goes: 'Everything will be okay in the end. If it's not okay, it's not the end.'[117]

Just having this perspective can bring a change of climate to our lives. Spring brings buds and blossom and, in the end, fruit. The fruits of the Spirit can begin to form: patience, kindness, goodness and love adorn the lives of those emerging from winter. Gregory of Nyssa interprets this: 'But then there came the One who works in us the springtime of our souls, the One who, when an evil wind was agitating the sea, said: "Peace, be still!" – and all became calm and still. Once again our nature began to flourish and be adorned with its own blossoms. But the blossoms that are proper to our lives are the virtues, which put forth flowers now but bear their fruit in their own time. The Word says: "The Winter is past." "You see," he says, the meadow is blooming because of the virtues. You see: that is self-control, the bright and fragrant lily; you see reverence, the red rose. You see the violet, the sweet smell of Christ.'[118]

Lifting your face and finding your voice

My dove in the clefts of the rock, in the hiding places on the mountain-side, show me your face, let me hear your voice; for your voice is sweet, and your face is lovely (2:14)

Many are those who, when faced with the intimacy of the divine romance and its challenge to transparency, react by hiding their faces and keeping quiet. It is like a bride who dare not lift up her face and speak to her husband; a sad story. The reasons for this tendency in human love relationships to hide ourselves may just be to do with upbringing – there may be embarrassment at expressing feelings to others. But there may also be low self-esteem, fear of failure or past pain – our own secret history. I have known many for whom just to become aware of this frozenness in their behaviour leads to action that enables them to warm up and be healed. I have been involved in some moving seasons in which people 'come back to their first love' and learn a new language of love.

Maybe I empathise because this kind of awakening is part of my own story. When I was aged fourteen, my parents got divorced. The news broke out of the blue and completely shocked me. I had not been aware of any difficulty in my parents' marriage. I appeared to recover and cope well through adolescence. But deep down there were consequences that did not come to the surface until I in turn entered my own marriage, when my wife found me almost incapable of expressing my feelings. I was gregarious in company, but at home, when it came to expressing what was going on under the surface, there was complete silence. My wife could have quoted these words from the Song to me literally: *My dove in the clefts of the rock, in the hiding places on the mountainside, show me your face, let me hear your voice; for your voice is sweet.* The healing came as she loved and coaxed me into communication, and frozen winter turned into spring.

In the divine romance, we may experience awe – and also shame. The beloved feels her unworthiness to be loved. This is the reaction of those confronted with theophanies in the Bible, whether Moses, Joshua, Job, Isaiah or Jeremiah; and it is appropriate to be speechless in the Presence. But the voice of God in such times is always saying, 'Fear not.' When this 'fear not' is heard, there can then be extreme loquacity, for example Mary's Magnificat, John's Revelation or the psalmist's torrents of wordy worship. The miracle is that the divine lover of our souls asks us to lift up our heads and to dare to speak. The Bride hides herself away and loses her voice. We need to hear the voice of the lover of our souls, who beckons us: 'Look up!'

Christians, or whole churches, can and need to learn to show their faces and let their voices be heard. If they will do so then, as in a marriage, there will be an exponential advance in the relationship.

When renewal occurs, it is often accompanied by fluency in prayer, in worship, in witness. Pentecost was accompanied by speaking in tongues. Justin Welby, Archbishop of Canterbury, recently said that for him, since his own experience of renewal, speaking in tongues became routine: 'It's just a routine part of spiritual discipline – you choose to speak and you speak a language that you don't know. It just comes.'[119] And there is a sense in which this essential lifting up of the head and beginning to speak is part of the 'discipline of intimacy'.

Let me hear your voice . . .

This verse provokes the question: is your voice one of those that is heard in heaven? I have travelled and seen the tear-stained faces of the suffering Church lifted up to heaven in constant prayer, particularly in Asia, in Africa, in South America. By contrast, in the UK and Europe and North

America, I sometimes feel Christ is like a bridegroom whose bride will hardly talk to him – she may sit quiet to listen; but will she let him hear her own voice? Will she lift up her face to speak, bringing transparency and healing and intimacy? A mark of renewal is that the language of prayer begins to flow.

The season of singing

With the sound of prayer comes the season of singing; the Song of Songs is after all a 'song'. This is the only place where singing is mentioned, but there is nothing strange in that; indeed, few songs mention the singing.

The singing here is brought about by the end to winter. It is drawn out by the voice of the Beloved saying, *Arise, my darling*. The fact that the rains are over and gone and flowers appear on the earth means that *the season of singing* is here.

Singing is a fascinating gift. Probably everyone has a song inside them – at least, everyone who has not been silenced. But even in times of trouble or imprisonment, there can be a song: negro spirituals emerged from suffering and slavery. People sing in their car, through pain and through joy, at weddings or funerals, at football matches and medals ceremonies. Lovers have 'their song'.

There is at this time an increasing popularity of song. In Britain a heart-stopping 'military wives' choir stole the small screen. In the United States, choral singing is the most popular of all arts-related participatory activities – across the country, 28.5 million people sing regularly, in one of 250,000 chorus groups. *The X Factor* is one of the most popular shows around the world.

Why the huge interest in karaoke? Why all the singing in the shower, in the car, in the chorus?

Researchers are beginning to discover that singing is like an infusion of the perfect tranquiliser – the kind that both soothes your nerves and elevates your spirits. 'The elation may come from endorphins, a hormone released by singing, which is associated with feelings of pleasure. Or it might be from oxytocin, another hormone released during singing, which has been found to alleviate anxiety and stress. Oxytocin also enhances feelings of trust and bonding, which may explain why still other studies have found that singing lessens feelings of depression and loneliness.'[120]

Michael Mayne, one-time Dean of Westminster Abbey, goes so far as to say: 'In the beginning was the Song: it is a concept as poetic and full of mystery as the story of creation in Genesis, or St John's affirmation: "In the beginning was the Word".'[121] The Christian writer J. R. R. Tolkien, at the start of *The Silmarillion*, imagines the dawn of creation for his 'Middle Earth' as one beautiful, developing, contested but perfect song.

The link between sexuality and singing is expressed by Janis Joplin who said: 'When I sing, I feel like when you're first in love. It's more than sex. It's that point two people can get to they call love, when you really touch someone for the first time, but it's gigantic, multiplied by the whole audience. I feel chills.'[122]

Apparently the hills are capable of singing together for joy (Psalm 98:8), the trees can sing too (Isaiah 44:23) and at the dawn of time, 'the morning stars sang together' (Job 38:7). It is not just the birds that sing, then – although their song is powerful too. Gerard Manley Hopkins wrote of the effect of their song: 'Nothing is so beautiful as spring – / when . . . / . . . thrush / through the echoing timber does so rinse and wring / the ear, it strikes like lightnings to hear him sing.'[123]

This 'lightning strike' of song is intriguing. Why should
it be so? Is there something vulnerable about singing, in
that the inner voice is heard in it? At any rate, in the exercises at the end of this chapter, I include the exercise of
composing and singing your own song. It is challenging,
but if you can cultivate a season of singing in your own life
it can be a deep thing. Sometimes singing is a yearning to
hope: 'Sing, barren woman . . . burst into song . . .' says the
prophet Isaiah (54:1), and we can do this even in times of
pain and darkness. As we do so, we will find the healing
power of song.

When I told the worship leader Martin Smith I was writing
a book on the Song of Songs, his immediate response was:
'What will that look like? Will a tune pop out each time you
open the book?' Now that is quite an idea: a book like some
of those birthday cards you can buy which play a tune when
you open them. But I guess the season of singing is a time
when a song emerges each time you open your heart.

The ruining foxes
*Catch for us the foxes, the little foxes that ruin the vineyards, our vine-
yards that are in bloom (2:15)*
'Foxes' could mean anything that ruins our relationship of
intimacy, on a human level and also in the Church. It may
be poor self-esteem, low thoughts, sin, habitual addictions
and temptations. These foxes need to be caught. We can
catch them but there needs to be effort and focused intention. Our relationships are often destroyed not so much by
big issues but by little ones – seemingly insignificant choices
and compromises. As Joyce Meyer writes: 'Watch the "little
foxes" in your life; forgive even the most minor offence so
that your heart stays clean, do not cut corners in your

finances or on the job when you think no one will notice, do not expose yourself to ungodly influences, thinking, *It won't hurt me if I do it just this once*. Little things add up to big things, and before you know it, little foxes can ruin a strong, healthy vine.'[124]

Anyone who has tried to keep chickens will know the reality of the war against the fox! Roald Dahl's *Fantastic Mr Fox* reversed the mythology and made a hero out of the fox. But in biblical terms (and on real farms), the fox always stands for the enemy. 'At that time some Pharisees came to Jesus and said to him, "Leave this place and go somewhere else. Herod wants to kill you." He replied, "Go tell that fox, 'I will keep on driving out demons and healing people today and tomorrow, and on the third day I will reach my goal'"' (Luke 13:31–32). Thus, as far as the Church is concerned, the fox is the old enemy who wants to kill the Christ.

Gregory again: '"Like a lion he lies awake in his lair" (Ps 9:30). He is the great dragon the Apostate, Hades which opens its mouth, the world ruler of the power of darkness, he who has the power of death . . . He is the one who seizes the inhabited earth as it were a nest and takes it up like forsaken eggs (Isa 10:14). He is the one who says his throne sits above the clouds and that he is like the Most High God (Isa 14:13–14). But how, I say, is this one named by the true and only Power? *He is a little fox!* And all those about, the army that is under his orders, are all disparagingly named in the same way by the one who urges the hunters to chase them down.'[125]

For Augustine, foxes are heretics: 'their fronts display a deceptive charm, but their rear ends are bound, that is sentenced. They drag firebrands behind them to burn up those who are seduced by them.'[126]

We can hunt our foxes down, though – through confession in community, through prayer and through a transformed lifestyle. The spiritual exercises at the end of this chapter explore this in practical ways.

My beloved is mine and I am his; he browses among the lilies. Until the day breaks and the shadows flee, turn, my beloved, and be like a gazelle or like a young stag on the rugged hills (2:16–17)

The chapter ends with an expression of exclusiveness appropriate to marriage: *My beloved is mine and I am his*. The evocative phrase *Until the day breaks and the shadows flee*, gives us hints perhaps of the shadows in life, in this time of a 'groaning creation'. Much of our experience is shrouded in darkness. But in this season, the Bride delights in the stag's strength and youthfulness. The phrase is repeated in 4:6: *Until the day breaks and the shadows flee, I will go to the mountain of myrrh and to the hill of incense*. For the Father's Son this had to do with the hill of Calvary and the incense and sacrifice for our sins offered up there. This is the same hill to which the Bride resolves to go.

We will return to this rich imagery, but for now we will close with exercises appropriate to the themes of this chapter.

Spiritual exercises for catching 'the little foxes that ruin the vineyard' and the season of singing

Ignatius's *Spiritual Exercises* concentrate for a week on the reality of sin and identifying what might be repetitive patterns. One exercise is as follows:

'I will call to memory *all the sins of a lifetime*, looking back on them from year to year or from one period to another. For this, three things will be helpful:

1. To see the place and house where I lived
2. The relations I had with others
3. The occupation in which I have spent my life.

To weigh these sins, considering the intrinsic foulness and malice of each deadly sin.'[127]

To record this in a journal is quite telling, especially if you are attentive to any 'little foxes that ruin the vineyard'. Spend some time repenting and turning from these sins one by one.

Then 'consider who God is, against whom I have sinned, going through his attributes and contrasting them with their opposites in myself: his goodness with my malice' etc.

Conclude with time spent considering mercy, 'conversing with God our Lord and thanking him for giving me life up till now, proposing for the future to amend my life with his grace'.

Find a place where you can speak out loud to God, remembering his call to you: 'O my beloved in the cleft of the rock: let me hear your voice . . .'

Write a song, however short, perhaps coming out of this meditation on his mercy, and then sing it to God.

'Take these words in. I say my friends and daughters of Jerusalem; for within this love there lives a deep desire. For my part . . . How many sleepless nights do you reckon I have spent watching him and hearing him? For the daytime was not enough to satisfy such a desire, but night by night on my bed and in my chamber I would cherish and adore . . . when in the midst of sweet conversations, by his eyes he filled me with the look of his divinity . . .'
Rupert of Deutz, writing between 1170 and 1229[128]

'This world has its nights – not few in number. I say the world has its nights, but it is almost all night, and always plunged in complete darkness.'
Bernard of Clairvaux[129]

CHAPTER SEVEN

Night Vision

*All night long on my bed I looked for the one my heart
loves; I looked for him but did not find him.*
*I will get up now and go about the city, through its streets
and squares; I will search for the one my heart loves. So
I looked for him but did not find him.*
*The watchmen found me as they made their rounds in the
city. 'Have you seen the one my heart loves?'*
*Scarcely had I passed them when I found the one my heart
loves. I held him and would not let him go till I had
brought him to my mother's house, to the room of the one
who conceived me.*
*Daughters of Jerusalem, I charge you by the gazelles and by
the does of the field: Do not arouse or awaken love until
it so desires.*

Song of Songs 3:1–5

Following the Bride's escape from winter, at the start of
Chapter 3 of the Song we come across the first mention of
'night' (3:1). The writer will bring us back to this theme for
a full description of what John of the Cross calls the 'dark
night of the soul' in Chapter 5, but for now there is an experience of darkness, of seeking that is not satisfied.

This yearning may occur in a marriage: when a couple
continually 'miss' each other and the result is pain, a longing
for reconnection. A degree of pain is part of any relationship,
of course, and if we are fortunate it can be a time of growth

– growing pains. This night of 'missing' each other can come through sadness, external pressures, tragedy. A joyful event, the arrival of children, can be followed by post-natal depression for some. Or it may be the sheer pace of life, lack of money, threat to employment, difficult neighbours, housing issues: the list of life-darkening possibilities is long!

In the Song, the Bride is unashamed in her desire and her searching. It is a fortunate husband who has a bride who will not settle for less than the best, however challenging this may be to him. This Bride is brave and courageous, admitting her dissatisfaction and longing. She is a contrast to many brides (and indeed husbands) who internalise their yearning and accustom themselves to a bleak, un-intimate relationship. We protect ourselves from rejection and maybe just stop seeking for better. By contrast, this Bride goes on looking, asking with vulnerability, and is rewarded eventually by finding 'him whom my soul loves'.

For the holy longing, commentators have almost universally landed on the idea of absence leading to increased 'desire'. Thus Bernard, interpreting this in what was his seventy-fifth sermon on the first twenty-five verses of the Song, says: '"On my bed night after night I sought him whom my soul loves." The Bridegroom has not returned when the Bride calls him back with cries and prayers. Why has he not? He wishes to increase her desire, test her affection, and exercise her faculty of love. He is not displeased with her, he is concealing his love.'[130]

This concept of the 'concealing of the love of God' is explored by C. S. Lewis in *The Screwtape Letters* when Lewis speaks of the strategy of God, after someone becomes a Christian, at a certain point to remove the sense of the 'experience of the presence of God', and to ask the person to continue to love God even in his apparent absence. Here the two tempters discuss what they take to be the way of God: 'Do not be deceived, Wormwood. Our cause is never more in danger than when a human, no longer desiring, but still intending, to do our Enemy's will, looks round upon a universe from which every trace of Him seems to have vanished, and asks why he has been forsaken, and still obeys.'[131]

I write this for those who are in Darkness. Darkness can be any suffering or trauma leading to absence. It can indeed be 'Darkness at Noon'.[132] Sometimes I sit listening with people who are in the night. It is as if the light they need to show the way is simply gone. I remember a teacher who winsomely told her children about the love of God while at the same time secretly questioning whether he existed at all, because of the suffering she saw in the world. Thankfully she came through this absence and darkness to find again the presence of God. I think of the film producer who just cannot break through into the presence of God, and simply has to hold on by an act of will as he walks through the darkness.

There is a demonic dimension to this darkness when the dominant voices of culture seem to speak out persuasively and seductively against Christianity. The much-repeated call from media platforms in the Western world seems to be: 'Admit it, there is no God – or if there is, don't take him too seriously; please at least make a joke about it.' More recently, the rise of a religion of terror has made such laughter doubly inappropriate.

I believe that we are in the midst of a season of darkness. Atheism is advertised on buses or broadcast on TV chat shows, the darlings of our culture are, by and large, godless, and the so-called New Atheism is ever more popular. It masquerades as scientific but is in fact merely soulless, and strident in its attacks against Christianity in all its forms.

This is the only thing new about the New Atheism: whereas before people could live in mutual respect of opinions held, it seems now that faith in God is to be hounded out of the public square by verbal scorn.

Darkness is not just a matter of philosophy or politics, of course; it is personal, and plunges real people into a private dark night of the soul where 'love grows cold'. Jesus speaks about this darkness: 'You will be hated by all nations because of me. At that time many will turn away from the faith and will betray and hate each other, and many false prophets will appear and deceive many people. Because of the increase of wickedness, the love of most will grow cold' (Matthew 24:10–12). If you are walking through the darkness of doubt, the very atmosphere that pervades our land may be contributing to stifle and throttle your faith too. It is into these experiences that the Bride speaks: *All night long on my bed I looked for the one my heart loves.*

Bernard writes of this general interpretation, widening it to include different eras of history:

> If you have no better explanation, I suggest this as a possibility. This world has its nights – not few in number. I say the world has its nights, but it is almost all night, and always plunged in complete darkness. The faithlessness of the Jews, the ignorance of pagans, the perversity of heretics, the shameless and degraded behaviour of Christians – these are all nights. For surely it is night when the things which belong to the Spirit of God are not perceived? . . . In those nights you will look in vain for the sun of justice and the light of truth, that is, the Bridegroom, because light has nothing to do with darkness . . .[133]

The fact in this passage also is that in the midst of darkness, the lover will be found by those who seek him. Humankind longs for God and looks for him.

In this section, it is interesting to note the progress the Bride makes:

> *I love him . . . (him whom my soul loves)*
> *I sought him . . .*
> *I found him not . . .*
> *I found him . . .*
> *I held him . . .*
> *I brought him home . . .*
> (ESV)

In a human love affair, there may in a time of crisis be a point where it is right to abandon decorum and go searching, even through the night. As a father might search for a lost teenager, so a bride might search for her husband through their night. Or a husband will go out into the city searching. It is a time of crisis, when nothing else matters.

In the divine romance, the Bride seeks her husband all night long; she goes about the city, and for the Fathers this was pictured as running throughout the 'design of the Divine Law', the Pentateuch,[134] seeking him. She asks the 'Watchmen', the leaders and gatekeepers of the Church, for help. Bernard continues: 'When he did not return at this call . . . then she who loved him became more eager and devoted herself eagerly and entirely to seeking him. First she sought him in her bed . . . Then she arose and wandered through the city . . . She questions everyone she meets, but there is no news; nor is this search and this disappointment confined to one night or one street, for she says, "I sought him night after night." How great must be her longing and her ardour, that she does not blush to rise in the night and be seen running through the city, questioning everyone openly about her beloved . . . Yet in all this she is still disappointed of her hope. Why? What is the reason for this long, unrelenting disappointment, which induces weariness, foments suspicion, inflames impatience, acts as a stepmother to love and a mother to despair? If he is still concealing his love, it is too painful.'[135]

Similarly, in the dark night of the absence of God we may also feel 'it is too painful'. Those in the darkness of the terminal illness of a loved one, or dealing with the more and more common darkness that is dementia, may join with Bernard in a contemporary cry of, 'It is too painful.' But this text encourages us: if we seek him, if we go about the city of God, if we go out and ask of 'the Watchmen', 'Have *you* seen him?' – if we humble ourselves, perhaps being helped through other traditions of the Church who have an understanding of theophany, contemplation and the capacity to see *him whom my soul loves* – we are on the right track. Then may it be that we in the end find him, and our finding will be all the sweeter for our faithful seeking of him.

> . . . *I found him whom my soul loves. I held him, and would not let him go until I had brought him into my mother's house, and into the chamber of her who conceived me. I adjure you, O daughters of Jerusalem, by the gazelles or the does of the field, that you not stir up or awaken love until it pleases.* (Songs 3:4–5; ESV)

In 1872, C. H. Spurgeon preached on what he felt was the meaning of these verses, namely: 'The Real Presence, The

Great Want of the Church'. Spurgeon was of course speaking not of a bodily presence but of the promise of the Holy Spirit in the Church: Christ has promised and assured believers of his presence – 'Lo, I am with you always'; 'Abide in me and I in you'; 'I will send another Comforter and he will be with you and he will be in you'. These promises are all experienced by the early Church from the day of Pentecost onwards. Again and again we read, 'Great grace was upon them all', or 'While they were worshipping, the Holy Spirit said . . .', and again, 'And the hand of the Lord was with them' – and so on.

Spurgeon speaks of this experience of God's presence through his Spirit as being the 'glory of the church', and I agree. I have known people join our church for many reasons but most often they stay because of one: the presence of God. There can be great good in discovering purpose and fruit in being a 'purpose-driven' church. But I often say to the flock I serve: 'Let us be a presence-led church rather than anything else.' With his nineteenth-century passion Spurgeon puts it like this: 'His presence is the glory of the church of God. When she is without it she is shorn of her strength; when she possesses it all good things ensue. Brethren, if a church be without the Spirit of God in it, it may have a name to live, but it is dead, and you know that after death there follows corruption, corruption which breeds foulness and disease . . . We must have Christ in the church, or the body which was meant to be the medium of the greatest good becomes the source of the grossest evil. Let the Spirit of God be in the church, then there is power given to all her ministries; whether they be ministries of public testimony in the preaching of the word, or ministries of holy love amongst the brethren, or ministries of individual earnestness to the outside world, they will all be clothed with energy, in the fullness of the power of the Lord Jesus.'[136]

In these verses from the Song, there is an energy to find the Presence of God again that is worthy of note both for our personal and our corporate lives. Thus we can say we must use all means to find him: heartfelt prayer; intimate, seeking worship; Scripture meditation, study, contemplation; fellowship, teaching, community; serving the poor and the lost, works of justice and so on. All these are to be used as the Bride seeks the Bridegroom.

Spurgeon continues: 'These ardent lovers of Jesus must diligently seek him. The chapter before us says that the spouse sought him, sought him on her bed, sought him in the streets, sought him in the broadways, sought him at last at the lips of the watchmen, sought him everywhere where he was likely to be found. We must enjoy the perpetual fellowship of Jesus. We who love him in our souls cannot rest until we know that he is with us. I fear that with some of us our sins have grieved him, and he has betaken himself to the far-off "mountains of myrrh and hills of frankincense".'

The great fact here is that *she* finds *him*: he can be found by us, and will be found. And when we do find him? We note that she is careful not to let him go. This implies he can be let go. But she brings him into the house where her mother conceived her – into the Church, as it were. She does not take him away to some new place or into a 'New Thing', but comes back to refresh and renew the known places – the ancient paths, the ancient future. Then, when he is there with her again, she takes care not to drive him away; not to 'awaken Love until it pleases'. James Durham compares this to Jacob's wrestling with the angel:

1. A holy kind of violence, more than an ordinary, wherewith the Bride strives and wrestles to retain him.
2. That Christ (as it were) waits for the believer's consent in this wrestling, as he says to Jacob, Gen. 32:26, 'I pray you, let me go:' which upon the matter seems to say, I will not go, if you will hold me, and have me stay.
3. An importunate adhering to him, and not consenting upon any terms to quit him.
4. Lastly the singular and inexpressible satisfaction she had in him; her very life lay in the keeping him still with her, and therefore she holds him, and cannot think of parting with him.

Durham concludes: 'A humble, ardent suing to him by prayer, with a lively exercise of faith on his promises (whereby he allows his people to be pressing) engages him to stay . . . as a little weeping child will hold its mother or nurse, not because it is stronger than she, but because the mother's bowels so constrain her, as she cannot almost, though she would, leave that child; so Christ's bowels yearning over a believer, are that which here hold him, that he cannot go; he cannot go, because he will not. Here we have ground to observe the importunateness of sincere love, which is such, as with an holy wilfulness it holds to Christ and will not quit him.'[137]

Misty Edwards puts this poetically and urgently in her song on this passage, 'My Soul Cries':

As the deer pants for the water, my soul longs for You
As the body dies without water, my soul dies without You
Take me to the place where You satisfy, take me to the river
They may say, 'Come on, get over it, everything is okay'

> They may say, 'Why the hunger?
> Why the thirsting? Why the mourning?'
> But my soul cries, my soul cries.

Misty is a worship leader with the International House of Prayer in Kansas City. Its leader, Mike Bickle, has made an appreciation of the Song of Songs part of the foundation of this work. Several of Misty's songs are sung expositions of the Song. Her cry is like that of a Hannah in expressing the desire of the Bride in this third chapter.[138]

I charge you by the gazelles and by the does of the field (v. 5)
In ancient times tamed gazelles were favoured companions of Eastern women: the gazelle might be standing near its mistress, fixing its loving eyes upon her, but if a stranger clapped his hands it would hurry away. The roes and hinds *of the field*, though, were even more sensitive; any sound would startle them, and the dangerous scent of a hunter on the wind would put them to flight. Spurgeon concludes: 'Even thus is it with Jesus. A little thing, a very little thing, will drive him from us.'

Spiritual exercises for seeing in the dark

> On my bed by night I sought him whom my soul loves; I sought
> him, but found him not. I will rise now and go about the city . . .
> (Songs 3:1; ESV)

This seeking of God at night is a frequent theme in Scripture. If you find yourself sleepless, remember that this may be God getting your attention. Psalm 77:4 says: 'You hold my eyelids open' (ESV).

For this exercise, simply note some of the psalmist's experience below and rather than counting sheep, talk to the Shepherd.

In the night watches, use the Lord's Prayer phrase by phrase as a ladder into Christ's presence (see Appendix 1). As you do this, remember these psalms:

> I bless the Lord who gives me counsel; in the night also my heart instructs me. I have set the Lord always before me; because he is at my right hand, I shall not be shaken. (Psalm 16:7–8; ESV)

> My soul thirsts for God . . . My tears have been my food day and night when I remember you upon my bed, and meditate on you in the watches of the night . . . My soul clings to you; your right hand upholds me. (Psalm 63; ESV)

> In the day of my trouble I seek the Lord; in the night my hand is stretched out without wearying; my soul refuses to be comforted. When I remember God, I moan; when I meditate, my spirit faints. Selah. You hold my eyelids open. (Psalm 77:2–4; ESV)

'She comes like "pillars of smoke;" and as smoke fleeing from kindled fire (especially new kindled) cannot but ascend, cannot but have smoke and that in abundance; so now the church being warmed, and of fresh inflamed and made lively with Christ's presence, cannot but send out a sweet savour, which discernibly ascends upward from the world (which is but a wilderness) as smoke doth from the earth.'[139]
James Durham

'Now when the turn came for each young woman to go in to King Ahasuerus, after being twelve months under the regulations for the women, since this was the regular period of their beautifying, six months with oil of myrrh and six months with spices and ointments for women . . . the king loved Esther more than all the women, and she won grace and favour in his sight more than all the virgins, so that he set the royal crown on her head and made her queen.'
Esther 2:12, 17

CHAPTER EIGHT

Wedding Preparations

Who is this coming up from the wilderness like a column of
smoke, perfumed with myrrh and incense made from all
the spices of the merchant?
Look! It is Solomon's carriage, escorted by sixty warriors,
the noblest of Israel,
All of them wearing the sword, all experienced in battle,
each with his sword at his side, prepared for the terrors of
the night. King Solomon made for himself the carriage;
he made it of wood from Lebanon.
Its posts he made of silver, its base of gold. Its seat was
upholstered with purple, its interior inlaid with love.
Daughters of Jerusalem, come out, and look, you daughters
of Zion. Look on King Solomon wearing a crown, the
crown with which his mother crowned him on the day of
his wedding, the day his heart rejoiced.

Song of Songs 3:6–11

In our church community in Oxford, there are numerous
weddings. A great deal of care goes into preparations: it is a
joy to behold the imaginative inventiveness that goes into
these events. You may have come across similar or been
involved yourself. There is the dress, the bridesmaids' dresses,
the hair, the nails, the flowers, bright colours, the groom's
and ushers' outfits, the decorations, the reception, the menu,

the service, the music, the programmes, the guest list, over-
night accommodation, the hen night, the stag night (a Song
of Songs concept, incidentally), to say nothing of finding a
marriage preparation course,[140] the future home, organising
the present list and so on. Preparation is an industry all of its
own and hence the job of 'wedding planner' has been
invented. I sometimes think the stress involved in wedding
preparation is an ideal preparation for life itself! If you are
reading this preparing for marriage, then may God give you
time and capacity quietly and carefully to get ready.

It is King Solomon who is well prepared here and men could
learn that it is not only for women to get ready but for them as
well. The necessary preparations for marriage are both outward
and internal. Here Solomon has a crown on his head, and
inside his heart there is 'rejoicing' (v. 11). He is leaving his
mother and cleaving to his wife in order to become one flesh.

I believe that Genesis 2:24, 'a man leaves his father and
mother and is united to his wife, and they become one flesh',
is reflected in this Song of Songs passage. It is a procession of
leaving. This idea is important enough to be quoted by Jesus
in Matthew 19:5, and by Paul in Ephesians 5:31. To 'leave' is
sometimes difficult for a man – leaving parents, mother, past
experiences; past pain perhaps, too. But without leaving, it is
hard for there to be the necessary cleaving. I find it helpful to
think of this process in the light of Solomon with his sixty
warriors here as a procession accompanied by friends. His
mother has 'crowned him' and this can be seen as a mother
letting him go and giving him his own authority, as she must.
If this is done, figuratively, during wedding preparations and
into the marriage, then this is healthy. Such are some of the
preparations, outward and inward, needed for a wedding.

But I often wonder: does as much care go into preparing

people (including you and me) for the coming of *the* Bridegroom? I wonder: have you chosen your clothes yet? Have you got your invitation? Have you got your oil for your lamp, in case he comes at night? Have you got your 'fine linen, bright and clean'? Are you ready? Are you in love? Do you talk to the Bridegroom? You can't make a phone call to him every day – but you can speak lovingly daily: you can be in constant communication with him; you can certainly prepare.

The book of Revelation speaks of this time when the marriage supper of the Lamb at last happens. There, Revelation says: '". . . his Bride has made herself ready. Fine linen, bright and clean, was given her to wear." (Fine linen stands for the righteous acts of God's holy people)' (Revelation 19:7–8).

For the rest of this chapter we will speak of the divine romance, so rich is the application. The passage here is about someone 'emerging from the wilderness' prepared, perfumed, processing, with 'daughters of Jerusalem' helping.

It can be read about the Bride (the Church) and it can also be read as being about the Bridegroom (Christ).

Contemplating Christ

Look on King Solomon . . .

Christ is the 'One greater than Solomon' who truly emerges from the wilderness of the world perfumed with myrrh. The New Testament shows us that Solomon is a type of Christ in all his wisdom and beauty: in *The Message*, Matthew 12:41–42 reads: 'On Judgment Day, the Queen of Sheba will come forward and bring evidence that will condemn this generation, because she travelled from a far corner of the earth to listen to wise Solomon. Wisdom far greater than Solomon's is right in front of you.'

The exhortations here are to: *Come out . . . Look at . . . Gaze on . . . him* (v. 11; ESV).

Puritan writer Thomas Brooks says: 'He is a jewel more worth than a thousand worlds, as all know who have him. Get him, and get all; miss him and miss all . . . The soul can crave nothing, nor wish for anything, but what is to be found in this Portion. He is light to enlighten the soul, wisdom to counsel the soul, power to support the soul, goodness to supply the soul, mercy to pardon the soul, beauty to delight the soul, glory to ravish the soul, and fullness to fill the soul.'[141]

In a passage very instructive to those learning about meditation on the Bible and *Lectio Divina*, C. H. Spurgeon urged his congregation to 'see the Lord':

'And behold King Solomon.' To-day let your eye rest upon him. Let your eye behold the head that to-day is crowned with glory, wearing many crowns. Behold, too, his hands which once were pierced, but are now grasping the scepter. Look to his girdle where swing the keys of heaven, and death, and hell. Look to his feet, once pierced with iron, but now set upon the dragon's head. Behold his legs, like fine brass, as if they glowed in a furnace. Look at his heart, that bosom which heaves with love for you, and when you have surveyed him from head to foot exclaim, 'Yea, he is the chief among ten thousand, and altogether lovely.'[142]

The book of Revelation talks to the lukewarm Laodicean church as needing to 'buy eye salve' in order to 'see' and not be blind. Spurgeon goes on, piling up image upon image in his exhortation to 'behold him' and the application for daily living that flows from that. 'Do not think that Christ has lost his former power. Behold him as he was at Pentecost, with the crown wherewith his mother crowned him in the day of his espousals . . . when the Church crowned him with her zeal, and the arrows went abroad, and three thousand fell slain by his right hand to be made alive by the breath of his mouth! Oh, how these early saints crowned him, when they brought of their substance and laid it at the apostles' feet . . .'

So, how do we look on him? People have different ways. Throughout this book I propose the time-honoured route of meditation and contemplation often known as *Lectio Divina*. *Lectio Divina* has been likened to 'Feasting on the Word'. The four parts are, first, taking a bite (*Lectio*), then chewing on it (*Meditatio*). Next is the opportunity to savour the essence of it (*Oratio*). Finally, the Word is digested and made a part of the body (*Contemplatio*). In Christian teachings, this form of meditative prayer leads to an increased knowledge of Christ.

Lectio: read

The first step is the reading of Scripture. However, it is generally recommended that we prepare for *Lectio Divina*, in order to achieve a calm and tranquil state of mind. As it says in Psalm 46:10: 'Be still, and know that I am God.' An example would be sitting quietly, and in prayer inviting the Holy Spirit to guide the reading of the Scripture that is to follow.

Following the preparation, the first movement of *Lectio Divina* is a slow and careful reading of the scriptural passage, perhaps several times over. In the traditional Benedictine approach the passage would be read slowly four times, each time with a slightly different focus.

Meditatio: meditate

Although *Lectio Divina* involves reading, it is less a practice of reading than one of listening to the inner message of the

Scripture delivered through the Holy Spirit. *Lectio Divina* does not seek information or motivation, but communion with God. The second movement in *Lectio Divina* thus involves meditating upon and dwelling over the scriptural passage. When the passage is read, it is generally advised not to try to assign a meaning to it at first, but to wait for the action of the Holy Spirit to illuminate the mind, as the passage is pondered upon.

The English word 'ponder' comes from the Latin *pondus*, from which we get the word 'pound', here relating to the mental activity of weighing or considering. To ponder on the passage that has been read, it is held and gently considered from various angles. Again, the emphasis is not on analysis of the passage but on keeping the mind open and allowing the Holy Spirit to inspire. We can also use smell, sight, sound, touch and hearing, allowing and let the five senses to be involved in our meditation.

Oratio: pray

Prayer is loving conversation with God, who has invited us into his embrace. Saint Ambrose stated regarding the importance of prayer in conjunction with Scripture reading: 'And let them remember that prayer should accompany the reading of Sacred Scripture, so that God and man may talk together; for "we speak to Him when we pray; we hear Him when we read the divine saying".'

Contemplatio: contemplate

Contemplation takes place in silent prayer that expresses love for God. The Catechism of the Catholic Church states: 'Contemplative prayer is silence, the "symbol of the world to come" or "silent love." Words in this kind of prayer are not speeches; they are like kindling that feeds the fire of love. In this silence, unbearable to the "outer" man, the Father speaks to us his incarnate Word, who suffered, died, and rose; in this silence the Spirit of adoption enables us to share in the prayer of Jesus.'[143]

In 3:11 of the Song we are encouraged to *go out . . . and look on him*, and as we do, we may think of different scenes of the life of the lover of our souls. For example, we are reminded that he comes out of the desert of obscurity to be baptised by John – and heaven opens: 'Come and look at what is happening . . .' Then we may think of him coming into Jerusalem on a donkey, with the crowd saying: Who is this? He is perfumed with myrrh ready for his sacrifice. We can consider and meditate on these scenes in the light of the passage before us:

> *What is that coming up from the wilderness like columns of smoke, perfumed with myrrh and frankincense, with all the fragrant powders of a merchant? Behold, it is the litter of Solomon!* (Song of Songs 3:6–7; ESV)

If we take the scene described in the Song of Songs 3:7, 9, we might imagine that, unlike the carriage made of the massive cedars of Lebanon, we have heard of one greater than Solomon carrying heavy wood for the True Cross that will bear the weight of the sin of the whole world! Let us come out and see him crowned. Matthew Henry put it thus: 'Some apply it to the crown of thorns with which his mother, the Jewish church, crowned him on the day of his death, which was the day of his espousals to his church, when he loved it, and gave himself for it (Eph 5:25); and it is observable that when he was brought forth wearing the crown of thorns Pilate said, and said it to the daughters of

Zion, "Behold the man!" [Then again] It seems especially to mean the honour done him by his church . . . When believers accept of him as theirs, and join themselves to him in an everlasting covenant, it is his coronation-day in their souls. Before conversion they were crowning themselves, but then they begin to crown Christ, and continue to do so from that day forward. They appointed him their head; they bring every thought into obedience to him; they set up his throne in their hearts, and cast all their crowns at his feet. It is the day of his espousals.'[144]

This is the first of three occasions when the phrase 'What is this?' (ESV) or 'Who is this?' (NIV) occurs in the Song. In Chapter 3, we read, *Who is this coming up from the wilderness like a column of smoke?* In Chapter 6:10: *Who is this that appears like the dawn . . . majestic as the stars in procession?* and in the final chapter we read: *Who is this coming up from the wilderness leaning on her beloved?* (8:5) The three-fold repetition of this rhetorical question adds weight to its importance. We can readily apply the first and second to Christ; but we can also apply all three to the Body of Christ: she comes up out of the wilderness of obscurity, covered in the aroma of Christ, terrible as an army with banners, having learned to lean on the Beloved in absolute dependence. This idea of the Bride who comes out of or emerges from the desert, 'The Real Emerging Church' if you will, is one that we can be nourished by and to which we will return.

Matthew Henry joins the Fathers in saying of 3:6: 'This is applicable to the Jewish church, when, after forty years' wandering in the wilderness, they came out of it, to take a glorious possession of the land of promise; and this may very well be illustrated by what Balaam said of them at that time, when they ascended out of the wilderness like pillars of smoke, and he stood admiring them: From the top of the rocks I see him. How goodly are thy tents, O Jacob! Num. 23:9; 24:5.' He adds: 'She is perfumed with myrrh and frankincense.

'Who is this? What a monument of mercy is this! The graces and comforts with which she is perfumed are called the powders of the merchant, for they are far-fetched and dear-bought, by our Lord Jesus, that blessed merchant, who took a long voyage, and was at vast expense, no less than that of his own blood, to purchase them for us. They are not the products of our own soil, nor the growth of our own country; no, they are imported from the heavenly Canaan, the better country.'[145]

Columns of smoke is an echo of the cloudy, fiery pillar in the Exodus, which led the people through the wilderness. This phrase is interpreted by the Church Fathers and countless commentators as having to do with the deaths of the Church's martyrs, the patient endurance of the saints. Wherever she goes, we might say the thick smoke of her suffering goes up to heaven. 'We are always delivered unto death,' said the Apostle Paul. The cause of truth involves a perpetual sacrifice. The fragrance also has to do with deeds of justice – 'the righteous deeds of the saints' (Revelation 19). Thus Spurgeon: 'Wherever the Church of Christ proceeds, though her pathway is a desert, though she marches through a howling wilderness, she scatters the richest perfume.'

Considering the nature of this 'richest perfume': if we survey the history of the Church as she has sought to bring justice on the earth, we might say that wherever the Church advances she shows the perfume of the knowledge of Christ – this is the fragrance of myrrh. People love Jesus; and love in the eyes of heaven is better than frankincense. Loving Christ they want to be like him, till patience, humility, brotherly-kindness, truthfulness, and all things that are honest, lovely, and of good repute, like 'powders of the merchant', are spread abroad throughout the whole earth.

In my research into my previous book, *Epiphanies of the Ordinary*, looking at the difference that contemplative encounters with God, or 'seeing salvation', made to people in church history, I concluded with a list of works of mercy – charities founded by Christians as a result of 'seeing the Christ': 'Many names spring to mind as examples of such love expressed in action: Tearfund, The Red Cross, Christian Aid, World Vision, The Leprosy Society, Open Doors, Amnesty International, Soul in the City, Betel, A Rocha, Viva Network, International Justice Mission. The Spirit of justice led Christians to pioneer the Socialist movement, the Feminist movement, the Peace movement, the Abolition of slavery movement, the Temperance movement. Wherever the love of God is invited – a passion for justice is ignited. If we just take a look through the lattice or window into the Church's great hall of fame filled with God's Spirit of justice, we see St Francis loving creation and pouring out his life on the poor; William Wilberforce shattering the chains of slavery and longing for a "reformation of manners" as he put it; Shaftsbury passing laws to protect children at work; Dr Barnardo loving the fatherless and giving the orphan a home; William Booth wresting prostitutes and alcoholics from the shadows; Hannah Moore seeking to educate the poor; Jackie Pullinger in Hong Kong building hostel-homes for addicts young and old and lovingly seeing them through the cold turkey night of deliverance with ceaseless loving prayer; Heidi Baker loving and feeding the poorest of the planet in Mozambique. This is a small list of a big group of people sacrificing their lives for others on the cesspits of society.'[146]

We can reasonably say that this is indeed the Church perfumed with all the spices of the merchants. The question to ask yourself is: am I part of this? What do I smell of? Do I have these 'fragrant powders of a merchant' on my garments? Often in my tradition, church can feel more like business and competition and striving to succeed, rather than the celebration of heavenly aroma, beauty, character and above all Christ-likeness. Take time with the exercises at the end of this chapter to examine your life and conscience and see what your aroma might be.

Sixty mighty ones armed against the terrors of the night

Around it are sixty mighty men, some of the mighty men of Israel, all of them wearing swords and expert in war, each with his sword at his thigh, against terror by night. King Solomon made himself a carriage from the wood of Lebanon. He made its posts of silver, its back of gold, its seat of purple; its interior was inlaid with love by the daughters of Jerusalem. (Song of Songs 3:7–10; ESV)

This chapter contains a graphic description of what are Solomon's desert troops (his 'Desert Rats'). The carriage has an armed guard: *sixty mighty men, some of the mighty men of Israel, all of them wearing swords and expert in war, each with his sword at his thigh, against terror by night* (3:7–8; ESV). This is an image of a highly trained, dedicated, armed and protected team of strong soldiers who act as bodyguards around this procession coming up out of the wilderness. These few lines are redolent of warfare and armour and intensive training.

Clearly, an application can be found in Paul's image of the

soldier at the end of Ephesians: he boldly states that our struggle is as a warrior Bride with rulers, authorities, cosmic powers over this present darkness, spiritual forces of evil in the heavenly places. It remains striking, emotionally charged language.[147] But as we enter the third millennium since Christ, far from this motif being archaic, it seems increasingly appropriate. Following the Second World War, British preacher Martyn Lloyd-Jones surveyed what he saw as 'the state of the world', with the following conclusion:

> It is my belief that the modern world and especially the history of the present century can only be understood in terms of the unusual activity of the devil and the 'principalities and powers'. In a world of collapsing institutions, moral chaos, and increasing violence, never was it more important to trace the hand of the 'prince of the power of the air', and then, not only to learn how to wrestle with him and his forces, but also how to overcome them 'by the blood of the lamb and the word of our testimony'. If we cannot discern the chief cause of our ills, how can we hope to cure them?[148]

It is from outside time and into this context that this Song of Songs text speaks to us. The parallel for Paul writing to the Ephesians is their need to 'put on the full armour of God'. The weapons he lists are: the belt of truth, breastplate of righteousness, shoes of the gospel of peace, shield of faith, helmet of salvation. The sword he ends his list of armour with is 'the sword of the Spirit which is the word of God'.

It is difficult to overstate the absolute necessity for the Church today to know the word of God, be trained in the right use of the word of God, be lovers of the word and the ways of God, be students of the word of God and to be, as it were, 'guardsmen' in the Church. When preaching on this in Oxford to students – a 'next-generation congregation' – I remember being moved as I looked out over these hundreds of future leaders, sensing the call on their lives to be part of this army of love going forth into what has aptly been described as an 'Age of Fracture'.[149] This passage speaks of mighty men, people who wear swords, those who are *experts in war*, those who are armed *against terrors by the night*. May a generation join up who are indeed armed against the terrors of the night.

What are these terrors? I believe they are anything and everything imaginable that this army of 'rulers, authorities, cosmic powers over this present darkness, spiritual forces of evil in the heavenly places' may throw at the Church. For Christ our captain this included the temptation to riches, to power, the accusation that he was mad or that he was demonically possessed, rejection by his family, rejection by those in leadership, betrayal by his close friend, abandonment by all his followers, torture and killing and darkness and the descent into hell. The terrors of the night today may include all of this; including the accusations we feel of pointlessness, pain, waste, madness.

To counter these threats, the Song gives an image of a set-apart, seriously trained, consecrated yet soldierly squad of lovers of God. As such they will be armed against the terrors of the night. How are we armed? By our training in the desert – training in the affections of God, which are powerful as our weapons, swords strapped on the thigh for us in this fight. It is impossible to avoid the desert. 'The desert is a place of revelation and revolution. In the desert we wait, we weep, we learn to live.'[150]

Thomas Merton, speaking of this inescapable passage through the desert for all who would live godly lives, said:

'This, then is our desert; to live facing despair, but not to consent. To trample it down under hope in the Cross. To wage war against despair unceasingly. That war is our wilderness. If we wage it courageously, we will find Christ at our side. If we cannot face it, we will never find Him.'[151] But the passage speaks of coming out of the desert. And many commentators believe this is happening for the Church in many parts of the world today. Tim Dearborn expressed the 'emergence from the desert' of this fully armed Church like this: 'Globally, we are in the midst of a transformation of the church that is far more substantive than the Protestant Reformation . . . The old structure of the imperial Western evangelical movement continues but is waning. The centre of Christendom has shifted to the South. This church bears marks that are trans-forming world Christianity, including that in the West. We stand in the midst of the intersection between the old and the new. Will Western evangelicalism allow itself to be transformed by these changes, or will it atrophy?' In his observation of the Church that is emerging, Dearborn describes the Church 'armed' with different attributes: 'Worship as a dramatic encounter with the power of God, rather than a passive and comforting moment of education and encouragement.

'Community as a gathering of people rather than a cluster of programs and activities.

'Mission as a daily encounter with the demonic and evil, conducted through spiritual battle, suffering and a holistic engagement with the world; for all of life is deemed as the domain of God, with social, economic and even political ministry integral to church life.'[152]

Perhaps the swords on the thighs of the warriors also speak to us about prayer. Prayer is not a walkie-talkie enabling us to discuss with friends where to meet up on the ski slopes, but a satellite phone connected straight to the throne room of heaven, to get our strategy for the battle in the war under God's standard that we have been drafted into. Thus this *sword at his thigh* that each soldier has may certainly apply to our training in prayer. Paul, speaking of the sword of the Spirit, which is the word of God, goes on in the next sentence to speak of the calling to 'pray at all times with all kinds of prayer and supplication'.

Veteran prayer writer E. M. Bounds says this about untrained soldiers in the spiritual battle: 'The great hindrance is in the preacher himself. There may be no discount on his orthodoxy, honesty, cleanness, or earnestness; but somehow the man, the inner man, in its secret places has never broken down and surrendered to God, his inner life is not a great highway for the transmission of God's message, God's power. Somehow self and not God rules in the holy of holiest. Somewhere, all unconscious to himself, some spiritual non-conductor has touched his inner being, and the divine current has been arrested. His inner being has never felt its thorough spiritual bankruptcy, its utter powerlessness; he has never learned to cry out with an ineffable cry of self-despair and self-helplessness till God's power and God's fire comes in and fills, purifies, empowers.'

Bounds speaks to the heart preparation of the Christian engaged in combat and it is not inappropriate to talk in these sacrificial terms when our task is to prepare the Bride. Bounds continues: 'Self-esteem, self-ability in some pernicious shape has defamed and violated the temple, which should be held sacred for God. Life-giving preaching costs the preacher much – death to self, crucifixion to the world, the travail of his own soul. Crucified preaching only can give life. Crucified preaching can come only from a crucified person.'[153]

Come out, and look, you daughters of Zion. Look on King Solomon wearing a crown, the crown with which his mother crowned him on the day of his wedding, the day his heart rejoiced (3:11)

We have been looking at Solomon's wedding preparations.

The book of Revelation speaks in a similar way in another passage concerning preparation for the wedding to come: 'They triumphed . . . by the word of their testimony; they did not love their lives so much as to shrink from death' (Revelation 12:11).

We will leave this crucial text reminding ourselves what it is about: wedding preparation. May we leave the wilderness having been thoroughly trained through it. May we come out of it leaning on the Beloved, perfumed with Christ-like character. May we be armed in prayer – may we play our full role in the wedding!

Spiritual exercises for wedding preparation

Check your perfume. Ask a friend, a spiritual director, your spouse: do I smell of Christ?

Spend time asking God specifically to reveal where you can grow in grace and character, remembering the fruits of the Spirit – love, joy, peace, patience, kindness, goodness, faithfulness, gentleness and self-control.

The Examen of Conscience

From Ignatius's *Spiritual Exercises*: this is sometimes called the 'Awareness *Examen*', or otherwise 'Daily Examination of Consciousness'.

Ask yourself these questions:

- Where and when did I miss living God's character in any of these areas yesterday? Spend some time asking for forgiveness and praying for change.

- Where and when did I meet Christ and have his aroma yesterday? Thank him and ask for more of his aroma tomorrow.

- Will I enlist to be one of these warriors armed against the terrors of the night? Ask God for training in the use of 'the sword of the Spirit which is the word of God'.

Spend ten minutes in 'Warfare Prayer', using the word of God as your weapon. See Ephesians 6:10–20.

Repeat these questions daily, asking to grow in Christ-like character.

'Dear Reader, the whole desire of the Divine Being can be described in a single sentence: God wishes to give Himself utterly to every creature that names His name. And He will do this, giving Himself to each one of us according to our individual capacity.

But alas! Man is a remarkable creature! How reluctant he is to allow himself to be drawn into God! How fearful, how remarkably fearful he is to prepare for divine union.
Jeanne Guyon[154]

'Jesus plans to bring his church – his divided, immoral, bitter church – to radiant glory . . . Jesus cherishes the church in order to take the stain of sin out of her soul.

'This method of changing his Bride is the only tested and proven way that works in history. Nourishing and cherishing is God's method to change people under our spiritual authority. The only way a man can change his wife, or a wife her husband or a couple their children is by nourishing and cherishing them. All of the Lord's discipline occurs as he nourishes and cherishes us.'
Mike Bickle[155]

CHAPTER NINE

Identity: 'How beautiful you are'

How beautiful you are, my darling! Oh, how beautiful!
Your eyes behind your veil are doves. Your hair is like a
flock of goats descending from the hills of Gilead.
Your teeth are like a flock of sheep just shorn, coming up from
the washing. Each has its twin; not one of them is alone.
Your lips are like a scarlet ribbon; your mouth is lovely.
Your temples behind your veil are like the halves of a
pomegranate.
Your neck is like the tower of David, built with courses of
stone; on it hang a thousand shields, all of them shields
of warriors.
Your breasts are like two fawns, like twin fawns of a gazelle
that browse among the lilies.
Until the day breaks and the shadows flee, I will go to the
mountain of myrrh and to the hill of incense.
You are altogether beautiful, my darling; there is no flaw in
you.
Come with me from Lebanon, my bride, come with me
from Lebanon. Descend from the crest of Amana, from
the top of Senir, the summit of Hermon, from the lions'
dens and the mountain haunts of leopards.
You have stolen my heart, my sister, my Bride; you have
stolen my heart with one glance of your eyes, with one
jewel of your necklace.

Song of Songs 4:1–9

This is the first of three soaring poems from the Bridegroom to the Bride, praising her to the skies and describing her physical glory and her beauty from head to toe – or from toe to head, in Chapter 6. The Bride responds in the next chapter with her counterpoint to this, describing the Bridegroom's glories in his turn.

As ever there is an application to love between a man and a woman and counsel for the divine romance.

In this affectionate, erotic, lyrical and passionate bridal love song, the Bridegroom delights in the Bride's eyes, hair, teeth, lips, cheeks, neck and breasts, with the conclusion: *You are altogether beautiful, my love; there is no flaw in you* (v. 7; ESV). There is no shame, but nor is there any suggestion of flaunting, prideful display; it is as if we are admitted into the genuine expression of affection from a man to a woman. As such, as well as enjoying the poetry, there are lessons for us to learn.

The human body, whether male or female, is one of nature's wonders. As I write this chapter, I sit before a seascape second to none, with wheeling birds and breaking waves and high winter tides threatening chaos and crashing against sea defences, all reminding me of the power of nature. The great glory of creation is before me. This chapter of the Song reminds us that woman (and man) is equally – if not even more so – a sign of creation's glory and power, its mesmerising fascination and its sheer beauty. The man's defences have been crashed into and have given way: *You have captivated my heart . . . with one glance of your eyes, with one jewel of your necklace* (v. 9; ESV). The body is the instrument on which is played a symphony of exquisite glory, and the man here has seen it. The text indicates in 1:5 that the Bride may not have been flawless according to Ancient Near

Eastern beauty standards – she was 'dark' or sunburned – but to the groom, in his eyes, she is perfect; because to look with love is to see whatever is pure, noble and beautiful. The lover is able to appropriate nature language that is familiar and everyday – doves, goats, ewes, pomegranate, fawns, twins of a gazelle – which is surprising language but it works.

For example: *Your cheeks are like halves of a pomegranate behind your veil* (v. 3; ESV). Cheeks are the indicator of emotion or affection: the pomegranate carries an aphrodisiacal reference, being fruit of redness or blushing – but the cheeks are veiled and discreet.

All husbands may do well to learn to praise their wife in their own way – yes, to praise her body, to find their voice and dare to use it, to write it, to meditate on and enjoy the beauty of the body and express this in words. If we are not gifted poetically, we may borrow another poet's words and make them our own. Certainly Solomon (or whoever the author of these Wisdom texts may have been) seems to have excelled at this.

It must be admitted that the language of the Song is hard to use when addressing a spouse today – the images feel impossible to handle and the comparisons seem strange: talking about *cheeks like halves of pomegranates, breasts like twins of a gazelle* may not be the best way to address your spouse! Nevertheless, we can learn wisdom from this gift of expression that may help us in the call to experience passionate, lifelong love. Whatever the stage of life of the Bride, evidently this is possible. Proverbs 31:10 speaks of a mature mother or Bride as someone whose worth is 'far more than rubies'. Her husband still praises her: 'Many women do noble things, but you surpass them all.' The conclusion is: 'Charm is deceptive, and beauty is fleeting, but a woman who fears the LORD is to be praised' (Proverbs 31:29–30). Lest this be read only as referring to a couple in a stage of life where they have left their physical relationship behind them, an earlier chapter of Proverbs reads: 'May your fountain be blessed, and may you rejoice in the wife of your youth. A lovely doe, a graceful deer – may her breasts satisfy you always' (Proverbs 5:18–19).

Apparently the Bible encourages these efforts: we can keep expressing affection, admiration, wonder. It seems we are to keep daring to express desire. As we do so, as we keep on finding our voice, love will return and grow and deepen. Enjoyment of the other will be rekindled. This is also sensuous imagery: *the hill of incense* is invoked, the wine of love brings welcome intoxication, the fragrance of oils involves the sense of smell, honey and milk are under the tongue for tasting. Husbands can learn love and its eloquent expression from this poet/Bridegroom, and wives can learn to be loved – how to keep being captivating – from this unabashed Bride.

This expressive affection evidently does the woman good. At the start of the Song she thought she was 'dark'; she said straight out: *Do not stare at me.* Now she has grown in confidence and security and does not mind being looked at. Indeed it seems to nourish and complete her: her response is not: 'Don't be silly', or 'Sorry, I am too busy', but rather: *Let my beloved come into my garden and taste its choicest fruits.*

In the same way that the woman is nourished and given confidence, so in the song of the soul, the Bride of Christ grows into maturity through the Bridegroom's nourishing words. Christ sees the end from the beginning. He sees the majesty of the mature Bride and names it, calling it forth as he does so. It is not conditional but actually describes what he sees with the eyes of faith: 'to present her to himself as a glorious church, without stain or wrinkle or any other blemish, but holy and blameless. In the same way, husbands ought to love their wives as their own bodies . . . they feed and care for their body, just as Christ does the church' (Ephesians 5:27–29). Paul taught that the Church will be 'radiant' (Ephesians 5:27). The joy of love makes the Church radiant. Feeling loved and loving Jesus back is the radiance of the Bride.

What does Christ see, then?

As I say, we need to allow a lack of precision that may frustrate some. Gregory describes this consequence of dealing with 'dark sayings':

> For Allegory supplies the soul separated far from God with a kind of mechanism by which it is raised to God. By means of dark sayings in whose words a person can understand . . . what is not his to understand, and by earthly words he can be raised above the earth . . . It should be noted that sometimes in sacred scripture the Lord calls himself 'Master', sometimes 'Father', sometimes 'Bridegroom' . . . Thus in this book the Lord and the Church are not called Master and Servant, but Bridegroom and Bride so that he may be served not only in fear, nor only in reverence but also in love and by exterior words, an inner affection may be stirred. In the Song of Songs, the contemplative life is given voice, for in them is expressed a longing for the coming of the Lord and for the sight of him in person . . .[156]

I think that receiving the encouragement from the 'cherishing heart' attitude of the Bridegroom creates a longing to see or contemplate his beauty in return. For the moment, he 'cherishes our budding virtues'.[157]

The Bride is seen as having 'dove's eyes'. I believe there is a link with Jesus' enigmatic saying in Matthew 6:22: 'The eye is the lamp of the body. If your eye is healthy [or "single"], your whole body will be full of light . . .' The context is that of laying up treasure in heaven and only serving one master. This, then, is perhaps Jesus' idea of the 'single' eye: looking straight, like a dove. Your eyes are seen as being somehow impacted by the Holy Spirit who, we read, descended like a dove: you have spiritual eyesight which gives light to your whole body.

The idea of goats may seem a surprising image for beautiful hair until you have seen the leaping *goats . . . of Gilead* – who are wild in their beauty. The idea of uncut hair is an echo of the dedication of Nazirites (like John the Baptist) who were completely devoted to God.

The reference to the Bride's teeth was taken by the Fathers to indicate the capacity to chew through ideas and arrive at good doctrine. Thus Gregory of Nyssa: 'Those who grind the divine mysteries up small by interpreting them more lucidly so that this spiritual nourishment can be take into the body that is the Church – these people carry out the work of teeth.'[158] Augustine, commenting on this passage, reflects on the enjoyment he finds in allegory: 'Why is it I ask that if someone should say there are holy and perfect men and women by whose life and conduct the Church tears away from their various superstitions those who come to it, and incorporates them into itself – Why is it I ask that it gives more pleasure to have this same idea expounded on the basis of that passage in the Song of Songs where it speaks of the Church in the language one would use to praise a beautiful woman: *"your teeth are like a flock of shorn ewes that have come up from the washing"*? To be sure one would not learn anything different without the help of the imagery. And yet somehow it gives me more pleasure to contemplate the saints when I see them as the teeth of the Church tearing away men from their errors and making them part of its body, breaking down their hardness by biting and chewing . . .'

Augustine's comments illustrate for us his attitude to the 'sport' of finding understanding for these images. He concludes: 'it is much more pleasant to learn such things through imagery and much more rewarding to discover meanings that are gained with difficulty'.[159]

The Bride has *lips like a scarlet ribbon* – we could say that her lips reflect the blood of the redemption of Jesus. In other words, that scarlet strand gives impact to her lips. The mouth is a powerful biblical theme; it can signify edifying speech that releases grace. Or in the book of James – when our lips are purified, then our lives are mature. Again, how we talk is an indication of the grace of God on our lives. Our words in prayer and worship, as well as our encouragement to others, are pleasing to God.[160] In 2:14, the lover said, *your voice is sweet, and your face is lovely.* The reason our voice is sweet is because the scarlet blood of Jesus covers us and causes our words to be accepted in the sight of God.

Your mouth is lovely, says the divine Bridegroom. He seeks the intimacy that has been described earlier like kisses. I am reminded of the transforming effects of the kiss in children's stories on the frog who becomes a prince, or on the sleeping beauty. Indeed, the Church has aptly been called 'Cinderella with amnesia' – having a royal destiny but now become a slave. The divine lover seeks to fill her with life, encouraging her: *your mouth is lovely.*

Next we read that *Your cheeks are like halves of a pomegranate behind your veil* (v. 3; ESV). I have already said that cheeks stand for emotion or affection, and the pomegranate speaks of redness or blushing. There is a subtlety involved, though, as these are 'veiled'. I believe the image speaks of how cheeks show the emotions of the Bride, impacted by the grace of God, that let it show even through the veil.

Your neck is like the tower of David (v. 4): the neck turns the head, and to be 'stiff-necked' is wrong. Here it is the opposite. The Bride's neck is strong; she has consecrated her free will to be completely obedient to the will of God, as was King David, whose towering example ushered in the golden age of Israel.

Your breasts are like two fawns (v. 5). When preaching through the Song, this is where I have to pause and admit to it being a stretch for modern readers to read this allegorically at all. And yet twenty centuries of interpreters have not had to pause in this way. Arguably, we might say this is because of our highly sexualised social context and our Freudian 'hermeneutic of suspicion', which is so stubborn. And yet, in the song of the soul – for the Fathers, the medieval commentators, the Puritans, the expositors of the Great Awakening and for revival preachers – this mention of 'breasts' has simply indicated power and beauty to edify and nurture others, especially the next generation.

Gregory the Great is one of the few who don't give pause at the language of the Song, but he nevertheless gives this verdict: 'For in this book . . . breasts are mentioned, cheeks are mentioned and the holy picture these words make is not meant for mockery . . . rather we should notice how marvellously and mercifully he reaches down to the vocabulary of our sensual love in order to set our heart on fire, aiming to incite in us a holy loving . . .'

For Durham these 'breasts' have to do with 'A believer's fitness to edify others . . . that believers being useful to others for their edification is a special ornament . . . the believer's warmliness and kindliness to Christ and those that are his, taking him and them (as it were) into their bosom.'[161]

So it is that in this passage Christ builds up his Bride: though we stumble in weakness, he defines us by our potential. We may feel the enemy has worn down the Church with accusation and condemnation. But here, by contrast, the Bridegroom cherishes us by affirming our willing spirit. We may typically define our lives by our spiritual struggles. But he doesn't define us by our present struggles. The Bridegroom defines the Bride by the longings he himself puts in her. It is not as if he doesn't see our sin. But he doesn't see only our negative struggle.

Many men struggle with the idea of being cherished, embraced and romanced by God. They too can take heart from this particular image. This is the same dynamic as the 'cherishing' of Gideon: when Israel was being attacked by the Midianites, Gideon hid in the winepress (Judges 6). He was filled with fear as the Midianite army sought to destroy Israel. The angel called him with the words, 'O mighty man of valour.' The Lord saw in Gideon's spirit a strength that he was not yet operating in. God named him a man of courage, when in the present he was frightened, running and hiding. Yet Gideon became one of the great leaders of Israel.

The Lord sees the end from the beginning. He sees the seeds of character in our life. He sees the budding virtue and has the authority to bring it to completion. Jesus speaks to Peter in this same way. Peter is filled with fear before a young servant girl as he denies the Lord. But just before that, Christ called Peter the rock, the unmovable one, somebody others could count on.

Here Christ says to his Bride: *You are altogether beautiful, my darling; there is no flaw in you* (4:7). The Song reads:

Until the day breaks and the shadows flee, I will go to the moun-
tain of myrrh and to the hill of incense. You are altogether
beautiful, my darling; there is no flaw in you. (4:6–7)

Because of Christ going to the cross in shame – the mountain
of myrrh – so we the Bride can be flawless, and without
shame. This verse speaks of the Bridegroom. And, as she is
joined to him through his suffering, it also speaks to the
Bride, as Gregory of Nyssa saw when writing just three
hundred years after Christ: '. . . indicating by myrrh his
suffering and by frankincense the glory of the godhead . . .
By these words he teaches that no one takes his life from him,
but that he has the power to lay it down and to take it up
again as he makes his journey to the mountain of myrrh,
accepting death on behalf of sinners, not as a result of any
deeds of ours but out of his own graciousness.' Gregory
concludes: 'this One is instructing us that the person who
shared myrrh with him will also fully share in his frankincense: for the one who suffers with him will be fully glorified
with him'.[162]

Other commentators hold that this is the Bride speaking.
It is a response from the Bride to the love expressed by the
Bridegroom, saying: 'I have decided: I will indeed go my
way through the shadows to take up my cross without
restraint or reluctance.'

The shadows whose fleeing we await may speak of the grey
areas, of weakness or compromise in a life. These shadows,
perhaps the same as those little foxes (2:15), are still present
in her life. *Until the day breaks* (or 'breathes' as the ESV has
it) may speak either of the day of eternity when we live in the
presence of God's full daylight, or of a time of victory where
we live in greater light on the earth. In either case, the Bride

is declaring that until more light comes, she will continue to embrace the mountain of myrrh, while praying for help on the hill of frankincense.

I will go: she commits to go to the mountain of myrrh, to leave her comfort zone, to embrace the sufferings of Christ. There is nothing that will keep her from complete obedience. You could say she agrees to embrace his death – as Paul says to the Philippians, 'I want to know Christ – yes, to know . . . participation in his sufferings, becoming like him in his death' (Philippians 3:10).

For Mike Bickle, 'This is one of the great verses in the book. Her life turns on this verse . . . These are great words to God. He wooed her. She responds, "I'll go! I want to be with the One who loves me this much." She rises up from her fear. It is such liberty to walk free from our fears, to walk out of our fears into the perfect will of God.'[163]

The Bridegroom's response is decisive:

You are altogether beautiful, my love; there is no flaw in you. Come with me from Lebanon, my bride; come with me from Lebanon. Depart from the peak of Amana, from the peak of Senir and Hermon, from the dens of lions, from the mountains of leopards. (4:7–8; ESV)

Lebanon, Amana, Senir and Hermon . . . Lebanon's mountains were dangerous places, though David found refuge there. Amana and 'Senir and Hermon' (one mountain with two names) are high peaks in Lebanon from which it is possible to see the Promised Land.

Hudson Taylor writes of the phrase *Come with me* in his *Union and Communion*. He gave up his life to go to the harvest fields with Christ and reach the people of China. In missiological terms, he knew what he was talking about, having left everything and having lost his wife and child in China – these were costly circumstances in which to remain courageous. For him, this is a call to mission. He writes: 'Come with me: It is always so: If our saviour says "Go and make disciples of all nations", he precedes it by: "All power is given to me" and follows it with "Lo I am with you."'[164]

For the persecuted but fruitful Chinese church that was his legacy, these verses about Lebanon, the peaks of Amana, Senir and Hermon are about spiritual authority (the heights) and spiritual warfare (dens of lions). One of Hudson Taylor's disciples was Watchman Nee, whose series of talks on the Song of Songs was published when he had been 'in prison for fifteen years under the persecutive communist regime of China'.[165] For him: 'Lebanon points to the high mountain top where the scented cedar is the most outstanding feature. The high mountains of scripture speak of our leaving the earth level to move up to a heavenly position . . . The believers' position should be on the mountain top. There are many who have failed and fallen down precipices but their original intended position in Christ is heavenly elevation. Amana means Truth . . . Shenir indicates flexible armour . . . Hermon denotes destruction and undoubtedly speaks of the cross and how the Lord Jesus, as the eternal Son of God, was manifested to destroy the works of the evil one.'[166]

At first blush this may seem tenuous. But others agree, thus Durham, speaking of spiritual warfare in the light of this verse, writes: 'There is nothing more unreasonable, bitter, cruel than a worldly atheist . . . they are lions and leopards. Believers should have their thoughts directed towards heaven and their affections should be fixed there.'[167]

Hudson Taylor continues: 'What are lions' dens when the

Lion of Judah is with us, or mountains of leopards when he is at our side? "I will fear no evil if thou art with me." On the other hand, it is while thus facing dangers and toiling with him in service that he says: "You have captivated my heart" . . .'[168]

As the Bride goes to the mountains of difficulty and into service with Christ whatever the cost, the Bridegroom's response is warm, deeply affected, and appropriate: *You have stolen my heart, my sister, my bride* (v. 9). This verse introduces the theme of God as a loving Father with feelings of tender affection – something we see more as the New Testament paradigm. To some extent this was a new emphasis in religious history in the days of Jesus, but there are strong hints of it in the Old Testament. The Jewish Pharisees held a paradigm of a holy God driven by religious rules. The Stoics had a paradigm of gods with no feelings at all, while the Epicureans believed in gods who were completely disinterested. For example, Plutarch preached that it was blasphemous to think of God as demeaning himself to be concerned and impacted by the affairs of this lower world. Into this context of the history of religious thought breaks the Christian paradigm of a God who deliberately underwent every human experience, and who deliberately submitted himself to pain, weakness and temptation. But this new paradigm finds its roots in the Song and other bridal passages such as Hosea.

You have ravished my heart, My sister, my spouse; You have ravished my heart With one look of your eyes, With one link of your necklace. How fair is your love, My sister, my spouse! How much better than wine is your love (4:9–10; NKJV)

This is a revelation of how lovely the Bride is to the Bridegroom. In the ESV this section starts: *You have captivated my heart* (4:9a). Meditating on this, we could say that this is a statement of his personality. He says, 'You – not your ministry, not your success, not the money you gave, not your track record of accomplishments – YOU have ravished or captured or captivated my heart.'

Now at this stage she has only said, *I* will *go to the mountain*. She hasn't yet gone. In this chapter she makes the commitment to go, but it is in chapter 5 that she actually goes to the mountain.

My sister, my bride

This is the first time the woman is called a sister or a bride, here in 4:8. Jesus calls us by a new name, his Bride. Being named his Bride speaks of his affectionate partnership for us. His heart is captured only by his Bride. *My sister* may speak of Jesus' human nature. To call us sister means that we are in the same family. He could not call us 'my sister' before the incarnation. He was not our brother until he took upon himself the form of a man. He relates to the brother–sister relationship because he partook of humanity. He 'is not ashamed to call them brothers and sisters' (Hebrews 2:11). Furthermore, Jesus endured indescribable humiliation to partake of human nature in the incarnation and it is in the light of this that he can call us 'my sister'.

He honours every glance of devotion to him (*with one glance of your eyes*, 4:9) – he counts every move of our heart towards him. We struggle to understand this only because we don't count every move of somebody's heart towards us. Every glance of our devotion touches him.

This is hinted at in the story in Genesis of the intimacy another woman, Hagar, experiences, through her seeing of the God who sees her. Although she is a nobody – foreign, a slave, unmarried, female and pregnant, the lowest of the low in ancient society – God sees her and takes account of her, and his heart is stirred by her. This is one of the very first theophanies in the Bible, and it speaks powerfully of the link between the eyes and the heart. Hagar calls the name of 'the LORD who spoke to her: "You are the God who sees me," for she said, "I have now seen the One who sees me" (Genesis 16:13). At the same time this experience of Hagar's is a sharp contrast to the woman in Proverbs 7:15, who uses her eyes not to see but to seduce and to lead astray.

With one jewel

Interestingly, in Ancient Near Eastern culture, there is a thing called an 'eye bead', a jewel worn on a necklace, often a white stone with agate in it to look like an eye pupil, and people wore these all the time as amulets of protection as well as for aesthetic purposes. The reference here to one jewel of a necklace compared with an eye may mean this sort of necklace.[169]

But in the sight of the lover of our souls, each individual response or glance of sincerity is also one link of the golden chain described in 1:10. It is not the whole necklace, but merely one link or jewel. However, every new link in her dedication moves his heart. He remembers every movement of our heart towards him. His heart is ravished by even one link, each new area of dedication.

This sense is similar to 6:5 – *Turn your eyes from me; they overwhelm me.* The eyes of the Bride are your eyes. This brings us back to contemplation and the knowledge that we need to look up, to gaze on him, to seek to see spiritually; to see mysteries . . . to see a door standing in heaven opened, like John in Revelation. Preaching on this, Spurgeon writes:

'Sometimes I find it good in prayer to say nothing but to sit or kneel quite still and look up to my Lord in adoring silence, realising him to be present and waiting to hear him speak until some precious word from his scripture comes into my soul spoken by those dear lips which are as lilies dropping sweet smelling myrrh.'[170]

So as we arrive at this halfway point in the Song, we dwell on the look of the Bride that stirs the heart of God. With the perfumes of myrrh upon her, I cannot help being reminded of the martyrs. Sometimes as they died, they cried: 'I see heaven opened.' So this passionate cry, *You have stolen my heart . . . with one glance . . .* is perhaps the look of the martyr witness who has had a heavenly vision like Paul: the 'connection of the eyes' like that of lovers, after which you are spoiled for the world. Archbishop and martyr Thomas Cranmer, at his death, went indeed to the mountain of myrrh. He achieved a final serenity: he fulfilled the promise he had made at his defence, crying: 'forasmuch my hand offended, writing contrary to my heart, my hand shall first be punished'. Foxe's book of martyrs puts it like this: 'And when the fire began to burn near him, stretching out his arm, he put his right hand into the flame, which he held so steadfast and immovable (saving that once with the same hand he wiped his face) that all men might see his hand burned before his body was touched. His eyes were lifted up to heaven and often he repeated: "this unworthy right hand" as long as his voice would let him, and using while he could the words of Stephen, first martyr, "Lord Jesus receive my spirit. I see heaven open and Jesus standing at the right hand of God." So it was that "in the greatness of the flame, he gave up the ghost".'[171]

The repercussions of that rainy Saturday have spread through the centuries like ripples of a stone thrown into the pool of history. But so I believe are the repercussions also for someone who knows that they affect the heart of God with one sacrificial glance upwards.

Spiritual exercises for 'going to the mountain of myrrh'
The 'two standards'

A helpful exercise for this halfway point in the Song is Ignatius's 'Meditation on the "Two Standards"'. This is part of the 'second week' of the *Spiritual Exercises*. Although the images evoked in this scene are somewhat medieval, the exercise is famous, ancient and worth exploring:

The two standards: Christ calls and wants all under His standard; and Lucifer, on the contrary, under his.

Seeing the Place: It will be here to see a great field of all that region of Jerusalem, where the supreme Commander-in-chief of the good is Christ our Lord; another field in the region of Babylon, where the chief of the enemy is Lucifer. (Ask for knowledge of the deceits of the bad chief and help to guard myself against them, and for knowledge of the true life which the supreme and true Captain shows and grace to imitate Him.)

1. Imagine as if the chief of all the enemy seated himself in that great field of Babylon, as in a great chair of fire and smoke, in shape horrible and terrifying. Consider how he issues a summons to innumerable demons and how he scatters them, some to one city and others to another, and so through all the world, not omitting any provinces, places, states, nor any persons in particular. Consider the discourse which he makes them, and how he tells them to cast out nets and chains; that they have first to tempt with a longing for riches . . . that men may more easily come to vain honour of the world, and then to vast pride. So that the first step shall be that of riches; the second, that of honour; the third, that of pride; and from these three steps he draws on to all the other vices.

2. *Imagine as to the supreme and true Captain,* who is Christ our Lord. Consider how Christ our Lord puts Himself in a great field of that region of Jerusalem, in lowly place, beautiful and attractive. Consider how the Lord of all the world chooses so many persons – Apostles, Disciples, etc., – and sends them through all the world spreading His sacred doctrine through all states and conditions of persons. Consider the discourse which Christ our Lord makes to all His servants and friends whom He sends on this expedition, recommending them to want to help all, by bringing them first to the highest spiritual poverty, and – if His Divine Majesty would be served and would want to choose them – no less to actual poverty; the second is to be of contumely and contempt; because from these two things humility follows.

3. There are to be three steps; the first, poverty against riches; the second, contumely or contempt against worldly honour; the third, humility against pride. And from these three steps let them induce to all the other virtues.[172]

Meditate on these two standards. The Bride chooses to *go to the mountain of myrrh and the hill of incense.* See if you are able to make the choice described above by Ignatius. Pray and talk to God about it.

'I don't know how to preach on this subject. Who can?
Is it a subject for exposition in a mixed assembly?'
C. H. Spurgeon[173]

'Very soon the shadow will give way to Reality. The
partial will pass into the Perfect. The foretaste will lead
to the Banquet. The troubled path will end in Paradise.
A hundred candle-lit evenings will come to their
consummation in the marriage supper of the Lamb.
And this momentary marriage will be swallowed up by
Life. Christ will be all and in all. And the purpose of
marriage will be complete.'
John Piper

CHAPTER TEN

Consummation and Presence

He

*How delightful is your love, my sister, my bride! How much
more pleasing is your love than wine, and the fragrance
of your perfume more than any spice!*

*Your lips drop sweetness as the honeycomb, my bride; milk
and honey are under your tongue. The fragrance of your
garments is like the fragrance of Lebanon.*

*You are a garden locked up, my sister, my bride; you are a
spring enclosed, a sealed fountain.*

*Your plants are an orchard of pomegranates with choice
fruits, with henna and nard,*
*nard and saffron, calamus and cinnamon, with every
kind of incense tree, with myrrh and aloes and all the
finest spices.*

*You are a garden fountain, a well of flowing water stream-
ing down from Lebanon.*

She

*Awake, north wind, and come, south wind! Blow on my
garden, that its fragrance may spread everywhere. Let
my beloved come into his garden and taste its choice
fruits.*

He

*I have come into my garden, my sister, my Bride; I have
gathered my myrrh with my spice. I have eaten my*

honeycomb and my honey; I have drunk my wine and
my milk.

Friends

Eat, friends, and drink; drink your fill of love.

Songs 4:10–5:1

The Song progresses. After the Bride's heady desire to kiss her beloved, she has found her voice and followed the path of the flocks to find him and be with him (Chapter 1). She has longed for her beloved and brought him into a place of resting and enjoyment of physical and spiritual love, a banqueting table under the banner of love. He has drawn her outside to come away in a springtime of energy – the 'foxes' which destroyed relationship are dealt with and in a state of a new openness she lifts her head and speaks to him (Chapter 2). She has experienced loss and absence in the night, which has only made her more zealous to 'emerge from the wilderness' and find her beloved. Once she finds him she clings to him and will not let him go. We are transported to a wedding procession – a triumphal entry – of Solomon or 'one greater than Solomon' in which all are exhorted to 'Go out', to 'look upon him' on this day of joy (Chapter 3). We have heard the Bridegroom's emphatic description of the beauty of the Bride, detailed from head to toe, and then her decisive resolve to get over mountains of difficulty or darkness. This in turn has ravished the heart of the Bridegroom (4:1–9).

His declaration continues thus:

How beautiful is your love, my sister, my bride! How much
better is your love than wine, and the fragrance of your oils than
any spice! Your lips drip nectar, my bride; honey and milk are
under your tongue; the fragrance of your garments is like the
fragrance of Lebanon. (4:10–11; ESV)

This is a celebration of the senses. The taste of the Bride is better than wine; her fragrance better than spices; her lips dripping nectar, honey and milk. This is a return to the erotic, passionate celebration of the other that began the chapter. Sight, smell, taste are rejoiced in here, as the sound of the voice and the touch of her lips are celebrated elsewhere. As one commentator puts it, 'The Song of Songs is a long, lyric poem about erotic love and sexual desire – a poem in which the body is the object of desire and source of delight, and lovers engage in a continual game of seeking and finding in anticipation, enjoyment and assurance of sexual gratification.'[174] There is too, though, a perfect balance in this chapter of the physical and allegorical. This is a chapter of both celebration of physical love *and* rich meaning concerning the bridal romance.

We now come to consider what can only be described as consummation: we have begun to consider her lips dripping nectar, honey and milk under the tongue. Now, at this halfway point in the Song, the Bride is described as a 'garden' and 'spring' and 'fountain' locked up or sealed, and there is an appeal to the 'wind' to awaken and blow in this garden so that its spices would flow. She responds: *Let my beloved come into my garden*; he responds, *I have come . . . I have gathered . . . I have eaten . . . I have drunk . . .* (5:1)

This is an image-charged description of love, with the anticipation of sexual enjoyment never far from the surface, but always discreetly or artistically described. The poem is never indecent, but it is also far from frigid or frumpy. One might say a perfect biblical balance is struck that celebrates, enthuses over and promotes an appreciation of sex within marriage that is truly remarkable. The poem is not hiding the lovers away, but concludes: *Eat, friends, and drink; drink your fill of love,* with the suggestion that all can rejoice in what is celebrated here: a healthy, sensual, heady, aroma-filled, fountain-flowing stream of sexuality within marriage. It goes beyond the lived experience of many, perhaps, but nonetheless it is there in the heart of the Bible, to be taken seriously and sympathetically. Catholic writer Dianne Bergant interprets this passage thus:

> The section ends with a declaration of consummation. The man's yearnings have been realized and his cravings have been assuaged. She has granted him access to her delights. He has taken pleasure in them . . . The poem invites everyone to drink deeply of this fountain of intoxicating love. The poem portrays human sexuality not only as natural but also as beautiful . . . The lovers are not warned about the overwhelming power that sexuality can wield. On the contrary it is this very power that is extolled.

We can also note the self-possession of the woman, her inapproachability, locked and sealed as he sees her. This is a positive quality. She is not ruled over by the man, but wooed. Her decision to *Let my beloved come in* is hers alone. She is willing to share her delights, but she decides when and with whom. The man in turn is ravished and undone. This is a mutual, two-way relationship of equals. Dianne Bergant concludes: 'Sexuality can open us to another, prompting us to share whoever we are and whatever we possess with the other. It can also draw us into the world of the other, then to marvel at the grace and beauty we find.'[175]

Married and courting couples do well to take this seriously and anticipate depth and richness in this part of their lives. Evidently the experience takes time: it is not to be come at lightly or without preparation; nor is it something that one of the two can afford not to have time for. There is a mutual enthusiasm and commitment here that couples will benefit from discussing and enjoying.

The very word 'garden' in Hebrew denotes a space that is enclosed or set apart from the rest of the natural world. There is a sense of tension between it being on the one hand a space that is organic and fruitful, but on the other, distinctive from the unruly natural world outside.

In the divine romance, these images are in fact quite easily translated into the language of spiritual affections. It is not that we are denying the erotic – far from it. But we are again applying the 'both/and' rule of interpretation.

'I don't know how to preach on this subject. Who can? Is it a subject for exposition in a mixed assembly?' Thus said Spurgeon in a rare admission of the intimate nature of the truths developed particularly in this chapter. He was about to expound the fact of 'Union with Christ' and 'knowing' the Lord. Even so, he hesitates – finding the subject matter tender, delicate and potentially shocking. 'I beg you O believers, let this choice subject saturate willing minds . . . If you are believers . . . He has brought you into a condition of the utmost conceivable nearness to himself: he has participated in *your* nature, and he has made you a partaker of *his* nature, and in so many words he says: "I will betroth you to me forever in righteousness . . . and you shall know the Lord." Can you grasp it? It will make your heart dance for joy if you can . . .'[176]

In another age, two hundred and fifty years earlier, people had no such scruples. The Puritans were perhaps the most given to expressing the 'ravishings' or faintings, the honey, the nectar, the well of living water, the flowing streams of enjoyment of Christ by the believer. In his Oxford study *Ravished by Beauty* Belden Lane calls this 'The surprising

legacy of reformed spirituality'.[177] Open a copy of the corre-
spondence of the great Puritan, Scottish covenanter Samuel
Rutherford (born in 1600) at almost any page and we find
him using Song of Songs language: 'I cannot but think it
must be up-taking and sweet to see the white and red of
Christ's fair face, for he is fair and ruddy and the chiefest
among ten thousand (Songs 5:10) . . . O that Christ would
break down the old narrow vessels of the ebb and flow soul
and make fair, deep, wide and broad souls, to hold a sea and
a full tide, flowing over all its banks of Christ's love.'[178]

Scottish divine Andrew Bonar's 'sketch of his life' concludes
of Rutherford: 'His description of himself is: "A man often
born down and hungry and waiting for the marriage supper
of the Lamb." He is now gone to the "mountain of myrrh and
the hill of frankincense", and there he no doubt still wonders
about the unopened, unsearchable treasures of Christ.' Bonar
concludes with the longing of his (and Rutherford's) heart for
revival in Scotland: 'But O . . . for his insatiable desires Christ-
ward! O for ten such men in Scotland to stand in the gap!
Men who all day find nothing but Christ to rest in, whose
very sleep is pursuing after Christ in dreams, and who intensely
desire to awake with his likeness.'[179]

We come therefore to what is really a revival passage as we
see an Edenic description of the Real Presence of Christ in his
Church. It is well described as a consummation. In this
'Union and Communion with Christ' moment, we revel in
the Bridegroom's delight in the lips dripping nectar – words
coming from her that are attractive, nourishing. Dispensing
honey and milk, the Bride has a nurturing role for others,
and the fragrance of her is again beautiful, the aroma of the
fruitfulness of all the choicest fruits. One might say that the
fruits of the Spirit are found in her: love, joy and peace,

patience, kindness, goodness and all the rest, and that these delight the affections of the Bridegroom. So it is that he speaks of the garden, the spring, the fountain that is the Church 'locked up' but so packed with potential and life.

At this point the wind is invited to blow – the south wind and the north wind: the *ruah* of God, the 'rushing mighty wind' of Pentecost, the 'breath' of which it was said to Ezekiel: 'speak to the breath' that it may blow and turn a valley of dry bones into a mighty army.

It is a spiritual picture of renewal, of revival, of restoration. But here above all the image is that of romance, the divine romance. The image of union, of Christ coming into his garden, is striking, daring, bold and brilliant. The Scriptures take us further than we had bargained, into territory that stretches our minds. Yet this is as it should be, for 'all scripture is God breathed' and as such is as challengingly expanding of our concepts of propriety as the incarnation itself.

Hudson Taylor wrote his little book *Union and Communion* because of this very verse: *I have come into my garden* (5:1). He concludes: 'We have, then, in this beautiful section, a picture of unbroken communion and its delightful issues. May our lives correspond! First one with the king, then speaking for the king; the joy of communion leading to fellowship in service, to a being all for Jesus, surrendering all for him and willing to minister all for him. Union with Christ has filled the heart, for all has been sealed and is kept for the Master's use.'[180]

Within the garden there is a fountain, to irrigate this garden but also *streaming down from Lebanon*. It is not an arid wilderness but a well-watered garden, and one whose potential is yet to be tapped. The psalmist feels the thirst of the Bridegroom: 'You, God, are my God, earnestly I seek you; I thirst for you, my whole being longs for you, in a dry and parched land where there is no water' (Psalm 63:1). Others have experienced this existential thirst. Famously, Malcolm Muggeridge, the British journalist and former communist who became a Christian, wrote of his discovery of spiritual water:

> I may, I suppose, regard myself as a relatively successful man. People occasionally stare at me in the streets: that's fame. I can fairly easily earn enough to qualify for admission to the highest slopes of the internal revenue. That's success. Furnished with money and even a little fame, even the elderly if they care to may partake of trendy diversions. That's pleasure. It might happen once in a while that something I said or wrote was sufficiently heeded for me to persuade myself that it represented a serious impact on our time. That's fulfilment. Yet I say to you and beg you to believe me. Multiply these tiny triumphs by a million, add them all together, and they are nothing – less than nothing – a positive impediment measured against one draft of that Living Water Christ offers to the spiritually thirsty, irrespective of who or what they are.[181]

Jesus identifies the Holy Spirit as the answer to existential thirst when he says: 'Let anyone who is thirsty come to me and drink. Whoever believes in me . . . rivers of living water will flow from within them.' As John says, 'By this he meant the Spirit' (John 7:37–39). When the Bridegroom speaks of the Bride as a fountain, a spring, a well or a flowing stream, we can thank God that the Holy Spirit of God indeed flows refreshingly in the lives of those who have come to him. This may be said to speak of a day when the Holy Spirit is powerfully flowing in the Church – a time of renewal, revival, restoration and romance that is not yet here with us but is already present in parts of the global Church.

The passage also speaks of the security and safety of the Bride. We are a *garden locked . . . a spring enclosed, a fountain sealed*. We may reflect on our safety and protection thanks to Christ. One idea attached to this notion of being sealed is that of ownership. When we are sealed, it indicates that we are owned by another. This should give us great joy and assurance.

Another idea attached to being sealed is that of security. When we seal something, we are making it secure, just like the Roman soldiers sealed the tomb of Jesus to make it secure, although of course it wasn't very secure against the actions of Almighty God. But when God seals you, then you are secure forever. For example, we may have heard amazing stories that even when a medical diagnosis brings terrible news, people can stand firm, saying, 'Yes, the news is bad, but I know I belong to God and therefore I am secure. No one is able to snatch me from his hand.' When God seals us, we will feel secure, because we know that no one – no person and no power in all creation – will be able to separate us from the love of God which is in Christ Jesus our Lord. That is the assurance of salvation we receive when we are drenched, sealed, irrigated – baptised – in and by the Holy Spirit.

Theologically, being sealed has to do with the power of the Holy Spirit – the fullness of the Holy Spirit in us. Some modern evangelicals say that we should not seek a 'baptism in the Holy Spirit' because the Spirit is already given when a person believes in Jesus Christ and redemption occurs.[182] I believe this is doctrinally correct, but that because of this reality, God wants to powerfully and repeatedly bring this fullness into our every experience – reminding us that we are *a spring, a fountain sealed . . . a garden fountain, a well of living water, and flowing streams . . .* (vv. 12, 15; ESV).

Though fullness of the Holy Spirit is a reality, the experiencing of its power is not automatic. Marriage and married bliss makes in fact a good analogy. People may be legally married – 'sealed' – yet in experience they may not know the intimacy and delight expressed in this chapter. In the same way, Christians may be recipients of grace but in fact have little experience of the power of grace poured into their life. Charles Simeon, writing in Cambridge in the nineteenth century, said, 'To many alas, this sealing of the Holy Spirit is mere foolishness but those who account it so speak evil of things that they do not understand. God is willing to bestow this blessing on all who seek it. And if we do not possess it, we should inquire what there is in us that has occasioned God to withhold it from us. We should beg God to take away the hardness of heart which incapacitates us for it and we should live more by the promises that by them it should be imparted to our souls.'[183]

Awake, O north wind, is the invitation. Many reading this may feel it is indeed time for the 'sleeping beauty' that is the Western Church to wake up. Some may feel they themselves are partly asleep, like the Bride in the next chapter: *I slept but my heart was awake* (5:2; ESV). It is a graphic, tragic image of a kind of drugged stupor – a 'sleepwalking into chaos' in our society that it seems we cannot shake off. This verse gives us a prayer that we can pray: *Awake, O north wind, and come . . .!* My prayer is that in my generation we would see a new Great Awakening, and so my prayer is: 'Awake, north wind.' It is not something I can drum up, but I can pray for it and I do so daily.

Finally, a word about his presence. The crowning glory of this sequence is the final sentence: *I have come into my garden.* I wonder how much we know today about this lovely, tender, sweet, powerful, mighty and much-longed-for healing presence of God in the Church. I wonder if you know the real, strong, transforming presence of Christ in your life. May we know it, ask for it, make room for it!

It is worth asking: can he be present and we not be aware of it? If we think of Mary Magdalene speaking with the not-yet-ascended Christ and thinking he was the gardener; if we think of those walking and talking on the way to Emmaus; then we can say assuredly: Yes! May our hearts be burning within us, like Cleopas and his companion.

Gordon Fee wrote a thousand-page analysis of the Holy Spirit in the writings of Paul and called it *God's Empowering Presence*. He writes this:

> Person, Presence, Power: these thee realities are what the Holy Spirit meant for the apostle Paul. Here we will know life and vitality, attractive life and vitality, in our personal lives and in the community of faith. Here we will constantly have the veil removed so that we might behold God's own glory in the face of Christ, so that we are constantly being renewed into his likeness. Here we will regularly expect, and see, both the working of miracles and the fellowship of his sufferings, without sensing frustration in either direction. If we do not have the Spirit, Paul says, we do not belong to God at all; my concern is that in our having his Spirit, we not settle for a watered down understanding that gives more glory to Western rationalism and spiritual anaemia than to the living God.

Elsewhere, he writes more about presence, calling it a 'delicious word'. He reflects: 'And the fact is: If you love someone, what you want more than anything else is that person's presence. Photographs are great. Telephone calls can be fantastic.

Letters have their power. But what you really long for is their presence.'[184]

May we, through meditating on the 'delicious word', know also the fact of his presence.

Spiritual exercises for inviting his presence

A garden locked is my sister, my bride, a spring locked, a fountain sealed . . . Let my beloved come to his garden, and eat its choicest fruits. (4:12, 16; ESV)

Imagine Christ outside the door of your life. The door is locked and bolted. Are you prepared to give Christ the key?

Recollection
Ask yourself: what areas of my past and my present (if any) are closed to God's presence? What parts of my life are barren? Where do I not experience his presence? Why not?

Quiet
Unlock, unbolt and open the doors of your life and each part of your past, and present the whole of it to him. Particularly welcome his word and presence in any area that seems barren or lifeless or challenging. What is his message to you about this, your garden? Remember, he is the Comforter who comforts us in our troubles.

Union and Communion
Jesus says: 'If anyone hears my voice and opens the doors, I will come in and eat with that person, and they with me' (Revelation 3:20). Experience union with Christ as he comes into your garden. Listen to his voice; let him hear yours.

'Often, I have felt that the bridegroom was drawing near to me and was as close as possible. Then all of a sudden he has gone away and I have not been able to find the object of my search. Once again I have begun to desire his coming and sometimes he returns. And when he appears to me I am holding him once more he escapes me, and when he has vanished I begin to seek him again. This happens often . . .'
Origen[185]

CHAPTER ELEVEN

The Dark Night of the Soul

She

I slept but my heart was awake. Listen! My beloved is knocking: 'Open to me, my sister, my darling, my dove, my flawless one. My head is drenched with dew, my hair with the dampness of the night.' I have taken off my robe – must I put it on again? I have washed my feet – must I soil them again? My beloved thrust his hand through the latch-opening; my heart began to pound for him. I arose to open for my beloved, and my hands dripped with myrrh, my fingers with flowing myrrh, on the handles of the bolt. I opened for my beloved, but my beloved had left; he was gone. My heart sank at his departure. I looked for him but did not find him. I called him but he did not answer. The watchmen found me as they made their rounds in the city. They beat me, they bruised me; they took away my cloak, those watchmen of the walls! Daughters of Jerusalem, I charge you – if you find my beloved, what will you tell him? Tell him I am faint with love.

Friends

How is your beloved better than others, most beautiful of women? How is your beloved better than others, that you so charge us?

She

> *My beloved is radiant and ruddy, outstanding among ten*
> *thousand. His head is purest gold; his hair is wavy and*
> *black as a raven. His eyes are like doves by the water*
> *streams, washed in milk, mounted like jewels. His cheeks*
> *are like beds of spice yielding perfume. His lips are like*
> *lilies dripping with myrrh.*
> *His arms are rods of gold set with topaz. His body is like*
> *polished ivory decorated with lapis lazuli.*
> *His legs are pillars of marble set on bases of pure gold. His*
> *appearance is like Lebanon, choice as its cedars.*
> *His mouth is sweetness itself; he is altogether lovely. This is*
> *my beloved, this is my friend, daughters of Jerusalem.*
>
> Song of Songs 5:2–16

The woman has gone to bed. She is lost in the thickness of sleep – but with her heart somehow awake. At her door there is the sound of her beloved knocking and calling to her – *sister, love, dove, perfect one* – her lover's head is *wet with dew* (ESV). But she is naked in her bed with her feet bathed – she hesitates at the effort of arising. As her lover puts his hand on the latch, she is fully awake and her heart begins to thrill within her. By the time she gets to the door to *open to her beloved*, her own hands are dripping with liquid myrrh. She opens, but her beloved has turned and gone! Her *soul failed . . . when he spoke* (ESV) and now he has gone. She calls, she looks, but he is not to be found. She gets up, goes outdoors and goes about the city. She is caught, beaten, bruised and exposed by the watchmen. She is *faint with love*.

This evocative cameo is a dramatic succession of sleep, arousal, two lovers missing one another, disappointment, frustration and eventual harm. It is a description of the turbulence of feelings where affectionate yearning and longing between a man and a woman end up in frustration and pain. As such it is a familiar portrayal of an intimate relationship. Love poetry describes what love itself experiences: the ebb and flow of strong feelings surrounding the possibility of encounter.

'There is excitement and great anticipation, yet there is also the possibility that the slightest detail can frustrate the lovers' plans. Lovers must allow themselves to be vulnerable if they are honestly to express the character and depth of their love for each other. However, emotions can be misread, intentions can be misunderstood and their vulnerability can make the lovers overly sensitive. This poetry concretely depicts this dimension of love.'[186]

The sequence is erotic, but suggestively rather than explicitly so: the man's desire for entry – for union – is evoked by his *head . . . wet with dew* and the insistent knocking: *Open to me, my sister, my dove, my perfect one* (ESV). As the woman describes herself 'naked and with her feet bathed' (some commentators read 'feet' as 'my most intimate parts'[187]), this has the effect of making him reach in through the latch.

The latch is the door opener, and for Longman, the 'door is clearly a euphemism for a woman's vagina and an open door denotes a sexually available woman. In the context of the Song of Songs' exclusive relationship, there is no question of promiscuity, just sexual openness.'[188]

Then it is the turn of the woman to feel arousal: her hands drip with myrrh – a symbol for sexuality all through the book so far (in 1:13; 3:6; 4:6, 14; 5:1). Hands dripping with myrrh, fingers covered with liquid, aromatic perfume; this is a strong symbol. But the encounter longed for by both never happens.

Is the whole passage a dream sequence, perhaps? If not, what are we to make of this 'missing' of each other for two people who in the previous chapter seem to have found perfect completion together? Is the woman downplaying her reticence here? Is she the one wavering and unable to make up her mind? It is not that she doesn't want him to come in, but initially her desire is not enough for her to get up and go to the door. She doesn't want to put the effort in to get dressed to let him in, and realises too late what her hesitation costs her and how it hurts him, hence the frantic pursuit. Or is it the man who somehow gets his timing wrong? Is he vulnerable or too sensitive, departing before he need lest he be confirmed in his fear of rejection? Is he simply too insistent and impatient? Is the whole passage in fact to do with the act of love itself – with its erotic references to hands and fingers 'dripping with liquid myrrh' – but forced to acknowledge dysfunction and disappointment?

The fact is that all the above can be read into this brief poem describing sudden failure in the midst of something that had been such a success: such truly describes the dance of sexual intimacy and the differences between men and women. The illustration is well worn and banal, but it is sometimes said that men are like gas stoves, igniting instantly but with the flame as instantly extinguished, while women can be more like electric stoves, warming up slowly but taking much more time also to cool down. Is this something of what is being described here – albeit much more poetically?

Perhaps the Bride herself is reluctant and forgetful, at fault for sleeping soundly when a rendezvous had been planned? This too is possible and such mishaps can easily happen in intimate relationship. We can understand different things from this short snapshot of disappointment for both parties.

At the same time, we can learn positive things from the awakening and the appetite of both. Certainly the Bride is not stereotypically uninterested in intimacy; quite the opposite. At the missing of this opportunity she says: *My soul failed me* or, 'I felt I was going to die.' (The same Hebrew expression is used of Rachel dying in Genesis 35:18.) The woman is overwhelmed by her yearnings, and places herself in jeopardy as a result. Love will cause people to cross land and sea to be with the other, as the cliché has it. It causes the Bride to forgo her comfort and to put herself at risk. There is a desire for intimacy that emanates strongly from the woman. She is not afraid of owning her love and, as we shall see, of speaking openly and articulately about it. She is not oppressed by or in fear of her man, and he is not taking her by force: he withdraws and does not insist. He waits without bitterness and in the end he is rewarded.

The beatings from the watchmen over this search for each other are difficult to interpret. Does the whole passage represent a dream sequence, as I mooted above and some commentators insist? Perhaps we can understand them as having to do with the negative attitudes (abuse even) of the watching world concerning the foolishness they see in the lengths to which lovers will go to connect? This is the unsympathetic public gaze versus the private intimacies of the couple. But the Bride is undeterred, does not take umbrage, does not question her beloved's actions, but pursues him with conviction and freedom. As such we might say with Solomon in Proverbs 31 that 'She is a priceless woman to be praised.'

The woman is asked: 'What's so special about this man?' She does not hesitate to enumerate his virtues, beginning with the fact that he is *outstanding among ten thousand* and concluding that he is *altogether lovely. This is my beloved, this is my friend.*

This is the only long physical description of the man in the Song, set against three long poems about the woman by the man. It is similar in technique, moving down from head, eyes, cheeks, lips, arms, body, to legs and back to the 'mouth most sweet'. In the song of the heart, it is an encouragement to lovers to find their voice and praise their beloved openly. As her description travels down his body from head to toe it is an encouragement to lovers to look at one another and to linger and to express poetically what they see. She sees a body that she loves and is enthusiastic about it – and we note that this is in the canon of Scripture, that this is seen as good.

This sequence can remind us of the way that public displays of affection ('PDAs') are often viewed critically in our culture, and how the same is true of religion. People don't mind religion in the UK, as long as it is private, kept hidden away out of sight, in the dark. But the idea that someone might pursue Christ against the conventions of culture, and risk a public disturbance thereby, receives strong condemnation and persecution.

That said, this could also be applied within the Church: when one individual is deeply pursuing Christ, it often stirs up discomfort or resentment in others who may feel that their own faith seems inadequate by contrast – yet, rather than adopting a more fervent attitude themselves, they instead turn on the individual concerned and accuse them of being 'over-emotional' about God.

Even commentators trying to avoid an allegorical interpretation of the Song at this point admit that the description is 'exalted, even holy . . . we note that this verse and the next reflect the language used in the description of resources used in the temple'.[189] This neatly brings us on to the divine romance. But it is not the only thing that does so; the idea of sleeping but having an awakened heart, *I slept but my heart was awake*, strikes deep: 'Here we find an unheard-of paradoxical union. We see from this how high the soul rises above itself . . . Enjoying the contemplation solely of that which is . . . the revelation of God in divine wakefulness. May we make ourselves worthy of it by attaining through sleep to wakefulness of soul.'[190]

The divine romance interpretation is here deepened with the graphic image of the head of *finest gold* (ESV), the lips dripping myrrh. The line *My beloved is outstanding among ten thousand* and the sure declaration that *This is my beloved, this is my friend* have rich resonance and an evocative energy in thinking about the Bride's love for Christ. Through all the centuries of the Church, the particular images in Chapter 5 have pressed those reading the Song to see this as yet another reason to apply the imagery, indeed the whole sequence, to the divine romance.

Jesus speaks of himself as the Bridegroom on various occasions in the Gospels. The prophets Hosea, Ezekiel, Jeremiah and Isaiah all use the imagery of Israel's relationship to God as being like a divine marriage. It may be a tempestuous relationship, sometimes faithless on the Bride's part. God the Bridegroom is utterly faithful; but he will at times 'hide his face'. But as Isaiah insists: 'For a brief moment I abandoned you, but with deep compassion I will bring you back' (Isaiah 54:7) – and Isaiah 62:4–5 prophesies: 'the LORD will take delight in you, and your land will be married . . . as a bridegroom rejoices over his bride, so will your God rejoice over you.'

This prophetic intent of the divine Bridegroom to take delight in his Bride receives a vocabulary here in the Song of Songs. But it is more particularly Isaiah's 'brief moment' of absence and sense of abandonment, along with the ensuing darkness, that can be said to be poignantly expressed in Chapter 5.

It is this fifth chapter of the Song of Songs that is the beating heart in Scripture for the concept of the 'dark night of the soul'. Aloneness, darkness and persecution: the dark night is the experience of the sleepy Bride who is slow to respond, who misses her beloved, who finds he is gone and who ends up beaten and with her protective veil removed.

As we have noted earlier, few escape times of darkness in their lives, and few Christian lives escape times of desert and absence. It may be circumstances of illness, barrenness, loss, bereavement, breakdown of relationship that we travel through. I write for all those navigating pain and loss, and I know these seasons myself. It may be an absence of the presence we have grown to love and recognise as God, lost completely for periods of time – times which may last longer than we feel we can bear.

As is the case here, these may well follow times of great 'presence'. An aching and a longing is felt for the blessedness once experienced almost tangibly. Like the Bride we get up to respond but find 'my beloved had turned and gone'. This is thick night, pitch-black.

What can come to help us in this context? What can help to lighten our darkness? Counter-intuitively perhaps, I believe that one source of comfort even in the worst times is the ancient idea of the 'dark night of the soul' itself. This Christian understanding was developed principally by John of the Cross, a sixteenth-century Spanish monk and friend of St Teresa of Avila. The insight he developed is that God will allow the Christian to travel through darkness – and that it is precisely in the darkness that we will learn to lean on God. There are invaluable lessons, he says, that can only be learnt in the darkness of suffering. So it is, paradoxically, that those who are wise will even welcome the darkness. Hence John of the Cross's poem:

> One dark night,
> fired with love's urgent longings – ah, the sheer grace! –
> I went out unseen,
> my house being now all stilled.
>
> . . .
>
> On that glad night,
> in secret, for no one saw me,
> nor did I look at anything,
> with no other light or guide
> than the one that burned in my heart.
>
> . . .
>
> O guiding night!
> O night more lovely than the dawn!
> O night that has united
> the lover with his beloved
>
> . . .
>
> I abandoned and forgot myself,
> laying my face on my Beloved;
> all things ceased; I went out from myself,
> leaving my cares
> forgotten among the lilies.[191]

This is evocative language. John's great contribution was to dare to call this a 'glad night'; he finds night 'more lovely than the dawn'. He calls it a guiding night that will get his heart burning with love for the lover of his soul. John of the Cross is drawing on the episodes in the Song of Songs where the Bride is sent out into the night. This is her experience in Chapter 3:

All night long on my bed I looked for the one my heart loves; I looked for him but did not find him. I will get up now and go about the city, through its streets and squares; I will search for the one my heart loves. So I looked for him but did not find him. The watchmen found me as they made their rounds in the city. 'Have you seen the one my heart loves?' Scarcely had I passed them when I found the one my heart loves. I held him and would not let him go . . . (Song of Songs 3:1–4)

She finds her beloved and clings to him and will not let him go. So, for us, night can be made helpful in (eventually) increasing the power of loving connection. But later (here in Chapter 5), she is again drawn out into the night and cannot find him. On this second occasion she tells how *The watchmen found me as they made their rounds in the city. They beat me, they bruised me; they took away my cloak, those watchmen of the walls!* (5:7). But she breaks through this negative experience into an even greater love for her divine lover.

This is the essence of John of the Cross's contribution. He writes in his Prologue to The Ascent of Mount Carmel: 'The darknesses and trials, spiritual and temporal, that fortunate souls ordinarily undergo on their way to the high state of perfection are so numerous and profound that human science cannot understand them adequately. Nor does experience of them equip one to explain them.' John goes on to say that his main guide will be the Scriptures. Later he talks of the fact that people in the dark night will frequently meet someone who 'in the style of Job's comforters, will proclaim that all this is due to melancholia or depression or temperament or some hidden wickedness, and that as a result, God has forsaken them'. He concludes, however, with this core idea: 'God is the author of this enlightenment in the night of contemplation.'[192] All this is for the encouragement of those in the darkness – may it help us gain a theology of suffering that works in the real world.

Those going through the trouble, sorrow and adversity that feels like this kind of darkness may well feel 'beaten'. The internet has brought a new aspect to this darkness. People are confronted with online attacks on social media or blogging against them which can be particularly vicious precisely because they are anonymous and unverifiable. Accusations are made and may be refuted, but the urban myths established thereby, whether on a national stage for political or religious leaders, or among friendship circles for individuals, especially younger people, may never die. This certainly also happens in the Christian arena. Such can be part of one's darkness. But it was ever thus. Jesus' saying: 'Woe to you when everyone speaks well of you' (Luke 6:26) is one word of paradoxical comfort from Christ to hold on to in such times.

Godly lovers of the poor speak of it too. Mother Teresa of Calcutta, according to letters released in 2007, provides a truly long-term case of travelling through the dark night of the soul, as she tells of her personal struggles, lasting from her first intimate call from God to found the Sisters of Charity in 1948, almost up until her death in 1997, with only brief interludes of relief in between. Franciscan Father Benedict Groeschel, a friend of Mother Teresa for a large part of her life, claims that this depression-like darkness left her only towards the end of her life.

In lands under persecution, there are real physical attacks that bring on this darkness – they could involve imprisonment, loss of work, separation from children, and the possibility of execution. Others have walked this way before, of course. Many of David's psalms testify to this sense of oppression, betrayal and real battle.

These times are important because they are when we have to realise that God wants us to trust him, to hold his hand in the darkness.

While we may have a simple plan for our life – to be happy, prosperous, successful and at peace – what God wants is for us to learn to trust him deeply and against the odds. Trouble comes for us when these two programmes are going in opposite directions, for God's is stronger and he will prevail. The Bride in the Song learns a deeper dependence; she is not offended. It is good when we decide not to be offended with God, not to accuse him of not knowing what he is doing, not to resist going down his path for us, but instead to trust him. This will prove transformational. We become someone who 'leans not on our own understanding'. We learn an eternal lesson. We can walk in his love – and give it away. The Bride in the Song, having been beaten up, when asked to tell what is so special about her beloved, says without hesitation: *My beloved is . . . outstanding among ten thousand* (5:10). She gives voice to a beautiful description as of Christ. That epiphany comes right after this darkness. There is now no hint of mistrust. She has broken through to maturity. And so may we, if we will persist in treading this road less travelled.

The Bible is shot through with epiphanies, revelations or unveilings, when God comes near. In a way what we see here is similar to what happens at the end of the Bible. In a time of darkness and exile, the Apostle John has what is named the Revelation. It contains the last word on Christ, his Church and the future of the world, and on the presence of evil in this present darkness. In Chapter 5 of the Song, we join the Bride who describes her beloved as *outstanding* (NIV), or *the chiefest* (KJV). The Church Fathers spent much time preaching on – unveiling, if you like – this revelation in Song of Songs, and we will join them in daring to speak of the different physical attributes of this prince, the fairest among ten thousand. All these outer attributes represent inner beauty of character. The Bride looks on her beloved from head to toe and gladly tells out the dazzling, outstanding beauty of her Bridegroom.

His head is purest gold (5:11)

Having this revelation of Christ as the head of the Church is full of consequences for our trust in his ways. His head is of purest gold, 'because of the goodness of the Deity, that is, the gold of the land of the living surpasses all things that have been made by him . . . for he is so brilliant that he cannot be seen by human eyes and those who live in the flesh'.[193] John of Ford has this: 'His head is the finest gold. He is in the heart of the Father where He peers into the depths of the riches of his wisdom and knowledge. He is in the soul of the Father, where he searches out the treasures of wisdom and benevolence. He is in the holy place of God's righteousness, penetrating all the depths of his judgements and the secrets of His decrees.'[194]

For me, his head being of 'purest gold' speaks of his leadership, which has been refined – made perfect through suffering – and can thus lead us also through painful refining. This is a great comfort to know, and we can trust him. 'He leads me beside quiet waters,' says the psalmist.[195] Some time ago I had to deal with some dark and difficult issues in the church body I was leading at that time. My former college principal, Alec Motyer, got to hear about it, and wrote to me: 'Your dear friends came by last Friday and let me know that you have passed through trying and stressful circumstance in the church . . . Please God the stressful times are becoming history. They may or may not be productive of evident blessing but, if the Lord should will to unroll the scroll of the eternal future, you will see that everything has not only worked for good but for very good indeed. The great thing – indeed, in ultimate terms, the only thing – is to keep our eyes turned on Jesus.' He went on in the same letter to speak in completely trusting terms of the recent, unexpected death of his wife: 'She slipped off Home bathed in the most perfect, even tangible peace. It was not that we expected this; it leapt upon us. Heaven came to earth. The gap left by her going is deep and wide. Life has but now no earthly focal point, but, otherwise is proving manageable – though I would be hard put to define what manageable means.' Here is a man who has absolute trust in the pure and perfect headship and leadership of Christ in his life. He trusts that *His head is purest gold*. Few perhaps are those who know it so deeply.

His hair is wavy and black as a raven (5:11)
The Bridegroom's wavy hair carries a nostalgic echo, or perhaps it is a prophetic fulfilment of a group of men set apart, the Nazirites of old, like Samuel or Samson or, later, John the Baptist, whose dedication was expressed in 'not letting a razor touch their head'. These were a company of dedicated servant leaders whose lives prophetically pointed forward to the One who was completely dedicated, sold out, given over to the purposes of God. There was no mixture or compromise in Christ, whose life flowed with holiness like his flowing hair.

Other medieval commentators have discerned that 'by saying black like a raven she points to the hiding place of veiled mysteries . . . concealed by great darkness as the prophet David said: "Clouds and thick darkness are round about him".'[196]

His eyes are like doves by the water streams (5:12)
We could spend a week meditating on his eyes. They speak of his knowledge, perfect and without deformity. They were single and strong; piercing like fire; yet limpid with love. 'Jesus looked at him and loved him', it is said of Christ's gaze on the departing rich young ruler.[197] Psalm 33:18 says: 'the eyes of the LORD are on those who fear him, on those whose hope is in his unfailing love'. The Bride has had an epiphany of what love looks like: she is saying, 'I know your eyes will see me. You haven't overlooked me. You have skilful discernment to know where I am.' It is important for us to know his omniscience. This keeps us from both fear and sin. But it also encourages us as we go through trials and tribulation. She knows his discernment about what she needs is absolutely perfect.

His cheeks are like beds of spice yielding perfume (5:13)
For James Durham – whose commentary (published in 1668) received a glowing commendation from John Owen[198] – the sweet-smelling cheeks 'must be somewhat whereby Christ becomes sensibly sweet and refreshful to the soul's senses than flowers of perfume are for the bodily senses; therefore his love is compared to ointment' (see 1:3). Mike Bickle says: 'His cheeks, his emotions are like "banks of scented herbs".' He comments that there are so many different types of emotions that are fragrant, that are pleasing to us. Many people think that the only emotion God has is joy when they become Christians, followed by anger when they

let him down. 'But His emotions are heaps of diverse, sweet fragrances to us. Jesus' emotional make-up is filled with passion and delight and longing for you. Jesus also has a passion for His Father, His creation, His holiness, His kingdom and so on.'[199] 'They are tremendous and dignified yet also with effervescent joy coming from Him.'[200]

It is noteworthy that the Bridegroom of the Song of Songs says of the Bride: *You have stolen my heart . . . with one glance of your eyes . . .* (4:9). It may take a personal epiphany, but we need to understand that although this is the maker of the universe, you or I can, it seems, affect his heart with one glance of our eyes of love and faith directed to him. This is no stoic deity without feeling, but a passionate lover of our souls. Thank God – and may we love him back!

His lips are like lilies dripping with myrrh (5:13)
Christ's words have the sweetness of lilies. We know that they are read more, quoted more, believed more and translated more than any others – because they are the greatest words ever spoken. Bernard Ramm has said about Jesus' words that 'Their greatness lies in the pure lucid spirituality in dealing clearly, definitively, authoritatively with the greatest problems that throb in the human breast . . . They are the kind of words and the kind of answers we would expect God to give.'[201] They are lilies dripping with myrrh. At the same time his words woo me out of a life of self-indulgence, as myrrh evokes death on the cross and thus death to self. These are words about redemption and the cross.

His arms are rods of gold set with topaz (5:14)
His arms, his powerful actions, are royal, golden and bejewelled. These are the works in which his power and skill are

shown. Especially perhaps Jesus' work in redemption, when he stretched forth his arms and hands on the cross, is a work of infinite skill, wisely contrived and exquisitely executed.

His body is like polished ivory decorated with lapis lazuli (5:14)
Older Bible versions (the KJV, for example) translate body as 'belly', giving us more of a sense of the deepest emotions of love. Even older translations give it as 'bowels'. It is the same Hebrew word as used in Isaiah 63:15 (KJV) to speak of the 'bowels of mercy' of God towards his people. It is again to be found in Jeremiah 31:20 (KJV), 'my bowels are troubled for him'. Durham relates this to the Bridegroom's depth of love: 'The words at first signify the intense love and tender affection wherewith our Lord Jesus (who is full of grace) is filled and stuffed (to say so) for the good of his people; no mother is so compassionately affected towards the fruit of her womb as he is for his own.' He concludes that 'this is the constraining, ravishing, engaging, and soul-inebriating consideration of Christ, conceiving him rightly in his admirable love'.[202] Such is the diamond-like nature of his love: it is tender but tough, like carved ivory, rare and expensive.

His legs are pillars of marble set on bases of pure gold. His appearance is like Lebanon, choice as its cedars (5:15)
God's eternal plan and the way he fulfils his divine purpose is durable and stable and beautiful like pillars of marble. His appearance is tall, stately, honourable and fragrant, like the cedar trees of Lebanon.

His mouth is sweetness itself (5:16)
With this idea, we return to what some hold as the 'main

idea' of the Song: the kiss of God. If we liken the kiss of God to a human kiss, it resolves everything. We remind ourselves of Hesse's brilliant lines quoted earlier:

> At that first kiss I felt
> Something melt inside me
> That hurt in an exquisite way . . .
> Everything was transformed and enchanted
> And made sense.[203]

Seventeenth-century Puritan Richard Sibbes spoke of the Spirit as 'the sweet kiss of the soul – experiencing spiritual ravishings, the beginning of heaven – heaven before its time'.[204] Samuel Rutherford, writing from a Scottish jail, speaks of 'a springtide of God's love'. He writes: 'My sweet Lord has taken off his mask and said "kiss thy fill" – the Bridegroom's love hath run away with my heart – Oh love, love, love.'[205]

In fact, the kiss is a universal symbol of intimacy, whether between friends or lovers. The kiss of God therefore is simply an experience of the presence and the love of God. I would say that the 'kisses of his word' are to be experienced daily. Someone said: 'Is not the kiss the very autograph of love?'[206] We kiss him but he kisses us also. It is not to be missed. This kiss brings transformation.

Such then is the Bride's vision of the beauty of Christ. It is so majestic that the Bride cries out in conclusion: *He is altogether lovely. This is my beloved*, adding, *this is my friend.* Deep calls to deep: it is intimate and challenging. This little book can help us to travel through the dark night, and help us as we do so to discover a vocabulary for loving God with all our heart, mind, soul and strength.

Spiritual exercises for the dark night of the soul

In Psalm 63 David says: 'I thirst for you, my whole being longs for you, in a dry and parched land where there is no water. I have seen you in the sanctuary and beheld your power and your glory' (vv. 1–2).

John of the Cross in *The Dark Night of the Soul* comments: 'David's teaching here is that the means to the knowledge of God were not the many spiritual delights he had received, but the detachments . . . of the dry and desert land . . . Also the way to experience and vision of the power of God did not consist in ideas and meditations about God . . . but in his inability to grasp God and to walk by means of any meditation: This inability is referred to as a land without a way. Hence the dark night with its aridities and voids is the means to the knowledge of God.'[207]

For this exercise, do not use any meditation but attempt simply to sit still before the Lord and contemplate him; silently 'behold him in the sanctuary'. Perhaps there will be revelation or visitation – perhaps not. But whatever the case, 'Be still'.

'The cities may be beautiful and comely, but they are
also awe inspiring . . . the animals and fruit . . . are
robust. The cosmic referents are clearly daunting. The
beauty here described does not conform to any
feminine stereotype of soft, crafted, fragile loveliness. It
is an open beauty, not protected or hidden from view. It
is an honest beauty, neither seductive nor in any other
way manipulative. It is an unpretentious beauty,
authentic and straightforward.'
Dianne Bergant[208]

'"Come, I will show you the bride, the wife of the
Lamb." And he carried me away in the Spirit to a
great, high mountain, and showed me the Holy City,
Jerusalem, coming down out of heaven from God. It
shone with the glory of God, and its brilliance was like
that of a very precious jewel, like a jasper, clear as
crystal. It had a great, high wall with twelve gates, and
with twelve angels at the gates. On the gates were
written the names of the twelve tribes of Israel. There
were three gates on the east, three on the north, three
on the south and three on the west. The wall of the city
had twelve foundations, and on them were the names
of the twelve apostles of the Lamb.'
Revelation 21:9–14

CHAPTER TWELVE

The Only One – 'My dove, my perfect one, is unique'

Friends

Where has your beloved gone, most beautiful of women?
Which way did your beloved turn, that we may look for
him with you?

She

My beloved has gone down to his garden, to the beds of
spices, to browse in the gardens and to gather lilies.
I am my beloved's and my beloved is mine; he browses
among the lilies.

He

You are as beautiful as Tirzah, my darling, as lovely as
Jerusalem, as majestic as troops with banners.
Turn your eyes from me; they overwhelm me. Your hair is
like a flock of goats descending from Gilead.
Your teeth are like a flock of sheep coming up from the
washing. Each has its twin, not one of them is missing.
Your temples behind your veil are like the halves of a
pomegranate.
Sixty queens there may be, and eighty concubines, and
virgins beyond number; but my dove, my perfect one, is
unique, the only daughter of her mother, the favourite of
the one who bore her. The young women saw her and
called her blessed; the queens and concubines praised her.

Song of Songs 6:1–9

The night has cleared and it is a new day – a new episode in the lovers' story. So glorious has been the Bride's description of her man, the *outstanding among ten thousand*, that the women of Jerusalem say: 'We want to see him too.'[209] She says, *My beloved has gone down to his garden* – this phrase was full of meaning for the Church Fathers. They always saw this as speaking of Christ's 'coming down to earth to be incarnate of the Virgin Mary and be made man . . .'.

In the song of the human lovers, the 'garden' certainly has suggestions of intimacy, enjoyment, closeness – with rich textures, the talk of beds of spices, grazing, gathering lilies. The last time we came across the garden, the Bride said, *Let my lover come into his garden and taste its choice fruit*, and the Bridegroom replied: *I have come . . .*

Here the Bride is enjoying her lover, it seems: she says, *I am my beloved's and my beloved is mine*. This is the language of growing relationship. It is slightly different from the *My beloved is mine and I am his* of Chapter 2. Some see progression in the relationship: confidence, a greater abandonment; less possessiveness and more trust, as is fitting. So it is that without restraint *he browses among the lilies*. There is a lingering loving enjoying that speaks of pleasure and peace and trust. This contrasts with the lurching drama of the dark night. This may relate to the seasons of peace and rest and joy that there can be and that are to be expected in a relationship. The woman is pleased that he should 'graze' or 'browse'.

He then speaks to her, comparing her to cities; there is a comparison to Jerusalem, putting us in mind of the glorious New Jerusalem of Revelation 21. The Bride is gorgeous like a city, but it is a complex picture – she is also like an army with banners. It is hard to picture this today – today's armies seem far from beautiful as they dress for the desert, and we are very aware that they defend us from bombs, terror and death but also dispense death and destruction. Yet at the time of the Song, there is no hesitation in ascribing great beauty to an army with banners. We may get a sense of it if we imagine the Trooping the Colour ceremony in London, which is watched by millions each year.

As Balaam saw amid the threat of war in Numbers 24:5–6, 8–9: 'How beautiful are your tents, Jacob, your dwelling places, Israel! Like valleys they spread out, like gardens beside a river, like aloes planted by the LORD, like cedars beside the waters . . . God brought them out of Egypt . . . May those who bless you be blessed!'

The Bridegroom then speaks of the power of the Bride's gaze, asking her to turn her eyes away from him, as he is overwhelmed. In a relationship a gaze, a look, a locking together of eyes can have a delightful, even devastating effect. We should not underestimate this and should strive never to lose our understanding of it. Shakespeare understood this, writing, for example, in Sonnet 17:

> If I could write the beauty of your eyes,
> And in fresh numbers number all your graces,
> The age to come would say, 'This poet lies;
> Such heavenly touches ne'er touch'd earthly faces.'

Here in the Song, the man is thus 'overwhelmed'. This is the second of three similar descriptions of the Bride, each speaking of eyes, teeth, cheeks. In fact there is a word-for-word repetition of 4:1–3. But here, for the first time, he concludes that 'my dove, my perfect one, is unique' or the 'only one' (ESV), leading us into the important theme of exclusiveness. This is 'the one'. There is no other.

This may, as we have said, be the story of the love affair between a young boy and a shepherd girl. This passage is one that adds weight to this interpretation.

Or the Song may be the story of Solomon at the start of his reign, when he asked for wisdom and received so much of the favour of God above and beyond that request. He wrote 1,005 songs, we are told – of which this may be the greatest.[210] But we also know that Solomon became promiscuous and fell into sexual sin – it may have been some kind of sexual addiction, such as we see diagnosed today. Later in his life he strayed far from the description in verse 9: *my dove, my perfect one, is the only one* (ESV). He abandoned the loving monogamy that this passage speaks of, with truly catastrophic consequences for the kingdom, leading to idolatry and so much loss.[211] This makes us pause and realise the weight of what is described here.

This disparity is one of the reasons why many commentators don't ascribe all of this song to Solomon. Another is that the Bride will soon contrast the love she has with her beloved with Solomon, and declares that even for the wealth of Solomon's house she wouldn't turn from it. Thus Solomon is held up to provide a contrast with the kind of love expressed here.

The practice of adultery and the straying from faithful relationship arguably led to the downfall of the monarchy and thus planted the seeds that ended in exile. This seems to begin in David's household in 2 Samuel, as he and then some of his sons act in sinful ways, which for a number of them leads to death. David and Bathsheba's child dies; Amnon rapes Tamar, which leads to Amnon's death. Absalom sleeps with his father's concubines as part of his rebellion – and then Absalom dies. Adonijah desires Abishag, which in turns brings him the sentence of death. Solomon's son Rehoboam's pride then leads to the loss of half the kingdom, and the death of the dream of a united kingdom in the Promised Land (1 Kings 12). One of the implications appears to be that unfaithful relationship is a reflection of the deeper issues of the heart. Adultery is linked to idolatry and turning one's eyes to the temptations of the world, rather than fixing them on God.

But to return to the Song itself: for this moment, for its author, the Bride is *the only one*. In a relationship, this is a key moment; one that changes everything. It is the day when a choice comes for commitment and love – a commitment which excludes all others, for she is *the perfect one, the only one*. A man will not only leave his mother and father, but will also leave and be dead to all other women. A woman will leave all other men. This exclusive relationship, or monogamy, is in the plan of God. We find it at the beginning, in the creation narratives. By the time of David and Solomon – for these kings at least – it had been replaced by polygamous and frequently disastrous royal liaisons.

But when Christ, the One greater than Solomon came, he repeated the Genesis mandate: 'A man will leave his mother and father and be united to his wife and the two will become one flesh' (2:24), concluding in Matthew 19:6, 'So they are no longer two, but one flesh. Therefore what God has joined together, let no one separate.'

Paul, in the same way, advises Timothy that an elder 'must be the husband of one wife'. There is a recurrent strand promoting the privilege of 'passionate monogamy' that we find expressed here in Songs 6. Cultures change and fashions influence our thought processes, but this couple lead us to value this aspiration that there should be 'an only one' – a freeing fact when we can recognise its truth. When this is declared, it brings security, confidence, intimacy and courage to travel through difficulty: 'For better for worse, for richer for poorer, in sickness and in health, till death us do part.'

In my journey as a pastor I have lost count of the number of marriages I have had the privilege of celebrating. But there has been one and only one occasion (in France, as it happens) when the bridegroom intentionally mis-repeated the vows I was leading him through, saying publicly, '. . . *pour le meilleur, mais pas pour le pire*' ('for better, but not for worse'. People were dismayed. He passed it off as a joke. But the chilling fact is that the marriage lasted about a month.

The truth is that even with the most godly intentions, some covenant marriages fail, and we have to acknowledge that – sadly, humbly and with sympathy and compassion. This is a mystery we should not enter into judgement over as there is already enough pain around in such a tearing apart of two people God has joined. May God help us nevertheless to understand and then, by his grace, to live out his covenant promises and purposes.

What does this passage say to help us in this journey to exclusive permanence? The passage speaks of that mutual enjoyment:

> *My beloved has gone down to his garden, to the beds of spices, to browse in the gardens and to gather lilies. I am my beloved's and my beloved is mine; he browses among the lilies.* (6:2)

This may speak of enjoyment of each other. A couple can learn from this about listening and looking. In the press of life, so many couples forget to browse among the infinite riches of the thought and insights of the other – and to take pleasure in this. A couple may do well to plan regular – daily and weekly – times alone, with no agenda but simply to listen and learn about the other's insights. These words may, though, speak also of lingering lovemaking: 'browsing among the lilies' has sensual echoes to it; this too will protect a couple's love from going cold.

And now, concerning the divine romance, what does this passage have to say to comfort and strengthen us on our journey of exclusive devotion to the holy lover of our souls?

The passage begins with the lover 'going down to the garden'. Christ came down when the whole creation was groaning and travailing in pain, and looking for the prom- ised saviour. He came down from his unspeakable majesty to take our lowly nature. He came down to his garden as the true gardener to plant God's field anew. Summing up the writings of the Fathers on this incarnation passage, Marvin Pope writes:

> He came to cultivate the garden again by planting virtues there . . . by the channels of His word to nurture the plants and especially the spice beds as those souls in whom the odours of holiness abound . . . His gathering of lilies was understood by some of the fathers as taking out of the world holy people who had attained to perfect whiteness . . . To do this, He went down into the garden tomb . . . Had He not gone down to overcome the sharpness of death, He could not have delighted in the holy feeding in the gardens, in the many churches of the faithful throughout the world . . .[212]

You are as beautiful as . . . (6:4)
The Bridegroom then breaks his silence to declare: *You are as beautiful as Tirzah, my love, lovely as Jerusalem, awesome as an army with banners* (6:4). He has been absent, but after

seeing her extravagant worship in 5:10–16, now he responds. If we, the Church, were facing a time of trial or dark night, we might say that Jesus was silent through it all. However, even in the difficulty the Bride boldly proclaimed: 'He's outstanding, he's dazzling, he's altogether beautiful. This is my lover and this is my friend.'

He now in turn describes her beauty in three ways – as Tirzah, as Jerusalem and as an army with banners. Some have asserted that this beauty was imparted to her through her trials and tribulations.[213] She ends up lovely, beautiful and worthy of admiration. He calls her *my love*. His first utterance communicates his affection. This phrase expresses how he feels about her. Augustine has said that the only praise to be desired and the only praise that is true, is praise that comes from God. God promises his redeemed such love through the prophet Isaiah: 'No longer will they call you Deserted, or name your land Desolate. But you will be called Hephzibah, and your land Beulah; for the LORD will take delight in you' (Isaiah 62:4).

It is interesting that each time Bride and groom address each other throughout the book they use the language 'you are beautiful' or 'my love' or 'my beloved'. We would do well to learn to do likewise in our human relationships of love.

The Bridegroom here celebrates the marvellous beauty worked in her by the Holy Spirit. Nine times in the Song, the Bridegroom affirms his Bride's beauty (1:15a; 1:15b; 2:10, 13; 4:1a; 4:1b; 4:7; 6:4; 7:7). Her beauty is the fruit of divine testing. She may feel herself bruised and battered by trials; but that is not how God sees her.

In a way, this beauty is the end product of her trials. All through the season of difficulty God may be said to be perfecting her heart for him. Romans 8:18 teaches that the sufferings of this age are not worthy to compare to the 'glory' or 'incomparable beauty' to be imparted to and revealed in us.

This is also true in a marriage relationship: the trials that each goes through can adorn and make beautiful. As strength of character grows through suffering, graceful looks grow too and the one can say genuinely to the other: *You are as beautiful as Tirzah.*

You are as beautiful as Tirzah, my darling . . . (v. 4)
Tirzah, in the Northern Kingdom of Israel, was so named because of its remarkable natural beauty. The word *Tirzah* literally means beautiful, or pleasant. Before Israel conquered the land of Palestine, Tirzah was a capital city. This can speak of the Bride as being beautiful in the midst of unbelievers. This is Mike Bickle's view: 'He is telling her that she will be effective in winning unbelievers. Her beauty would not only be seen by God, it would be beautiful enough to win the cynics and those that were blinded and darkened of heart.' This may seem a lot to read into this, but there is a mystery and beauty here that certainly is winsome.

you are . . . as lovely as Jerusalem (v. 4)
God ordained Jerusalem as the national centre of worship. His presence, the Shekinah glory of God, dwelt in Solomon's temple in Jerusalem. In a sense Jerusalem became the most significant city in the whole earth, because it was the only city where the Shekinah glory of God dwelt.

you are . . . as majestic as troops with banners (v. 4)
Again, Bickle writes: 'An army with banners speaks of a victorious army. When an army returned victorious from war, it marched down the streets with banners. We can say

she came through the test of the dark night as a victorious army with banners. She didn't give in to the devil by accusing God. She didn't lose her life in God when everything went wrong circumstantially. But she said, "I love Him! He's dazzling!" He responds, "You are like a victorious army. You endured the most difficult test possible and you came forth in spiritual victory." In a time of testing, the Holy Spirit poured loyal love into her heart for Jesus. He is declaring, "You are to Me as a victorious army. You have conquered the sinful passions of your own heart by the Spirit. You have struggled and defeated the enemies of your soul."'[214]

I believe this is a helpful reading in the light of the many trials believers can face. It is not that we *may* face trials in the life of love into which the believer is called, but rather that we *will* inevitably face trials. Sometimes they are completely beyond our power to cope with or understand, like the beating that the Bride has gone through in the night. It is of great comfort that God sees and affirms the Bride's beauty in these times – times which come because the whole of creation is groaning.

Early on (2:4) she said, *Let his banner over me be love*; now she is marching in victory with the banners of the love of God.

Overwhelming eyes

Turn your eyes from me; they overwhelm me (6:5)

This has been described as one of the most dramatic passages in the Bible. For Jesus to say, 'you overwhelm me', shows us how God is overwhelmed by weak people who are submitted to the Holy Spirit.

By her 'eyes' we can understand that this refers to her love for him sustained during testing. Her eyes were fixed on the

Bridegroom through the testing of 5:6–7. We might think of great parallel Scriptures like: 'fixing our eyes on Jesus, the pioneer and perfecter of faith. For the joy set before him he endured the cross, scorning its shame' (Hebrews 12:2). Or: 'We do not know what to do, but our eyes are on you' (2 Chronicles 20:12).

I believe that fixing our eyes in contemplation and gazing on Christ do in some sense prevail over his heart. The passage suggests her single-minded 'dove's eyes' of devotion are irresistibly beautiful to him. His response, *Turn your eyes from me*, means to turn the gaze of your devotion away. Jesus was not asking for her literally to look away – it was a statement depicting the hold she had upon his heart. We find it hinted at in other Scriptures such as when the Lord told Moses, 'Leave me alone' (Exodus 32:10). Moses had a hold on the heart of God. Similarly, Jacob wrestling with God says, 'I will not let you go unless you bless me' (Genesis 32:26).

Here, for me, it is as if the Lord Jesus could not withstand her gazing affection any more than one man could stand against an entire army. He says, 'Your eyes have overwhelmed me.' This is what God says to people on the earth who feel nothing spiritually and yet stay true to him. She is serving him for him, not just in order that her earthly circumstances should get better, but for himself.

This comes close to the insights of Ignatius's famous exercise of considering the two standards, which we considered in a former chapter: he challenges the believer to enlist not under the standard of the god of this world, but to '"Consider Christ our Lord taking his stand in a great plain in the region of Jerusalem in a lowly attractive spot". Christ chooses people to spread his "sacred doctrine among people of every state and condition." The one wanting to follow Christ more

THE SONG OF SONGS

closely is to consider the speech delivered by our Lord to his servants and friends as he sends them out on this enterprise: "He commends them to seek to help all men and women by attracting them first to the highest spiritual poverty . . . and secondly to the desire for humiliation and contempt. For from these two things follows humility . . ."[215]

She is enlisted as one who does not mind being 'poor in spirit'. It seems that this kind of devotion conquers his heart. So it is that the love of the most fallen, broken people overcomes him. We do not easily understand the heart of Jesus being overwhelmed. Another fruitful exercise might be to picture in your mind the uncreated eternal God speaking in such a way to people on the earth. Yet this passage helps us see that he is overwhelmed by weak, broken people who love him. What overwhelms him? We know that the stars do not, the seas do not, and the armies of history do not. No army can overwhelm him. He steps into time and the armies of God are with him. The demonic powers and principalities cannot conquer him. He is the ultimate warrior.

But he is conquered by the devotion of his Bride. One thing has subdued him: the gaze of his Bride.

> *Your hair is like a flock of goats descending from Gilead. Your teeth are like a flock of sheep coming up from the washing. Each has its twin, not one of them is missing. Your temples behind the veil are like the halves of a pomegranate.* (6:5–7)

Jesus describes her maturity, highlighting three aspects of her character that were first affirmed in 4:1–3. He then moves on to the important statement: *There are sixty queens and eighty concubines, and virgins without number. My dove, my perfect one, is the only one* (6:8–9; ESV). Jesus is describing the

pre-eminence of his Bride (v. 8). He uses a three-fold comparison: his Bride has more honour and excellence than queens,
concubines and virgins.[216] The book of Esther speaks of many
women in the king's court, being prepared for the king
(Esther 2:12–17). The queen was one of many in the royal
courts, but distinguished among all others. The Venerable
Bede (in the eighth century) takes this as referring to immature and imperfect servants of God being described and
compared to the true Bride. 'But the universal Church herself
by right excels all of these. She it is who in these same believing members praises the name of the Lord "from the rising of
the sun to its setting" from the beginning to the end of the
age.' In praise of her he says most beautifully: *My dove, my
perfect one, is the only one,* 'for she does not allow of that division that schism brings'.

Expounding on this word 'one', Bede's concern is unity
and the true catholicity which he finds in Acts 9:31 where it
is said: 'So the church throughout all Judea, Galilee and
Samaria enjoyed a time of peace and was strengthened. Living
in the fear of the Lord and encouraged by the Holy Spirit, it
increased in numbers.' The words 'throughout all' here are
from the Greek *kath holés,* hence 'catholic'.

A. W. Tozer writes of this unity of the Church in a chapter
entitled 'The Art of True Worship' (which could be a subtitle
for the Song of Songs): 'It is rarely that we find anyone aglow
with personal love for Christ . . . This love, as a kind of moral
fragrance, is ever detected on the garments of the saints. The
list of fragrant saints is long. It includes men and women of
every theological shade of theological thought within the
bounds of orthodox Christian faith. This radiant love for
Christ is, to my mind, the test of true catholicity, the one
sure proof of membership of the Church Universal.'[217]

These are challenging comments to reflect on. Am I 'aglow with personal love for Christ', like the Bride in the Song for her lover? Am I part of *the only one of her mother, pure to her who bore her* (6:9; ESV)? Theodoret of Cyrus, writing along the same lines in the fifth century, interprets this, 'Let us understand the Bride stands for those that undergo the hard work of practising virtue solely for the love of the Bridegroom. And choose both to do and to bear all things . . . it is souls of this sort that are possessed only by a longing for Christ that fill the role and rank of the Bride.'[218]

My dove, my perfect one, is the only one, the only one of her mother (6:9)
Perfect, of course, also means mature. God's ultimate design is that the Church would be filled with the maturity that belongs to the fullness of Christ (Ephesians 4:13). His Church will eventually become perfected in love. His Church will be glorious and radiant, without any spot or wrinkle (Ephesians 5:26–27). Part of this perfection will be her unity, for which Jesus himself prayed. She may be made perfect or brought to maturity because she's gone through testing. She's been assaulted by the powers of darkness. He calls her 'my mature one'. Of all the attendants around the throne of God, there are none in the same category as her. She is unique, completely set apart – the essence of the definition of holiness.

The fact may be that the Church has never been mature at any time in history. The church seen in the book of Acts was not a mature church. It had moments of glory for a small amount of time, in one city or another. And the Church across the world, the whole Church worldwide, has never been mature together at any one time. However, the Bible hints that before Christ returns, the Church will have substantial maturity. She will somehow 'make herself ready'.

The Church will enter into the measure of the stature that belongs to the fullness of Christ (Ephesians 4:13). We don't yet know what that will look like. But God will finish what he began. The gates of hell will not prevail against her: she will arise and become prepared.

Spiritual exercises concerning 'the only one'

This chapter has a poem from the Bridegroom describing the Bride (6:4–9), while the previous chapter is a love song from the Bride to the Bridegroom – the only one in the Song (5:10–16). This exercise is a simple encouragement to creative composition:

First, spend some time in quiet contemplation of Christ.

Then write a love song or poem to him. See if you can make it twenty-four lines long, so that there is substantial content, as we find in Chapter 5 of the Song.

Finally, read it out loud as a prayer.

'I do not mean the Church as we see her spread out through all time and space and rooted in eternity, terrible as an army with banners. That, I confess, is a spectacle which makes our boldest tempters uneasy. But fortunately it is quite invisible to these humans.'
C. S. Lewis[219]

'How beautiful are your tents, Jacob, your dwelling places, Israel! Like valleys they spread out, like gardens beside a river, like aloes planted by the Lord, like cedars beside the waters . . .'
Numbers 24:5

CHAPTER THIRTEEN

'Who is this that appears like the dawn?'

Friends
> Who is this that appears like the dawn, fair as the moon,
> bright as the sun, majestic as the stars in procession?

He
> I went down to the grove of nut trees to look at the new
> growth in the valley, to see if the vines had budded or the
> pomegranates were in bloom.
> Before I realised it, my desire set me among the royal char-
> iots of my people.

Friends
> Come back, come back, O Shulammite; come back, come
> back, that we may gaze on you!

He
> Why would you gaze on the Shulammite as on the dance of
> Mahanaim?

Song of Songs 6:10–13

It is interesting that Lewis, in *The Screwtape Letters*, assumes
this passage speaks of the Church. But then, those attempt-
ing to read the Song only literally are hard pressed here to
find a meaning that fits the fast-moving images of this brilliant section of the Song. Certainly the Bridegroom is reaching
for extravagant comparisons: a Bride *awesome as an army
with banners* (ESV) or *majestic as the stars in procession* (NIV).

We have already mentioned Fernand Dumont, who writes of 'a woman not yet seen, but whose perfume accumulates on the horizon like a storm cloud'.[220] And this just about captures the captivating woman described here.

On a personal level this metaphor speaks to the way that – like a military force appearing on the horizon to besiege a city – a lover has the power to demolish all of our walls of defence, and lay siege to the heart. In love, above all things, we are made vulnerable to the conquest of another who overrides even our greatest defences. This is a thrill, but terrifying too, because letting somebody in is like flying a white flag and trusting that once you surrender yourself to them, they won't hurt you with the power they now have over your heart.

The rest of this section is obscure for those seeking a literal love-affair interpretation of the poem. 'The next verse is considered the most difficult in the entire song,' says Bergant. Similarly Longman: 'commentators agree on the incredible difficulty of the text'.[221] But in this section it is when we move to consider allegory that the meanings locked up begin to reveal powerful truths buried inside them. So for the rest of this chapter we will be reading allegorically, exploring the divine romance.

John Donne's brilliant sonnet, which I referenced in the first chapter of this book, links the love of God to an army invading his personal city:

> Batter my heart, three-person'd God, for you
> As yet but knock, breathe, shine, and seek to mend;
> That I may rise and stand, o'erthrow me, and bend
> Your force to break, blow, burn, and make me new.
> I, like an usurp'd town to another due,
> Labor to admit you, but oh, to no end . . .

In this section the Bride is again *terrible as an army with banners* (KJV) in her effect on the Bridegroom and on the watching world. The seventeenth- and early eighteenth-century Puritan commentator Matthew Henry effortlessly interprets Songs 6:10 in this way: 'Who is she that looks forth as the morning? This is applicable both to the church in the world and to grace in the heart. They are amiable as the light, the most beautiful of all visible things. Christians are, or should be, the lights of the world. The patriarchal church looked forth as the morning when the promise of the Messiah was first made known, and the day-spring from on high visited this dark world. The Jewish church was fair as the moon; the ceremonial law was an imperfect light; it shone by reflection; it was changing as the moon, did not make day, nor had the sun of righteousness yet risen. But the Christian church is clear as the sun, exhibits a great light to those that sat in darkness.'[222]

Who is this who looks down like the dawn, beautiful as the moon, bright as the sun, awesome as an army with banners? (ESV). This is a rhetorical question affirming the place of pre-eminence that the Bride has in the created order. The Holy Spirit asks these rhetorical questions at three critical times – 3:6, 6:10 and 8:5 – as the Bride comes to maturity.

Who is she who looks forth as the morning . . .
The day has finally come. We are reminded of 2:17 and 4:6: *Until the day breaks and the shadows flee.* Now the day is breaking and the shadows of compromise have left, darkness is gone and the sun is breaking forth in a new day. In her current condition, she *shines forth like the dawn*, the shadows spoken of earlier are now gone. The morning light has finally

come and the doubts are gone. This speaks of the mature Church being like a source of light in a dark and fallen world.

Fair as the moon (NIV/KJV) or as beautiful as the full moon (NASB)
The moon is ordained as a source of light in the night-time. The moon does not have its own light. The mature Church is like a source of light in a dark and fallen world. The moon only receives and reflects the light of the sun, thus providing light in the night. The Church is typified as the moon shining in the darkness of a fallen world. We are shining in the darkness of this age. All of our beauty comes from the light of Jesus Christ.

Who is she who looks forth as bright as the sun? . . . terrible (KJV) or majestic (NIV)
The mature Bride is like a majestic army that eventually experiences great victory over the powers of darkness. As she triumphs over her own sin, she becomes a terrifying weapon in God's hand against Satan's kingdom.

Matthew Henry moves on to his second application, drawing on the Church Fathers: 'The gospel-kingdom looks forth as the morning after a dark night; but it is scarcely perceptible at first. It is but fair as the moon, which shines with a borrowed light, which has her changes and eclipses, and her spots too. But, when it is perfected in the kingdom of glory then it will be clear as the sun, the church clothed with the sun, with Christ the sun of righteousness.' Henry continues in a passage that reflects the Puritans' confidence and convictions about the future of the Church. 'The beauty of the church and of believers is not only amiable, but awful as an army with banners. The church, in this world, is as an army, as the camp of Israel in the wilderness; its state is militant; it is in the midst of enemies, and is engaged in a constant conflict with them. Believers are soldiers in this army. It has its banners; the gospel of Christ is an ensign and the love of Christ. It is marshalled, and kept in order and under discipline. It is terrible to its enemies as Israel in the wilderness was (Ex. 15:14) . . . When the church preserves her purity she secures her honour and victory; when she is fair as the moon, and clear as the sun, she is truly great and formidable.'[223]

This is one of the great themes of the Song: the Bride emerging from obscurity in the wilderness, leaning on her beloved and growing to maturity and power. This is how God sees the Church, even though we may not (yet) see her thus. Spurgeon's sermon on this text, entitled 'The Church as God sees her', has to do with the Church's preaching of the gospel, her being armed with the sword of the Spirit which is the word of God, and particularly the word of the gospel. He illustrates: 'There is a story of an officer who was rather awkward in his manners, and, upon some great occasion, almost fell over his sword in his haste. His majesty remarked, "Your sword seems to be very much in the way." "So your majesty's enemies have very often felt," was the reply.'

Spurgeon goes on: 'We are now to observe, that the chief glory and majesty of the church lies mainly in the banner which she carries. What cause for terror is there in the banner? We reply, the enemies of Christ dread the cross, because they know what the cross has done. Wherever the crucified Jesus has been preached, false systems have tottered to their fall. Rage the most violent is excited by the doctrine of the atonement, a rage in which the first cause for wrath is fear. The terribleness of the church lies in her banners, because those banners put strength into her. Drawing near to the standard of the cross the weakest soldier becomes strong: he who might have played the coward becomes a hero when the precious blood of Jesus is felt with power in his soul. Martyrs are born and nurtured at the cross. It is the blood of Jesus which is the life-blood of self-denial; we can die because our Saviour died.'

This way of referring to the Church, her banners and her destiny, is another key theme in the Song. We see that the Bride, the Church, becomes ever more radiant and powerful. She is emerging like the dawn, like the moon, like the sun, she is *terrible as an army with banners*. It may be that this is hard for us to believe in Europe in the present day. It may be that looking further afield – given the tragically increasing contexts of persecution – that it is even harder to see the Church as progressing, taking ground, being 'terrible' or 'awesome'. And yet the book of Revelation speaks of her making herself ready with 'fine linen, which is the righteous deeds of the saints'. Perhaps she makes herself ready precisely through the varied sufferings of persecution. Perhaps her 'righteous deeds' indicate her capacity to keep on loving and serving the poor through suffering and thus procure this 'fine linen'.

But this text is also about the victorious Church that Jesus prophesied into being when he said: 'I will build my Church and the gates of hell shall not prevail against it' (Matthew 16:18; ESV). It is about the promise that she *will* grow up into maturity, unity and effectiveness. We may ask: what is the secret or 'key' required for this to be possible? According to the Song, the answer must be emphatic: passionate love for Christ. As she is lovesick, faithful, intimate, devoted even in darkness, so she appears like the dawn and becomes awesome.

This is my constant prayer for her.

The next verses, which speak of the Bride's going down to the orchard to look at the blossoms, happen in a sequence when the Bride finds herself transported with her desire into Christ's chariots, like Elijah taken home in the chariots of the fire of God. These are enigmatic pictures but perhaps show the Church coming to love the work of the kingdom – becoming fascinated to see whether the vines are in bloom and, as she does see them, experiencing Christ's glorious presence. Rather like the three disciples on the Mount of Transfiguration suddenly confronted by Jesus in his glory, it is true that as we become involved in serving people with the gospel, in serving the poor or even in dazzling worship, so in spiritual terms we are taken up into the heavenly realms, and seated with Christ.

Return, return, O Shulammite, return, return, that we may look upon you (6:13; ESV)
The Hebrew word for *Shulammite* is most probably a feminine form of 'Solomon'. If so then 'Solomon' may indeed be her Bridegroom's name. The beloved Bride takes her husband's name in a feminine form, a version of Shalom, peace. The king has put his name upon her. He is the Prince of Peace, and she is the Daughter of Peace. Previously she was called *the fairest among women*; now she is espoused unto her Lord, and has a fullness of peace. So it is that here she is called the Peace-laden, or the Peace-crowned.

Return, return, O Shulammite; return, return, that we may look upon you. Why should you look upon the Shulammite, as upon a dance before two armies? (6:13; ESV)
'As the house of Israel is among the nations like a burning torch in dry stubble, so also is the spiritual Israel. Voices will

cry after the Bride of Christ, "Return! Return! Return! Return!" A pilgrim bound for the Celestial City cannot go through the world, even through the worst part of it, such as Vanity Fair, without being noticed, and questioned, and sought after, and if possible ensnared.'[224]

When do these tempting voices come? Their sound is heard often. 'Return' is repeated four times here. They come so often. The book of Hebrews is right to say of those seeking their heavenly homeland: 'If they had been thinking of the country they had left, they would have had opportunity to return' (Hebrews 11:15). These opportunities to return to the world's ways come in our way everywhere, and at all times. If you wish to stop being a Christian, if you wish to follow the world in its pleasures or in its labours, the doors are always open. The world will be wonderfully forgiving of our time of spiritual enthusiasm if we but stop protesting against it.

So it is that people may turn back. They may be drawn away by their nearest and dearest. Particularly for those coming to the one true God from other faith backgrounds, the conflict can be indeed, or close to, a fight to the death. I have seen bullet wounds in the leg of one convert from Islam, received as he fled from those wishing to kill him. I have known people disinherited because of their love for Christ, but staying true until the end. In my work as a pastor in Paris, I remember a young Jewish boy coming to faith in Christ: his parents banned him from any and every contact with the church in his street. I remember a gorgeous young Muslim mother becoming a strong, beloved member of our cohort of young Christian mums – before being drawn back to her family, finally leaving the church one Ramadan season, saying: 'It is just too lonely.'

I have seen rude and devastating ambushes inflicted on those falling in love with Christ: 'Many a man has been wooed from the ways of holiness by her that lay in his bosom. Samson had his Delilah. Oftener still, the professing Christian woman has been solicited to forsake her Lord by him who should have helped her in her noblest aspirations. Children have been misled by parents, friends by friends, for Satan hath many servitors, and many who do his bidding almost unwittingly. It is a fight to reach to heaven, and few there be to help us in it, but the path to hell is downward, and multitudes thrust out their hands to urge us to the infernal deeps. These cries are borne to us by every gale, in tones both loud and gentle, "Return, return."'[225]

I have known sacrifice and saintliness as people resisted the call to 'Return'. Hebrews describes these heroes of the faith: 'they would have had opportunity to return. Instead, they were longing for a better country – a heavenly one. Therefore God is not ashamed to be called their God, for he has prepared a city for them' (Hebrews 11:16).

These have responded to a call but not to return to the world. So it is that at the same time as voices calling the Bride to return to the world, there is a voice that calls to our spirit to come Home. Thus 'Return' may have another meaning at the same time. This is another voice crying to people to return, but in a completely different direction; a voice which cries: 'Return, return!' But this is a call to 'Return, O prodigal, to the Father': to go to Christ, to go to heaven, to go towards holiness. It is a 'Return!' addressed to all God's people; for all people are originally his children. Though we are prodigals, and have gone into a far country, we always were his children; even when we spent our substance in chaotic living we were still his sons, and each of us could speak of 'My Father's house' if we but knew it. To come to Christ, and holiness, and heaven, is to return. When the Israelites came out of Egypt to go to Canaan they were not going to a strange land; they were returning to what had always been their inheritance according to the covenant; they were going out of the house of bondage, and they were returning to the land that flowed with milk and honey, where their fathers had sojourned before them.

'My Father is in heaven, my Saviour is on the throne; many brethren have gone before; all my heart is with my treasure, therefore I hear the shining ones crying to me every day, "Return, return, O Shulammite; return return!": come nearer to Christ, nearer to God, nearer to holiness. You are saved; seek to be like your Saviour. You did enjoy splendid days at first, in the love of your espousals; return to them; walk always in the light as God is in the light. You were once in the banqueting-house, and the banner over you was love: return to that house of fellowship.

'Return, return, to greater heights of holiness, to deeper self-denial, to braver service, to intenser love, to more burning zeal, to more of the Godlike and the Christlike. "Return, return." The holiest and the best call us that way. Every saint in heaven cries, "Return"; every child of God on earth who is full of the inner life entreats us to return, and chiefly, that dear voice, which once for us cried, "My God, my God, why hast thou forsaken me?" is always calling to us, "Return, return".'[226]

This is the same call to 'Come back to your first love' of the risen Christ to the Ephesians. This is the call, 'Simon son of John: "Do you love me?"' of the Risen Christ to his wayward disciple. This is the chance to come back, to return, for all of us. Maybe today some reading this will want to 'Come Back', even if it is for the first time in their awareness.

Come back to a deep love for Christ, a hunger for his word, a love for his people expressed in spending time with them, a love for lost people who have not yet found Christ. Come back to intimacy. Come back to the spiritual disciplines. Remember the height you have fallen from; repent and return to your first love.

Why should you look upon the Shulammite, as upon a dance before two armies? (6:13; ESV)
The NIV has here *as on the dance of Mahanaim*, which literally means 'two camps' and the background to which is rich. Among other things, it is the place where the angel confronted Jacob.[227] It is where David had insults hurled at him by Shimei; and it is the place of war between the houses of David and Absalom. As such, it is a place of contestation, of conflict between the people of God; some say also of inner conflict. It is this inner conflict that we will explore briefly.

The Bride, like the individual Christian, is a person who battles in a kind of perpetual dance to get free to godliness. There is both heart-breaking disappointment and a drama that is beautiful to watch as the Bride struggles and breaks free. Hence this enigmatic verse.

The disappointment is seen in the scheming of Jacob against his brother. It is echoed in the betrayal of Joseph by his brothers, and right down to the tragedy of Absalom, who fought his father and his brothers and died doing so. This is a wearisome and warlike 'dance' of two camps that, whether we like it or not, is a part of salvation history. But the Bride can and must emerge from it.

Spurgeon built on this to say that the Christian has a battle-dance to fight their way through, one which may last most or all of their life. He speaks of the fact of 'two armies in every Christian'. We see it in the Song of Songs. The Bride is *dark but lovely*. She is sleepy and misses her companion in the night, and ends up being beaten. In the book of Psalms, where again and again we are enmeshed in this 'dance', it is the soul that is asked: 'Why are you disquieted within me?' and then exhorted to: 'Hope in God!' (Psalm 42). Psalm 73 speaks of the psalmist being 'plagued and punished all day' and feeling that 'In vain I have kept my heart pure . . .': there is a loss of hope, 'Until I entered the sanctuary of God' – at which point everything changed.

The Apostle Paul is the same. He lives with internal conflicts and contrary desires to the extent that he asks, 'Who will deliver me from this body of death?' (Romans 7). John Bunyan's book *Holy War* describes God conquering the town of 'Mansoul', which is then attacked from within and without. Richard Sibbes' book, *The Soul's Conflict with Itself*, has this as its theme.[228] This is the battle that the Bride, and you and I as a part of the Bride, will have to wage.

This is the now and the not yet of the Christian life. This is what 2 Corinthians 1 means in speaking of 'such pressure that we despaired of life itself'. This is *the dance of Mahanaim*.

This dance is in part the fight against the world and the devil, but just as much it is the fight against the flesh. We read of Christ what is true of ourselves: 'Then the devil left him until an opportune time.' The origin of the fight is clear: it is the fight with the old nature that Christ came to free us from, the result of the derailment of God's good purposes at the beginning by demonic design. Whether it accuses us in our thinking or has us locked up physically, it is a real and not an imaginary fight. It is a dance that comes and goes. But it often comes back with greater intensity when we least expect it. Sometimes the flesh is subdued, sometimes it fights back strongly. The frequent fall of leaders today in the Church and in society and in history right back to David shows us the drama that is this dance.

The effect of this dance, though, is – if we will hold to him – to make us lean on God. Life is a battle and the battle makes us cry out. We would rather it weren't so, but the dance of dependency on God is one that angels will come out to watch and look on. We may say with the Bride: 'Why would you gaze on the Shulammite?' But it is a dance that will prove captivating in its intensity and beauty when we can get heaven's perspective on it.

The effect of this conflict may, paradoxically, be to save us from ourselves: 'Doubtless it is best as it is,' says Spurgeon, 'and when the winding up of the chapter comes perhaps we shall see that our sins committed have been the means of saving us from other sins that would have been our ruin. Many believers would have grown too proud to be borne with if some infirmity had not plucked the plume from their helmets and made them mourn with brokenness of heart before God. God can bring good out of evil by his over-whelming grace, while on the other hand our good works have often puffed us up and led us into pride . . .'

Will this dance go on for ever? How and when will there be an end of it? Clearly it will not go on for ever. It is our destiny in this now-and-not-yet season. But the Bride, and we ourselves, are nonetheless being changed from one degree of glory into another as we behold and contemplate the beauty of the King. The Bride is becoming beautiful and pleasant. She is making herself ready. She is growing in stature, in perfection. She is fruitful. The dance is training her. But it is to this developing perfection that the author now turns his attention for the seventh chapter of the Song.

Spiritual exercises for a dance before two armies

One of the gifts of the contemplative tradition to the Church has been the capacity for solitude. For this exercise, we will explore this gift. Solitude is essentially time away from everything in order to make a time and place for God. To bring solitude into our lives is one of the most necessary but, for many, also the most difficult of disciplines. Even though we have a deep desire for solitude, we may find it completely impossible to keep quiet with God.

'As soon as we are alone, without people to talk to, books to read, TV to watch, or phone calls to make an inner chaos opens up in us. This chaos can be so disturbing and so confusing we can hardly wait to get busy again.'[229] Nouwen wrote this before the internet age, and we may now say that solitude has become even more rare. Young people particularly find it almost impossible to close off all their screens and be still before God alone. Arguably, this turning towards God in quiet is part of the 'dance before two armies' in which we tune in to God and dance before him alone.

Our exercise therefore for this passage is simple:

Prayer of Recollection: Where have I missed God and where have I met him? (Ten minutes.)

Prayer of Quiet: Listen to the voice of the beloved speaking. (Ten minutes.)

Contemplation: Love and worship and see him in the sanctuary, beholding his power and his glory. (Ten minutes.)

Let this lead to a time of '*Union and Communion*'.

'Marriage is, before anything else, an act of contemplation. It is divine pondering . . .

'Marriage is living with glory. It is living with an embodied revelation, with a daily unveiling and unraveling of the mystery of love in such a way that our intense yet shy curiosity about such things is in a constant state of being satisfied, being fed, yet without ever becoming sated. It is living with a mystery that is fully visible, with a flesh and blood person who can be touched and held, questioned and probed and examined and even made love to, to our heart's content, but who nevertheless proves to be utterly and impenetrably mysterious, infinitely contemplatable.'
Mike Mason, *The Mystery of Marriage*[230]

CHAPTER FOURTEEN

The Body of the Beautiful Bride

He

How beautiful your sandalled feet, O prince's daughter!
Your graceful legs are like jewels, the work of an artist's
hands.
Your navel is a rounded goblet that never lacks blended
wine. Your waist is a mound of wheat encircled by lilies.
Your breasts are like two fawns, like twin fawns of a gazelle.
Your neck is like an ivory tower. Your eyes are the pools of
Heshbon by the gate of Bath Rabbim. Your nose is like
the tower of Lebanon looking toward Damascus.
Your head crowns you like Mount Carmel. Your hair is like
royal tapestry; the king is held captive by its tresses.
How beautiful you are and how pleasing, my love, with
your delights!
Your stature is like that of the palm, and your breasts like
clusters of fruit.
I said, 'I will climb the palm tree; I will take hold of its
fruit.' May your breasts be like clusters of grapes on the
vine, the fragrance of your breath like apples,
and your mouth like the best wine.

She

May the wine go straight to my beloved, flowing gently over lips
and teeth. I belong to my beloved, and his desire is for me.

Song of Songs 7:1–10

Following the question: *Why should we look upon the Shulammite?* (ESV) in Chapter 6, we are treated to a panning shot of the Bride, upwards from toe to top – in a reversal of previous directions – with a graphic lingering over feet, thighs, navel, belly, breasts, neck, head, hair and *all your delights* (ESV). The lover then enjoys *your stature . . . like a palm tree* (ESV), and *your breasts . . . like its clusters* (ESV), before saying he will climb the palm tree and lay hold of its fruit.

This is indeed a glorying in the beauty of the body of the other. Again and again, the Song has no hesitation in delighting in contemplation of bodily beauty. It is as if these two are back in the garden, knowing no shame.

It is worth acknowledging that this portrayal may well be more graphic than many would be comfortable with. Despite our sexualised society, sex is nonetheless often an unmentionable subject. Of course, this may partly be a healthy discretion and modesty. But it is interesting how, for all its emphasis on purity before marriage, Hebrew thought is more than comfortable with this highly erotic body imagery. This leads us to reflect on what this means for our attitude to the body.

'I cannot help thinking', said General Gordon, 'that the body has much to do with religion.'[231]

'If indeed the flesh possesses no useful function, why did Christ heal it?' So says Justin. He continues: 'How moreover, did he raise the dead? Was it souls or bodies? Clearly it was both together . . . At his own resurrection . . . He rose with his body, convinced that the promise concerned it too . . . He asked to eat with them. Thus he proved that the resurrection would come to our actual fleshly bodies.'[232]

Through this passage we come to understand more of this 'theology of the body'. It is a healthy, unembarrassed contemplation. This section is erotic at moments, but again never inappropriately graphic. The images invoked (*pools of Heshbon, tower of Lebanon, a mound of wheat encircled by lilies, head . . . like Mount Carmel*) are noble and evocative.

If the body is good, its dance movements are good as well. If we take a literal approach then from the last verse of Chapter 6 it may be that she is dancing: *Why should you look upon the Shulammite, as upon a dance before two armies?* (ESV). Perhaps the woman is dancing in a way that shows off her *rounded thighs . . . like jewels* (ESV); perhaps indeed her clothing has jewels hanging from it as one might imagine in a traditional Middle Eastern dance costume. The dance, if dance it is, might well be provocative, perhaps revealing or suggesting parts of her body normally hidden. She is not embarrassed by her sexuality, but nor is there any aspersion that she is flaunting it. She is at home in her flesh and blood – her body. She is living out our calling to be fully human, literally embodying a godly glory, and not 'merely spiritual'.

The dance is seen from the man's point of view: his appreciation of navel, belly, breasts and tresses of hair like flowing purple royal tapestry that hold the king captive. 'There is nothing in his preoccupation that can be considered lewd,' writes Dianne Bergant of this scene: 'He does not fantasize about how the woman's body can satisfy his sexual desires . . . Like the woman, the man is neither inhibited by his sexuality nor obsessed by it.' She rightly concludes: 'This sexuality is a reality of human maturity, and though it influences the character of the relationship between women and men, it is not portrayed as an overwhelming drive that neither can control.'[233]

The Song takes us again into territory where the body is affirmed as good and intrinsically worthy of contemplation, rather than seen as in any way contemptible. The false dualism seen in some seasons of the history of the Church, alleging that body is bad and spirit is good, is contradicted by the affirmation of and delight in the body (both male and female) in the Song, which we see in this chapter perhaps above all.

The idea that in order to be spiritual the body and its appetites must be denied is turned on its head by the positive pictures in the Song. These pictures have much to do both with the body and with human sexuality.

This has been the burden of more recent Catholic thinking, particularly that of Pope John Paul II in his work on the Theology of the Body. He preached a total of 129 'Wednesday audience addresses' during his papacy on this subject, believing that an understanding of human embodiment is a key to 'the new evangelisation'. He believed that a key to addressing a post-Christian world in crisis was to help modern men and women understand the meaning of their bodies.

'Sexuality', John Paul II affirmed, 'is by no means something purely biological, but concerns the innermost being of the human person as such. A person's "sexuality," therefore (his maleness or femaleness), in some way is "constitutive of the person," not only "an attribute of the person."'

Christopher West, commenting on this, says: 'This means our sexuality is not merely one aspect of our humanity. Rather, our sexuality illuminates the very essence of our humanity as men and women made in the divine image . . . because the truth is that a person is human only insofar as he is bodily, only insofar as he is man or woman. Hence, the question of sexuality has high stakes: nothing less than the reality of the creature. For "every human being is by nature a sexual being."'[234]

In Chapter 7 the woman and the man are at ease in their bodies and their sexuality. Again we see pointers here for how, in different seasons of life, but particularly here at the start of married life, a full appreciation of the body of the other is not only sanctioned but should be the norm for human flourishing.

The Mystery of Marriage is the title of Mike Mason's masterly book on the subject: 'Marriage is living with glory. It is living with an embodied revelation, with a daily unveiling and unravelling of the mystery of love . . . with a flesh and blood person who can be touched and held, questioned and probed and examined and even made love to, to our heart's content, but who nevertheless proves to be utterly and impenetrably mysterious, infinitely contemplatable.'[235] This is something of what is being described in Chapter 7 of the Song: the 'infinitely contemplatable' beauty of the Bride.

Several commentators, for example Cheryl Exum, see in this section of the poem a certain level of exaggeration and even playfulness in the use of these metaphors – metaphors which at times can seem 'too much', for example comparing a nose to a tower. She suggests that there could be a teasing, affectionate tone to this section, in the same way that Shakespeare plays on love poetry and ridicules its extremes of language in Sonnet 130, while nevertheless affirming his beloved.[236]

As far as the divine romance is concerned, from the Church Fathers onwards there have been imaginative applications for this passage: over-imaginative perhaps, but they are always interesting and illuminating. Here are some extracts from the writings of Nicholas of Lyra (d.1340): '"How lovely are your steps" – they go in the way of evangelical counsels . . . "Your navel" . . . By the navel beneath which the foetus is conceived and by the womb in which it is nourished before birth is meant the Church's fruitfulness in bearing sons to Christ himself . . . "Your two breasts", that is, the two covenants from which is sucked the milk from which sons begotten in Christ are nurtured and make increase, see 1 Peter 2: "Like newborn babes long for the pure spiritual milk by which you may grow up to salvation." "Your neck" – meaning faith shaped by love which joins the body of the Bride to Christ her head . . . "Your head", that is to say: Christ's divinity. From it there flow the understandings and impulses of the spiritual life, into the humanity of Christ first of all, and after that to all the members of the Church . . . From all that has now been said, a conclusion is drawn: "How beautiful you are."'[237]

For Theodoret, monastic Bishop of Cyrus writing in the fourth century, a thousand years earlier, similar themes are evoked: '"Your two breasts are like fawns, twins of a gazelle" for the founts of your teaching, which pour forth new streams, teach sharp-sightedness and spiritual insight, for the gazelle takes its name from its sharp sightedness and the word "fawn" signifies something new. "Your neck is like an ivory tower", for by taking my yoke upon it, it is set free of its pitch dark colour and made white. It is also, like a tower, fearsome to enemies and, for its shining, much desired by friends.'[238]

Summing up these and other interpretations, we might tentatively see ten affirmations here of the Bride and her beautiful body, as follows:

Beautiful . . . feet, O prince's daughter. Her success in evangelism. The Church is a family – a Royal Priesthood.

Your rounded thighs are like jewels, the work of a master hand (ESV). We are God's workmanship. God charts out a course of preparation for our lives. It is not haphazard or arbitrary but the work of a master craftsman, our sovereign God.

Your navel is a rounded bowl that never lacks mixed wine (ESV). Our inner life nourishes us with a full range of spiritual nourishment to bring maturity.

Your belly is a heap of wheat (ESV). This phrase is full of the promise of fruitfulness: the idea of the belly – or womb – full of wheat. Some have seen this as 'a powerful statement about the great harvest at the end of time in which the Church is extraordinarily fruitful'.[239]

Your breasts are like two fawns. The youthful strength to edify and nurture a next generation as the Church reproduces and is fruitful and multiplies.

Your neck is like an ivory tower. A resolute commitment of our will to be in line with that of Christ and hence because of this for the Church to be a place of safety and refuge.

Your eyes are the pools of Heshbon by the gate of Bath Rabbim. ('The gate of Bath rabbim' literally means 'in the gates of the daughter of the many'.) Clear faith and revelation that has been cleansed by receiving the teaching and insight flowing from the prophets.

Your nose is like the tower of Lebanon, looking towards Damascus. Her spiritual discernment guarding the king's property, facing the main enemy of her life – Damascus was Israel's fiercest enemy at the time.

Your head crowns you like Mount Carmel. The Bride's thought-life has grown to be mature as Christ has become her head and as her thinking has been submitted to his ways: her wisdom is thence like a fruitful and beautiful mountain.

Your hair is like royal tapestry; the king is held captive by its tresses. Hair again brings us to think of a Bride wholly given, consecrated like the Nazirites of old who would not let their hair be cut. In the same way, Jacob in his wrestling, Moses in his interceding for Israel, and (in particular senses) Noah, Job and Daniel, are among those who have somehow, mysteriously, 'held' the Lord of Glory captive. This captivates and 'holds' even the King of kings, whose heart can be moved deeply and so permits himself to be 'held captive' by the beauty of the Bride when she emerges from the wilderness of captivity.

These are ten attributes of the Bride that have moved the Bridegroom – and when seen in us they may move him today. He pauses for breath and sums up his appreciation, saying: *How beautiful you are and how pleasing, my love, with your delights* (v. 6).

Climbing the palm tree

We come now to another effortless but challenging image in the Song: the analogy between the consummation of a human love relationship and the image of Christ going to the cross to win his Bride, the Church.

> *I say I will climb the palm tree and lay hold of its fruit. Oh may your breasts be like clusters of the vine, and the scent of your breath like apples, and your mouth like the best wine.*
> **She**
> *It goes down smoothly for my beloved, gliding over lips and teeth. I am my beloved's, and his desire is for me.*
>
> (6:8–10; ESV)

As an earthy love poem, this is a description of consummation and lovemaking involving the intent of the lover – *I will climb the palm tree* – and the encouragement of the beloved – *I am my beloved's*. The palm tree is slender below but fruitful above; its fruits can be tasted and enjoyed. The lover proceeds to take possession and climb the tree. Dates are mentioned, along with grapes – both sweet to the taste – and the scent of the beloved's breath is likened to apples and the taste of her mouth to the best wine . . . Passionate kissing is meant as part of this picture for the Bride who, after all, began the Song with the statement of intent: *Let him kiss me with the kisses of his mouth. For your love is more delightful than wine.*

In the song of the soul, the *mouth like the best wine* and *the scent of apples* also speak of divine union and communion. The book began with the expression of longing: *Let him kiss me*, and continues here in the same vein. There is a parallel with Songs 2:4–5: *He brought me to the banqueting house, and his banner over me was love. Sustain me with raisins; refresh me with apples, for I am sick with love* (ESV).

Writing of this passage, Gregory of Nyssa says: 'Her thirst has become so strong she is no longer satisfied with the cup of wisdom . . . She asks to be taken to the wine cellar itself and apply her mouth to the rim of the vats themselves that are overflowing with intoxicating wine . . . She aspires still more highly. She asks to be put under the banner of love. Now Love, John says, is God.'[240]

Some commentators (but far from all) in different ages have found this image of climbing the palm tree hard to assimilate or spiritualise.[241] But it is a powerful idea, that there exists a parallel between the moment of greatest intimacy between two lovers – the sexual act – and the place where we gain intimacy with Christ and all walls are broken and veils torn down and heaven and earth can finally meet – at the cross. We could say that true love is found not in sex, but at the cross. Daring though it is, the Church Fathers did not hesitate to equate the climbing of the tree with Christ going to the cross to win his Bride. Augustine and others give this interpretation, as does the historian of early England, the Venerable Bede writing in the eighth century: 'As to the Bridegroom's words: "I will mount the palm tree, I will grasp its fruits", they fit the era when . . . in the many voices of the prophets the Lord promised that he would come in the flesh to redeem the human race, when he predicted that he would, dying of his own free will, *mount the tree and return victoriously to life* when the reign of death had been destroyed. The fruits of the tree moreover which he said he would lay hold of mean the later glories that followed after his ascent of the cross, that is to say, the splendours of his resurrection and ascension into the heavens, the advent of the holy Spirit and the salvation of the believing world . . .'[242]

The wine goes down smoothly

In this interpretation, thinking of cross and redemption, what of the wine that *goes down smoothly* (7:9; ESV)? It is not much of a stretch to remember Jesus' question to the sons of Zebedee: '"Can you drink the cup I am going to drink?" "We can," they answered. Jesus said to them, "You will indeed drink from my cup"' (Matthew 20:22–23).

For the Bride, then, the wine going down smoothly has been thought to speak of a submission to the way of Christ – of becoming conformed to him even in his death, as Paul said – a drinking of his cup if this is given to us to do, as it was for the apostles. It is a prophetic calling to potential martyrdom, as it was for the sons of Zebedee in the Scripture we have quoted. It speaks to us of the gladness of obedience even unto death. As such it reminds us of heroes of the faith such as Bishop Ridley who went to his death in Oxford. On the eve of his death he was, it is said, in the best of spirits, saying he regarded his martyrdom the next day as his marriage. He said he hoped his jailors would all attend his 'marriage feast', remarking: 'Though my breakfast will be somewhat sharp, my supper will be all the more pleasant and sweet' – a living proof that the wine *goes down smoothly*.

In our own lives it can speak of the availability of the Bride as a living sacrifice. But the most immediate reference to which this lovely little verse points is of course the Communion Service and our own glad drinking of the cup: 'This cup is the new covenant in my blood; do this, whenever you drink it, in remembrance of me' (1 Corinthians 11:25).

The Bride gladly does this, drinking it in remembrance of him through all time and throughout the world, whenever she gathers for this purpose. As she does so, she anticipates the Marriage Supper of the Lamb, saying in spirit: 'The wine goes down smoothly for my beloved.'

Spiritual exercises for a theology of the body

We have seen the truth of General Gordon's remark: 'I cannot help thinking that the body has much to do with religion.' Prayer also has much to do with the body. In Ignatius's *Spiritual Exercises*, the fourth week recommends 'three ways of praying'. I recommend them here. They are:

First, to pray through the Ten Commandments, resting or 'strolling about' and asking for grace to know our failings concerning them. This will help us earth in our bodily life our progress (or lack of it) in Christ-likeness.

Second, to meditate and pray through the Lord's Prayer phrase by phrase, staying with any that seem particularly meaningful (see Appendix 1). Ignatius recommends that 'one should spend an hour on the whole of the Our Father'.

Third, and this is a thing that may in a small way help us to begin to be truly aware of our bodies: 'The Third Method of Prayer is that with each breath in or out, one has to pray mentally, saying one word of the OUR FATHER: so that only one word be said between one breath and another, and while the time from one breath to another lasts, let attention be given chiefly to the meaning of such word, or to his own baseness, or to the difference from such great height to his own so great lowness. And in the same form and rule he will proceed on the other words of the Our Father.'[243]

This slow meditation, involving the awareness of our own breathing, will bring us some consciousness of our own body (as well as enabling us to connect with the content of the prayer) and as such is at least a beginning in this practice of theology of the body.

'The open heavens above me, the prospect of the adjacent fields with the sight of thousands, some in coaches, some on horseback, and some in the trees and at all times affected and in tears was almost too much for me, and quite overcame me.'
George Whitefield[244]

'For he went into the field of the nations through the coming of the Holy Spirit who . . . at once changed the night of ignorance into the light of morning by knowledge of the truth . . . In these ways he did indeed go out into the field, that is the life-world of the nations . . . from the city where "he came to his own and his own received him not".'
Apponius, writing in the fifth century[245]

'Our multicultural city is a mission field in which we share the gospel of Jesus Christ in word and deed.'
People's Church, Toronto[246]

CHAPTER FIFTEEN

Romance in the Fields

I belong to my beloved, and his desire is for me.
Come, my beloved, let us go to the countryside, let us spend
the night in the villages.
Let us go early to the vineyards to see if the vines have
budded, if their blossoms have opened, and if the pome-
granates are in bloom – there I will give you my love.
The mandrakes send out their fragrance, and at our door is
every delicacy, both new and old, that I have stored up
for you, my beloved.

Song of Songs 7:10–13

In our church, like many others, we put on courses for marriage enrichment and marriage preparation. Over seven sessions, we provide a candlelit dinner each week as our stunning church building (a mix of medieval and Victorian styles) is transformed into a restaurant for thirty couples – each at their own table – as a kind of date night.[247] Each week there is an interview with a different couple on the team. For a few years the absolute highlight, on the evening devoted to speaking about 'good sex', was the testimony of a couple, then in their seventies, who would always include a story about making love in the open air. I remember my jaw dropping when I first heard the wife – who is a pillar of our church – speaking about this, as did everyone else's, including that of her husband. But what made the most impact was that it was such a gently told, matter-of-fact story. She would begin by saying: 'I was a virgin when we got married and had a lot to learn in this area. But I have to say that this intimate part of our lives has always been so precious to me – and still is today.' She then went on to encourage couples to be adventurous as well as discreet. Here was a woman who gave herself to care for the poor and the elderly ('to look after orphans and widows in their distress', to use James's description of 'religion that God our Father accepts'[248] in his eponymous letter) testifying to another side of life and seeing absolutely no contradiction. She was correct in this. It was part of the maturity evident in her.

The Bride's invitation to her lover is to come away with her – *Let us go out into the fields*, with the promise: *There I will give you my love* (ESV). This is an invitation to get away from it all. Whether it is, as some say, an invitation to make love in the open air, in the country, or an invitation to head to some country lodging, clearly the Bride is innovative and uninhibited. The woman is taking the initiative, not the man, and not for the first time. She is at home in her body, and at ease in her love affair with her beloved. She adds in sensual details – such as vines budding, blossoms opening, pomegranates in bloom and mandrakes giving their fragrance. All these have been images of sensuality already in the Song apart from mandrakes, but the aphrodisiac connotations of these are found elsewhere in the Bible (see Genesis 30:15). Verse 13, detailing *every delicacy . . . that I have stored up for you, my beloved*, is again a sign of a bride who is preparing for lovemaking. It is, it seems, 'always on her mind', which shows a focus on sensual things in the woman. Perhaps in popular culture this seems more usually to be the preoccupation of the man. But times are changing and it seems this is no longer so much the case. At any rate, in the Song there is a view of woman which is bold and unabashed even for women and men who read this today.

The line *I am my beloved's, and his desire is for me* (7:10; ESV) sees a maturing of the Bride's love affair. At the start of her journey, she declares, with a perhaps possessive ring: *My beloved is mine* (2:16). At the same time she makes the lament, *they made me take care of the vineyards, my own vineyard I had to neglect* (1:6). But here at last the Bride, having taken care of and tended her vineyard, having caught the little foxes that were ruining it, having gone through darkness and winter and desert, has emerged leaning on her beloved, and her concern is now not selfish but outwardly focused.

In the song of the Bride of Christ, *I am my beloved's, and his desire is for me* (7:10) can indicate a further maturing in the Bride's confidence in the Bridegroom, meaning: I belong to Christ and I am sure of his desire for me. He is concerned for me, he desires my affections, he wants relationship. This in turn releases us into freedom and confidence and enables us to enter fully into the adventure of the fields.

As part of this awareness that 'his desire is for me' is the fact that we have to do with a jealous God: 'For the Lord your God is a consuming fire, a jealous God' (Deuteronomy 4:24). 'I am jealous for you with a godly jealousy. I promised you to one husband, to Christ, so that I might present you as a pure virgin to him' (2 Corinthians 11:2). 'How can I give you up, Ephraim? How can I hand you over, Israel? . . . My heart is changed within me; all my compassion is aroused' (Hosea 11:8). These texts show that he is a loving God who wants to be with us and who desires relationship with his Bride. This is just like a bridegroom who seeks 'quality time' with his bride – he does not anticipate that she will be always weighing up other options and never available to him, never talking to him. At this point in the Song the Bride has grown through the night and the winter and is able to finally say 'Yes' to the 'wine' of sacrifice. She is saying: I accept and I belong to my beloved completely. This is the wholeheartedness spoken of in Romans 12 where the Bride presents herself as a living sacrifice to God.

One of those who see the Song as relating the progress to maturity of the Bride is Hudson Taylor, who writes in this way: '"I am my beloved's and his desire is for me", she gladly exclaims. Now it is none of self or for self, but all of thee and for thee. And if such be the sweet fruits of going down to the nut orchard, and caring for his garden with him, she will need no constraining to continue in this blessed service: "Come my beloved, let us go forth into the field, let us lodge in the villages."'[249]

For James Durham this verse speaks of a desire for unbroken communion, a desire to be with him both at home and away from home: 'Going forth into the field: She desires not to go out of doors without him . . . A desire to go away with him, that she might be alone in his company, as a wife going abroad to the fields alone with her husband, as Gen. 24:63, it is said that "Isaac went out to the fields to pray:" that is, that he might be the more retired in that duty . . . .where desire of fellowship with Christ is right, it breathes after a walk with him every where, at home and abroad, they cannot endure to go out of doors, or to the fields without him . . . Delight in Christ's company seeks to be gone aside with him, to be alone with him, to be freed from all other companies, and abstracted from all distraction, the more freely to be solaced with him.'[250]

The fields of mission

The Church Fathers and many others since have seen this beautiful passage as speaking of the mission fields. Thus Apponius writes in the fifth century: 'Therefore this soul . . . would desire to go out from the dwelling place of the synagogue and the city of the Hebrew nation . . . into the field of the great multitude of the peoples, for the sake of redeeming the other nations – the nations that did not see him in the flesh . . . : "I do not pray for these only but also those who will believe in me through their word."

'By these words he urges him in particular to go out into the uncultivated field, the thorn-ridden world of the nations, to dwell among the ruined villages . . . which now, with Christ the Son of the living God living among them . . . have become villages that are built up by the teaching of the apostles . . . assemblies of truth, homes for Churches where God now dwells . . .'[251]

Spurgeon declares this passage to be 'A call for Revival', saying, 'A loving Church spontaneously puts herself upon widened service. She has a large heart towards her Lord and longs to see Him reign over all mankind. She does not wait to hear again the Macedonian's cry: "Come over and help us", but she is prompt in mission enterprise. She does not tarry until forced by persecution to go abroad everywhere preaching the word, but she sends forth her champions far and wide . . . She says, "Let me go to the regions beyond to break up the fallow ground and cause the wilderness to blossom."'[252]

Chinese church leader Watchman Nee adds to this idea of the growth in maturity of the Bride: '"Let us go forth into the field." Now she is no longer acting alone, and the Lord is no longer acting alone. There is a joint work of "us." . . . Since she is liberated from herself, she is also delivered from all narrowness and pettiness. Her focus is no longer on her meeting, her work, her church, or her group. Her attention is the field, the world. She has a world view, not just an "unworldly" view . . . The whole focus is turned to the field.'

I believe that there is something of the adventure of mission that can be 'caught', if not 'taught', here. The promise, *There I will give you my love*, along with the sweet smells of the blossoms and the heady atmosphere of the presence of God, is clearly available to be experienced in the mission fields as perhaps nowhere else.

Watchman Nee continues: '"There will I give thee my love." What does "there" mean? It means the fields, villages, and vineyards, that is, the Lord's work . . . How wonderful this is! In the past, because of much serving, the maiden would lose the fellowship at His feet. To an immature believer, work does not improve his love to the Lord. On the contrary, it puts a barrier between him and the Lord. This is a sign of an imperfect union. But by this time, her experience has reached the stage of perfection, and she is able to relate the Lord's work to the Lord Himself and able to relate even the world to the Lord . . . She can make her work an expression of her love to Him.'

For a period of ten years my family moved out of our culture, out of our comfort zone, into another language and people group, so that all our preaching, evangelising, counselling had to take place in another language. All our friendships had to be conducted in a language that was not our own. All our public praying and worshipping and community building needed to be undertaken in the language of that mission field. In our case, we moved from leafy suburbs to the inner city, from lots of room to a constrained space . . . We learnt to lean on God and to give him our love there in the field. Although we were apprehensive of it, it was the richest, most stimulating, most captivating aromatic atmosphere of love relationship and reliance on the Beloved that we could possibly have imagined. I would not trade that experience for the world. I recommend 'going to the fields' as a rich invitation to experientially discover the provision, protection and presence of the living God.[253]

Where are these fields of mission today? They are spread out throughout the world. On every continent, there are crying needs and extraordinary opportunities. Those reading this will already have, or can ask God to give them, a burden for a people group that he longs to see revived. It may be Muslim-background people groups, it may be China, it may be the Indian sub-continent, or the unreached people groups of Africa.

My own love affair has been with Europe: beloved, beautiful Europe, which sent missionaries to the nations but which has become post- or even anti-Christian in parts and seemingly closed to allowing the gospel into the public square.

But I believe there are signs that the ice age may be ending. This continent of seven billion inhabitants in the EU alone is faced by massive challenges: financial meltdown, a crisis of integration of cultures, an ever-present terrorist threat – to name but a few. The ageing of society represents a major new demographic challenge. The average life expectancy of a new-born baby in the world as a whole was estimated at 67.9 years for the period 2005 to 2010. In the EU, life expectancy at birth stood at 79.7 years in 2009. The UN's population projections suggest that the number of older persons in the EU will increase to such an extent that there will be fewer than two persons of working age for each person aged 65 or more by the year 2060. Financial projections suggest this will bring a pensions and tax crisis. But where there is crisis there is opportunity. Churches have traditionally focused on youth, aiming to build 'the Church of the future' – but now we must come to be aware of older people as a mission field with just as great a potential. Who will give their life to it?

For myself at any rate, I long to see the empty cradles of Europe, her churches and cathedrals, light up with a new generation of believers.

I have a stirring, an aching and a longing for the re-evangelisation of Europe. For me it is genuinely a romantic kind of hope, remembering the Song of Songs: There *I will give you my love* . . .

Carl Jung said: 'The Christian missionary may preach the gospel to the poor naked heathen, but the spiritual heathen who populate Europe have as yet heard nothing of Christianity.'[254] There is no doubt that Europe is a strategic place for Christians to get involved and give their lives.

Days of apparent darkness can be the days of greatest opportunity. In Paris, our family's 'field' for those ten years at the turn of the century, I saw a French-speaking church come to life as it developed and expanded before my very eyes. In the space of ten years, a group of forty became a family of four hundred. These cosmopolitan Parisian believers were drawn from many nations – and such must be the Church in Europe now – from Lebanon, Egypt, Israel, Morocco, Cameroon, Togo, Benin, Rwanda, Nigeria, Algeria, the DRC, Madagascar, Brazil, USA, Columbia, Guadeloupe, Dominican Republic, Haiti, Ireland, Portugal, Britain, Germany, Switzerland, Sweden, Norway, Austria, Russia, Iran, China, New Zealand, Philippines, and of course France. Watching them worship God together in Paris was like a 'foretaste of heaven'.[255] As the

Song says: *at our door is every delicacy both new and old, that I have stored up for you, my beloved* (7:13). In this case, these choice fruits represented all the nations.

It was as if in this city of Paris, one of Europe's world-class cities, we had become a house of prayer for all nations – and in God's good grace, he had given us the chance to see it, to bring those peoples together. The Song says: *let us go to the countryside . . . spend the night in the villages . . . There I will give you my love* (7:11–12).

There is nothing like this adventure, when joined to the Holy Spirit's power. I will give the last word on this to Apponius, speaking from the fifth century, and with whom we began this section: 'For he went into the field of the nations through the coming of the Holy Spirit who by the fire of his own power and the lustre of the apostles at once changed the night of ignorance into the light of morning by knowledge of the truth . . . In these ways he did indeed go out into the field, that is the life-world of the nations . . . from the city where "he came to his own and his own received him not".'[256]

May this happen again in our generation.

Spiritual exercises for Romance in the Fields

In the fourth week of the *Exercises*, Ignatius advises on what he calls 'The Contemplation to Attain Love'. The exercise that follows has to do with the call to the fields, or at least out of our regular field of activity into who knows where. The following is the prayer he gives for us to make our commitment to that. Consider whether you can say it: 'Take, Lord, and receive all my liberty, my memory, my intellect, and all my will – all that I have and possess. Thou gavest it to me: to Thee, Lord, I return it! All is Thine, dispose of it according to all Thy will. Give me Thy love and grace, for this is enough for me.'

If you can read this prayer, as having to do with 'the fields', and say this challenging prayer at all, then say it over four times.

Give God your 'liberty', then your 'memory', then your 'intellect' and lastly your 'will'.

This links up to Romans 12:1–3 where Paul invites us to similar commitment: 'Therefore, I urge you, brothers and sisters, in view of God's mercy, to offer your bodies as a living sacrifice, holy and pleasing to God – this is your true and proper worship. Do not conform to the pattern of this world, but be transformed by the renewing of your mind. Then you will be able to test and approve what God's will is – his good, pleasing and perfect will.'

Pray through these verses, moving through the Quiet and into the Union and Communion.

'We should not underestimate the dreadful, irrational, chthonic power and terror of *eros*.'
Philip Seddon[257]

'Every love story is a potential grief story.'
Julian Barnes[258]

CHAPTER SIXTEEN

'Place me like a seal'

She

> *If only you were to me like a brother, who was nursed at my mother's breasts! Then, if I found you outside, I would kiss you, and no one would despise me.*
>
> *I would lead you and bring you to my mother's house — she who has taught me. I would give you spiced wine to drink, the nectar of my pomegranates.*
>
> *His left arm is under my head and his right arm embraces me. Daughters of Jerusalem, I charge you: Do not arouse or awaken love until it so desires.*

Friends

> *Who is this coming up from the wilderness leaning on her beloved?*

She

> *Under the apple tree I roused you; there your mother conceived you, there she who was in labour gave you birth.*
>
> *Place me like a seal over your heart, like a seal on your arm; for love is as strong as death, its jealousy unyielding as the grave. It burns like blazing fire, like a mighty flame.*
>
> *Many waters cannot quench love; rivers cannot sweep it away. If one were to give all the wealth of one's house for love, it would be utterly scorned.*

Song of Songs 8:1–7

Last but not least, the epic eighth chapter of the Song contains some of the most loved and quoted lines in all literature: from the evocative *Many waters cannot quench love* to the enigmatic *love is as strong as death* and the realist *jealousy [is] as unyielding as the grave* to the tender *place me like a seal over your heart.*

The chapter begins with the Bride yearning to be able to be more expressive and expansively affectionate in public.

> *Oh that you were like a brother to me who nursed at my mother's breasts! If I found you outside, I would kiss you, and none would despise me.* (8:1; ESV)

This is a parallel passage to her earlier public display in front of the watchmen, when she seemed almost recklessly abandoned, going out in the night asking, *If you find my beloved . . . tell him I am sick with love* (5:8). Here her attitude is more mature. She wants to be discreet in public, but she is still desirous to give public expression to her affection:

I would give you spiced wine to drink, the nectar of my pomegranates (v. 2).

Verses 2 and 3 return to the sensual imagery of spiced wine and *the nectar of my pomegranates*, and also tell us the Bride's position – that she is being held by his left hand and caressed by his right hand. There is an associative ring that brings depth and power to these images.

The woman is, at the start and at the finish, the leader in the dance of love that is this poem, the Song of Songs. She it is who asks for more intimacy; it is she who is suggestive and imaginative. She initiates and she invites. In the development of sexual activity within marriage, this defines a bolder approach than that sometimes adopted by women. Despite a

culture where women have been 'liberated', completely transformed from more prudish times as it may seem, many
women in relationships may still not be as relaxed and keenly
demonstrative, or have such appetite for physical connection,
as does this bride. In the Song the other women are also
comfortable and at ease with this woman's approach.

The Bride of the Song wants to go to *my mother's house*,
showing that she wants this not to be an illicit affair but a
passionate and yet appropriate marriage in that it can be celebrated there. In verse 5 the Bride takes the initiative again:
Under the apple tree I roused you. She is perhaps referring to the
earlier scene in 2:3. The idea that *there your mother conceived
you* connects the new love that is theirs both with the continuity of life and the idea of new life.

Dietrich Bonhoeffer, imprisoned then martyred during
the Second World War, wrote about this 'office' of marriage
in a letter from prison to his niece on the eve of her
wedding: 'Marriage is more than your love for each other.
It has a higher dignity and power, for it is God's holy ordi-
nance through which he wills to perpetuate the human
race till the end of time. In your love you see only your two
selves in the world, but in your marriage you are a link in
the chain of the generations, which God causes to come
and to pass away to his glory, and calls into his kingdom.
In your love you see only the heaven of your happiness, but
in marriage you are placed at a post of responsibility
towards the world and mankind. Your love is your own
private possession, but marriage is more than something
personal. It is a status, an office.'[259]

I believe this centrality of family in society and the status
of marriage is of vital importance to the continuity of our
culture.

Coming home

I would lead you and bring you to my mother's house (v. 2)

In the song of the Bride of Christ, 'my mother's house' previews Paul's 'Jerusalem that is above is free, and she is our mother' (Galatians 4:26). This phrase thus masks a longing for heaven, which is our true home, from which we are alienated because of sin, but for which we are perpetually homesick because we are designed to belong there. This becomes therefore a portrayal of the joys that are to come.

My mother's house links to the core concept of Home. Julian of Norwich speaks of this 'Home' in heaven in her sixth Revelation of Divine Love, which may expand our understanding of this image:

> mine understanding was lifted up into Heaven
> where I saw our Lord as a lord in His own house, which hath
> called all His dearworthy servants and friends to a stately feast.
> Then I saw the Lord take no place in His own house, but I saw
> Him royally reign in His house, fulfilling it with joy and mirth,
> Himself endlessly to gladden and to solace His dearworthy
> friends, full homely and full courteously, with marvellous melody
> of endless love, in His own fair blessed Countenance.[260]

In the fifth century, Theodoret of Cyrus wrote: 'For what is the house of the all-holy Spirit if it not the divine temple that images the "Jerusalem that is above". Those who enter it engage in free and frank converse with the Bridegroom because they have assumed the status of the Bride.'[261]

Awakening love

Daughters of Jerusalem, I charge you: Do not arouse or awaken love until it so desires (9:4)

As before, this phrase has at least two important interpretations.

One meaning is to do with the latent power of love and the warning not to become awakened to it before it is time, or before we have the capacity to know how to respond to it. Philip Seddon, using the language of psychology, rightly comments: 'We should not underestimate the dreadful, irrational, chthonic power and terror of *eros*: its power to rip spouses and families apart. *Eros* is not a moral agent, it is simply a power – the power of creation. When we isolate sex, we idolize it. The Song is aware of that, and we need to be: *love is strong as death, jealousy is fierce as the grave. Its flashes are flashes of fire, the very flame of the Lord.* The pulsating power of *eros* is clear. Hence the repeated entreaty of the Song: "Do not stir up love until it is ready" (2:7; 3:5; 8:4). Childhood, virginity, innocence are not vacuous words: they reveal the essence of tender respect for the integrity and preciousness of the younger other which motivates all genuine love.'[262]

Spiritual awakening can in fact be just as strong as the physical awakening described above by Seddon. Writing of her spiritual awakening, Thérèse de Lisieux describes her own experience of being 'ripe for love' as she puts it: 'I was at the most dangerous time for young girls, but God did for me what Ezekiel recounts: passing by me, Jesus saw that I was ripe for love. He plighted his troth to me and I became his. He threw his cloak around me, washed me with water and anointed my head with oil and I had matchless beauty and he made me a queen. Jesus did all that for me. Jesus did all that for me.'[263]

This happened to Thérèse on Christmas Eve in 1886,

when she was fourteen years old. This was an experience that transformed her life. From then on, she writes, her powerful energy and sensitive spirit were turned towards love, instead of making herself happy. At fifteen, she entered the Carmelite convent in Lisieux. Living a hidden, simple life of prayer, she, like Julian of Norwich, was gifted with great intimacy with God. Through sickness and dark nights of doubt and fear, she remained rooted in God, leaning on his merciful love. This is of course part of her appeal to people even today: steadfastness despite suffering. After a long struggle with tuberculosis, she died on 30 September 1897, at the age of twenty-four. Her last words were the story of her life: 'My God, I love you!'

The world came to know Thérèse through her autobiography, *Story of a Soul*. She described her life as a 'little way of spiritual childhood'. Anticipating Mother Teresa of Calcutta, 'What matters in life', she wrote, 'is not great deeds, but great love.' Thérèse lived and taught a spirituality of attending to everyone and everything well and with love. She believed that just as a child becomes enamoured with what is before her, we should also have a childlike focus and totally attentive love. And it all began with this timely awakening.

Her story of the 'awakening of love' – a love which is not put out by the waters of suffering – has been remarkable in its influence. Today Lisieux Basilica is a place of prayer for over one million pilgrims each year, and especially attracts the young. It shows what can happen if love is awakened when it is ready.

The other main interpretation of this text, as we have already seen, is that once connected to the beloved, the Bride does not want to be disturbed *until it so desires*. The text becomes a plea for prolonging intimacy, a yearning that the moment of communion should not stop – at least until it is the right time. This could have to do with the afterglow of intimacy, which is not to be broken and may be prolonged. It has therefore to do not so much with foreplay as with 'afterplay', which can be equally rich, perhaps involving rest and quiet, peaceful union and a gentleness from which it is good not to awaken until ready.

In the divine romance, Pennington makes a helpful link here to the Sabbath rest that we are exhorted to enter into – see Hebrews 4 and Psalm 95: 'It is a mighty thing to create heaven and earth, but the work of the Sabbath takes preference over it. It is a great thing to work for the common good and to be the truly devoted servant of the salvation of many, a task truly salutary and very fruitful. But to gaze silently on the Word is a task literally angelic, or rather divine. The other days with their tasks have an evening. But the Sabbath Day, with its task, namely Contemplative Repose in God – is never brought to an end by evening. All other work . . . suffers an element of obscurity. But work of the vision of God and His eternal praise, which is the true work of the Sabbath . . . never fades into an evening.'[264]

Leaning on the divine lover

Who is this coming up from the wilderness leaning on her beloved? (v. 5) This is the third repetition of this phrase pregnant with meaning, *Who is this coming up from the wilderness?* For additional meanings, see sections on 3:6 and 6:10 where we have spoken of the Church perfumed with the courage of the martyrs and the Church armed in a day of battle.

But here she is 'leaning' – as though to suggest that Christ is calling the Bride to be completely dependent. In Scripture we can discern some key moments where 'leaning' is described. John the apostle leaned on Jesus' breast at the Last Supper: 'One of them, the disciple whom Jesus loved, was reclining next to him' (John 13:23). You could say this is a picture of the Church fulfilling Song of Songs 8:5.

At a previous supper, Mary Magdalene poured out oil on his feet in her love for Jesus. Here is a picture of a woman in the New Testament leaning on and loving Jesus. Perhaps in our day the Holy Spirit is preparing a Bride with a loving and a leaning heart. Mary has had an experience a little like that of Jacob. She has wrestled, and now she limps. She is leaning, limping and loving.

Applying this to daily life, it is possible trouble comes when our plans and his plans are different. Our personal plan, if we are honest, is often simply to be happy on the earth. But his plan is that we would come up out of the wilderness, leaning on the One we love. The Lord's plan and goal is to see in the Bride an attitude of utter dependency on him.

The history of God's people reveals that we find it hard to lean and love in the midst of blessing. Eventually, we try to stand in our own strength, becoming our own source. We may use the blessings of God to further our own ends. The heart of fallen man is not prone to lean. Our hearts are prone to self-assertion and independence. In salvation history, when God prospers Israel, she ends up not leaning. Take the example of Uzziah, of whom it is said: 'But after Uzziah became powerful, his pride led to his downfall' (2 Chronicles 26:16). Pride came before a fall.[265]

It is a fact of redemptive history that many individuals who start out anointed end up snared in sin and pride. First Saul and then so many other kings of Israel did not lean upon God in the seasons of blessing. This is what distinguished King David.

Similarly, in the wonderful and terrible history of Pentecostal revivals (wonderful because glorious in God, terrible because so often flawed), a leader may start by humbly, urgently, crying out for God's blessing and holiness. Then when the blessing of God does indeed rest on them, it seems that one way or the other, too often 'something happens'. One common problem is that a leader gives in to temptation or becomes unaccountable to others when he or she prospers. Often such leaders lose their sense of dependency on God. Terrible character flaws can emerge and go unchecked, and then disaster strikes. Financial indiscretion, marriage breakup, a drift into heresy or cultish manipulation of others are just some of the dangers of not leaning.

This text encourages us that it is God's plan to give people the urge and the capacity to lean, especially in a time of blessing.

At any rate, at the end of the Song this Bride has an understanding of her inadequacies and weaknesses. In the wilderness season of testing you could say God revealed to her the weakness of her flesh. Walking in the knowledge of our weakness is a great sign of maturity. Her first confession in Song 1:5 was: *Dark am I, yet lovely.* Now perhaps she has come to mature understanding. *Who is this coming up . . . leaning?* (ESV). Similarly, even at the end of his life, Paul the apostle said, 'I am a chief sinner.' This does not mean that he sinned more than others. It means that he had more revelation of his sin.

Here are some areas of life in which we can lean upon Jesus:

For salvation
For attaining victory
For wholeness

(The Bride in the Song has depended upon him with genuine vulnerability. In the same way, he is working in our lives to bring us to a discovery of our own inadequacies.)

For direction
For provision

(God arranges circumstances in such a way that it is obvious he alone is her source of supply. The Bride, whether as an individual, as a whole Church or denomination, or a movement, may need to understand this afresh today.)

I see this kind of provision in the moving stories of saints of old such as George Muller or Hudson Taylor. In order to prepare himself for service in China, even though he was a doctor and therefore relatively wealthy, Hudson Taylor did without money and food, and sometimes heating fuel for his rooms in England, so that when the time came he could truly lean in China where he was alone without the comfort of a regular salary – and plagued with 'intermittent supply' from home. His sole comfort lay in leaning on the Beloved.

Sometimes, adverse circumstances crash in on us – but this can help to give us such a dependence on God: we face illness; disappointment in a relationship; betrayal; financial hardship; persecution. This small phrase *coming up . . . leaning* can be a key to unlock our hearts as we ask what our reaction is to all these things. Do we try to escape them and use our worldly savvy to get out of trouble, or will we, like that remarkable man Job, learn to lean? Can we dare to say: 'Though He slay me, yet will I hope in him' (Job 13:15).

If God is blessing us, though, the question is still: will we keep leaning? I believe Jesus looks for a Bride who voluntarily remains in her weakness even as she feels the power of the Holy Spirit on her. This is how Jesus walked with God on the earth. May we voluntarily choose to submit our strengths or resources to the Holy Spirit in weakness rather than use them to establish ourselves in strength in natural things. Mike Bickle calls this 'voluntary apostolic weakness'.[266] This is the kind of apostolic weakness that Paul embraced: 'Therefore, in order to keep me from becoming conceited, I was given a thorn in my flesh, a messenger of Satan, to torment me. Three times I pleaded with the Lord to take it away from me. But He said to me, "My grace is sufficient for you, for my power is made perfect in weakness." Therefore I will boast all the more gladly about my weaknesses, so that Christ's power may rest on me' (2 Corinthians 12:7–9).

I believe the Christian world (and the world in general, perhaps) is tired of hype, pretence and exaggerated claims. May we learn to lean.

To apply this to the Church – whether our particular expression of the universal Church is formal or informal, traditional or more Pentecostal – the Bride who leans will voluntarily embrace weakness in the way she uses her spiritual influence with people who desire to receive from her.

She will not take advantage of people.
She will refuse to direct people using her spiritual authority.
She voluntarily embraces weakness in the way she uses her spiritual influence with people who resist and oppose her.
She will not use her position of power and influence to fight her enemies.
She will not use anger and strife to pay back those who oppose her.

She will refuse to manipulate in ministry contexts, avoiding hype and pretence.

She will avoid worldly exhibition, showmanship and theatrics in her ministry style.

She will be modest.

She will continue in her call to serve among the poor, recognising that she herself is poor even if abundant finances are available as a result of the anointing on her life.

She will continue in the fasted lifestyle in the midst of any economic prosperity on her ministry – we could and should imagine a bride who voluntarily embraces weakness in the way she spends her money.

Network or movement?

We may add a word here on the temptations to power in 'becoming a movement'. 'Of the making of many movements, there is no end', to misquote Ecclesiastes.[267] Often, as soon as there is blessing on a network of friends who love God and have experienced his power and see people gathering, a mysterious change occurs and hey presto, the network has become a movement. The motivation may be pure: we want more people to embrace the good things experienced by this network of friends who have been impacted by the grace of God with this particular emphasis. This emphasis may be any good thing, for example: Kingdom Theology and Practice / Intercessory Prayer / Bible Exposition / Works of Justice / Mission / Creation Care / Church Planting – and so on. We just want more people to understand this good thing, this 'godly vision'; and so we create a movement. Movements are no doubt needed. But those who lead them are wise if they do all they can to keep leaning on God and not begin to rely on their own power. This is a subtle thing when day to day you are trying just to survive, not go bankrupt and certainly striving to be wise. But it is my view that as soon as there is talk of distribution networks, as soon as corporate thinking comes in and marketing techniques are discussed, a tacit agreement to silence concerning others doing almost identical things, a failure to give away power, we have in my view stopped leaning and become less than God's best. We so easily become market-driven or ambitious for worldly success. It is still today so challenging to those movements that are 'powerful' or churches that are large (and I include my own) to remember how Jesus so ruthlessly cleared out the marketplace behaviour, criticising the traders for turning his Father's house into a den of thieves.

So this is indeed a verse to meditate on and to pray into – that we may learn to lean.

Who is this coming up from the wilderness leaning . . .? (v. 5)
So much for a detailed allegorical exploration of the idea of leaning for the Church. What, we may ask, does this phrase mean for a physical relationship?

The song of intimate relationship speaks here about emerging from the desert of uncertainty or winter and barrenness with a Bride leaning on her lover. For all the initiative, leadership and innovation taken by the Bride, we can see now that there is also a time to lean. A beautiful balance between leading and submitting is needed in any relationship.

This attitude of leaning, relying on, being supported by one's partner is an important part of love. It is the 'for better for worse . . . in sickness and in health' of the marriage service – which I believe to be a 'deep calling to deep' moment – that can be seen here.

It sets the stage for the next verses, which many commentators regard as the climax of the Song.

The covenant seal of marriage

Set me as a seal upon your heart, as a seal upon your arm (v. 6; ESV)
Recently I attended a wedding in the French Alps, just near Geneva. Before the Church Blessing, the day began, as French weddings do, with *La Civile*: the civil ceremony. I was reminded just how formal and legal the marriage ceremony is, even in a secular state. At the end of the reading out of extracts from French law, the mayor of the town handed over a signed and sealed document and said: 'You are now married!' to the applause of all.

In the song of intimate love relationship, and also in the divine romance, the seal of which we read here represents what the Bible calls a Covenant. In the Bible the main word for the structure of relationship between a saving God and a saved people is exactly this word 'covenant' (*berit*). The word does not in fact occur in the Song, but 'seal' comes close. For Eugene Peterson, commenting on the Song: 'Covenant in effect means that humanity cannot understand life apart from a defined and revealed relationship with God . . . The Song provides an instance of understanding and realizing the experience of covenant, from the inside, using not the objective language of international treaty making, but the subjective language of personal love-making. In this way it provides one of the most vivid, biblical expositions of the inner content of covenant that we have.'[268] The Bridegroom is asking the Bride: *Place me like a seal over your heart, like a seal on your arm*. I want Covenant Relationship.

The covenant seal is one thing. But here, the Bride asks for her very self to be set as a seal on heart and arm. 'Over the heart' refers to affections and 'On the arm' covers all actions for the future: a complete 'seal' on all that she is. The implications of this are profound: asking to be 'set as a seal on the heart' means 'The woman is asking to be identified with the man's very identity . . . She wants the relationship between herself and the man she loves to be as intimate, as inseparable and as distinctive as the link between the man and the personal seal that marks his identity.'[269]

A seal on our hearts and on our arms

Place me as a seal over your heart, like a seal upon your arm, for love is as strong as death (8:6)

Both of the two great commandments are spoken of here in this lovely phrase. The seal of love on the heart speaks of the Bride's affections as she lives out the first commandment, 'You shall love the Lord God with all your heart.' The seal of love upon the arm speaks of her ministry as she lives out the second commandment, 'You shall love your neighbour as yourself.'

Sealing has to do with the power of the Holy Spirit – as Ephesians 1:13–14 says, 'And you also were included in Christ when you heard the message of truth, the gospel of your salvation. When you believed, you were marked in him with a seal, the promised Holy Spirit, who is a deposit guaranteeing our inheritance until the redemption of those who are God's possession – to the praise of his glory.' 2 Corinthians 1:22 runs on similar lines: 'Now it is God who makes both us and you stand firm in Christ. He anointed us, set his seal of ownership on us, and put his Spirit in our hearts as a deposit, guaranteeing what is to come.'

In Chapter 10 we looked at the phrase *a fountain sealed*. This verse addresses the same theological idea, with the sealing focused on the heart and the arm.

The seal has to do with ownership, security and authority, as I have said; theologically, this idea of sealing has to do with the power of the Holy Spirit. Through the Church's history many have spoken tellingly of this: Blaise Pascal, Thomas Aquinas, Martin Luther, George Whitefield, John Wesley, Jonathan Edwards, John Flavel, Charles Simeon, and many more. It is important that we pursue the fullness of the Holy Spirit – it is not automatic. I have already quoted Charles Simeon: 'God is willing to bestow this blessing on all who seek it. And if we do not possess it, we should inquire what there is in us that has occasioned God to withhold it from us. We should be asking God to take away the hardness of heart which incapacitates us for it and we should live more by the promises that by them it should be imparted to our souls.' Some of these impediments may include hidden sin, compromise and love of the world, fear of man, or fear of the consequences of utter abandonment to God.

Verse 6 – *Set me as a seal upon your heart, as a seal upon your arm* (ESV) – I take to be a request from the Bridegroom for absolute closeness to his Bride. He asks her to set him over herself as a seal. Her decision to do this is not to be taken lightly. It is giving her everything. But if required it will take her even through the waters of death.

As we come near the end of the Song, which speaks to all currents in the Church, it is interesting to see how the spirituality of three quite different writers combines here – evangelical A. W. Tozer and the Catholic Ignatius, as well as the Methodist John Wesley. All three knew great spiritual fruitfulness, and all three speak of complete consecration as a key to that fruitfulness. I believe this is what is meant here by setting him as a seal. At the start of his *Exercises*, Ignatius calls for 'indifference' to success or failure, fame or disgrace, provided we live to 'praise reverence and serve God our Lord'. The endeavour of the entire *Spiritual Exercises* can be seen as being to help us arrive at this detachment from ambition and attachment to Christ.

John Wesley, founder of Methodism (another form of 'spiritual exercises', if you like), has his own heart 'strangely warmed' in a moment reminiscent of this heart: *it burns like blazing fire* here in Songs 8. John Wesley's famous 'Covenant Prayer' urges the same detachment from the world and consecration to God. This prayer is prayed on New Year's Eve by Methodists each year and is as challenging as the decision of commitment in Ignatian spirituality:

I am no longer my own, but thine.
Put me to what thou wilt, rank me with whom thou wilt.
Put me to doing, put me to suffering.
Let me be employed for thee or laid aside for thee,
exalted for thee or brought low for thee.
Let me be full, let me be empty.
Let me have all things, let me have nothing.
I freely and heartily yield all things to thy pleasure and disposal.
And now, O glorious and blessed God, Father, Son and Holy
Spirit,
thou art mine, and I am thine.
So be it.
And the covenant which I have made on earth,
let it be ratified in heaven.
Amen.

This is indeed sealing on the heart and on the arm.

We have considered Ignatius of Loyola and John Wesley. Evangelical A. W. Tozer's description of the filling (or 'sealing') with the Holy Spirit involves just the same kind of commitment. He writes: 'After a person is convinced that they can be filled with the Spirit, they must desire to be: Are you sure that you want to be possessed by a Spirit who, while

He is pure and gentle and wise and loving, will yet insist upon being Lord of your life?

'Are you sure you want . . . One who will require obedience to the written Word? Who will not tolerate any of the self-sins in your life: self-love, self-indulgence? Who will . . . reserve the right to test you and discipline you? Who will strip away from you many loved objects which secretly harm your soul?'

Tozer concludes, tellingly: 'Unless you can answer an eager "Yes" to these questions, you do not want to be filled. You may want the thrill or the victory or the power, but you do not really want to be filled with the Spirit.'

This arguably encapsulates the whole journey of the Bride in the Song. It is this that marks out her progression from immaturity to a leaning 'Union and Communion'. Tozer continues: 'If, on the other hand, your soul cries out for God, for the living God, and your dry and empty heart despairs of living a normal Christian life without a further anointing, then I ask you: Is your desire all-absorbing? Is it the biggest thing in your life? Does it . . . fill you with an acute longing that can only be described as the pain of desire? If your heart cries "Yes" to these questions you may be on your way to a spiritual break-through which will transform your whole life.'[270]

This has been and always is the Bride's journey, beginning with the cry: *Let him kiss me with the kisses of his mouth.* It is continued through darkness and through winter, through sleepiness and through opposition. Always she is spurred on by affection, by longing for union, by intimate tenderness. She does not give up, and in the end she is rewarded.

Love is strong as death (v. 6)
In the spiritual realm the writer is realistic in describing love's strength as *strong as death*, meaning that as death conquers,

so true love will also inevitably conquer. The fact is that the love of Christ will on the last day be shown before everyone in just the same way that death surely will touch everyone.

Mention of death moves the poet on to speak of love's jealousy, which he speaks of as being as *fierce as the grave* (ESV). We see this sentiment in the truism: 'Hell hath no fury as a woman scorned' – the famous line coined by William Congreve, albeit only now quoted in abbreviated form.[271] (A blogger wrote: Nothing is more ferocious than a woman who's been rejected in love, as evidenced by the hammer thrown through my windscreen late last night. Hell hath no fury.)

Men, of course, are guilty of as bad or worse acts of violence as women, as Shakespeare's study in jealousy, *Othello*, brilliantly shows:

> For that I do suspect the lusty Moor
> . . . the thought whereof
> Doth, like a poisonous mineral, gnaw my inwards;
> And nothing can or shall content my soul
> Till I am even'd with him . . .

As we know, the jealousy of Iago and the jealousy provoked in Othello leads in the end to the murder of the beloved by the lover. And real life too often reflects such fiction.

Love is jealous because it arises from a longing for an exclusive relationship with the other which by definition cannot be shared with a third person. Attempts may be made in nearly every generation to throw off these 'shackles' of exclusiveness. But they fail, since this jealousy as *fierce as the grave* emerges and unwillingness to share the beloved with another overtakes any endeavours to be counter-cultural, to break the shackles of tradition or to revolt against Christian mores. We may wonder why this is; ultimately it may be that we are simply built this way. I believe there is a healthy jealousy where each partner makes and receives a promise to 'forsaking all others, be faithful to you as long as we both shall live'. From this ensues the expectation that each will not dream of looking at another person lustfully, will not agree to be in an intimate environment such as a lunch *à deux*, or even an email conversation that is in any way 'flirty', or any other inappropriate exchange. A couple may do well if in doubt to discuss 'what would make you jealous?' – in order to flee from it for dear life as the wise son in the book of Proverbs, who is advised to flee 'from the adulterous woman, from the wayward woman with her seductive words, who has left the partner of her youth and ignored the covenant she made before God. Surely her house leads down to death and her paths to the spirits of the dead. None who go to her return or attain the paths of life' (Proverbs 2:16).

Certainly the love relationship here is a picture, an image of a deeper love relationship between Christ and his Church, or between God and his people, and the God of the Bible is a jealous God.

The Ten Commandments insist that humankind should have no other God but the Lord. Later, Moses is even told that one of the names of the Lord is 'Jealous' – 'Do not worship any other god, for the LORD, whose name is Jealous, is a jealous God' (Exodus 34:14).

Its flashes are flashes of fire, the very flame of the LORD. Many waters cannot quench love (vv. 6–7; ESV)
The Bible as usual is tersely realistic in its warnings. We should be true to love to avoid what the Song rightly calls the

flashes of fire, the very flame of the LORD. The fact is that eros, this fiery yearning for union, will not be put out even by the tsunamis that can crash over us in life. People in love remain true; they do not forget even if physically overwhelmed. Furthermore, neither can they be bought off. As verse 7 (ESV) says: *If a man offered for love all the wealth of his house, he would be utterly despised.*

Love and death

Many waters cannot quench love; rivers cannot sweep it away (v. 7)
This passage depicts the love so strong that it is able to travel through the deep waters of death and up out from the grave: the Lord Jesus Christ going down into the waters of death and proving stronger than death, the last enemy to be destroyed. When he travelled down into the grave it was like the floodwaters – Psalm 18:4 links the two concepts: 'The cords of death entangled me; the torrents of destruction overwhelmed me.' In another messianic psalm, we read of the depths of torment that were embraced by Christ – 'My heart is in anguish within me; the terrors of death have fallen on me' (Psalm 55:4).

It is good to pause and wonder at the courage of Christ, whose love is truly as strong as death. In the agony of abandonment and nailed to that deathly instrument of torture which was the cross, he went down to the grave.

But the waters of death did not and could not put out the fire of his love. He rose triumphant. He lives forever, and we can only shake our heads in wonder at the burning fire of his inextinguishable love.

If one were to give all the wealth of one's house for love, it would be utterly scorned (v. 7)

These words end this famous section. Money cannot buy love; and what may be easier for us to understand and relate to than if someone truly loves another they will not count the cost of being able to be with them? I remember one couple where the bride was prepared to lose a considerable inheritance in order to marry someone not approved of by her father. She considered the consequences carefully and was prepared to give up all the wealth of her house to avoid losing the one she loved. Here is another illustration: a couple are in love and get married; the bride contracts a serious, life-threatening illness. There is a possible cure, but it is very expensive. The couple sell all they have. Finally, as the cure must be pursued abroad, they sell their home and use the proceeds to travel and to pay for this cure that may just work. In the end the bride comes through.

When the husband is asked: was it worth it? His reply is 'Yes, yes, a hundred times over. I scorn all this money compared to having that which was lost – my healthy wife – restored to me.' Such is the strong-as-death power of love.

Spiritual exercises for leaning and sealing

One of the key ideas of the Ignatian *Exercises* is that of 'indifference' or 'detachment'. Ignatius felt that for a person to follow God, he or she should so love and reverence and honour him that they become detached from or indifferent to ambition for wealth or power or preferment. They should put aside any desire for success in this world – including family attainments. Instead they should lean on Christ fully. This is a concept rarely applied today but of great value for all who pursue it. This exercise considers our levels of leaning on Christ for happiness.

Check your happiness levels! Jesus says: 'Happy [or 'Blessed'] are the poor in spirit.' Can you say that you are happy in God, for who he is and who you are? This is not to say that there are no challenges or sadnesses in your life, but that you are glad to love God, and know and enjoy his presence.

Hand over to God any aspiration for people or for position and leave the matter completely in his hands. Do this in a prayer of consecration and try to let each situation go into God's hands.

Enjoy the love of God: come back to your 'first love', taking time to be a lover of God alone. Ask the question: *Who is this coming up from the wilderness, leaning on her beloved?* See if it might be you.

'Our lives begin to end the day we become silent about the things that matter.'
Martin Luther King[272]

'Don't let the noise of other people's opinions drown out your inner voice.'
Steve Jobs[273]

'A voice is heard in Ramah, mourning and great weeping, Rachel weeping for her children and refusing to be comforted, because her children are no more.'
Jeremiah 31:15

CHAPTER SEVENTEEN

'Let me hear your voice!'

Friends

> We have a little sister, and her breasts are not yet grown.
> What shall we do for our sister on the day she is spoken for?
> If she is a wall, we will build towers of silver on her. If she
> is a door, we will enclose her with panels of cedar.

She

> I am a wall, and my breasts are like towers. Thus I have
> become in his eyes like one bringing contentment.
> Solomon had a vineyard in Baal Hamon; he let out his
> vineyard to tenants. Each was to bring for its fruit a
> thousand shekels of silver.
> But my own vineyard is mine to give; the thousand shekels
> are for you, Solomon, and two hundred are for those who
> tend its fruit.

He

> You who dwell in the gardens with friends in attendance,
> let me hear your voice!

She

> Come away, my beloved, and be like a gazelle or like a
> young stag on the spice-laden mountains.
>
> Song of Songs 8:8–14

After the heights attained in the first part of Chapter 8, these
final verses of the last chapter of the Song may seem

something of an anticlimax. Some commentators believe that the Song really ended with the previous poem in praise of love. For them it is a given that the verses that follow are an addition and not to be given the same weight as the rest.[274] But there are nuggets here if we dig for them. And they bring the Song to an epic end, as we shall see when we come to explore the last verse in the next (and our final) chapter.

We have a little sister speaks of the family's concern that the Bride's happy experience should also be shared by her sister. The concern for the joy of the Bride to spread to another who experiences the same journey in the future is natural. After all, when we attend a wedding, flowers are traditionally thrown at the end. The one who catches them is said to be next in line to get married.

If she is a wall, we will build towers of silver on her. If she is a door, we will enclose her with panels of cedar (v. 9)
The speakers – perhaps the girl's brothers – have an understandable concern for her marriageability. This is expressed in the quite natural desire for adornment and beautifying – *If she is a wall*. A wall is strong and confident, able to withstand pressure. *If she is a door* perhaps envisages a situation where she is more vulnerable to attempts at entry, and should that prove the case their resolve is to protect her and board her up – the implication is that this will be 'until love is ready'.

I am a wall, and my breasts are like towers. Thus I have become in his eyes like one bringing contentment (v. 10)
This surprising, graphic image has to do, I believe, with someone who is confident. She will carry herself with her head up and shoulders back. Again, the Bride has developed from someone hiding away, saying *don't look at me* (1:6)

– the one to whom the lover needs to say: *Show me your face, let me hear your voice* (2:14). All this has been replaced now by *I am a wall*, someone strong and defended and ready.

In the divine romance, the idea of the 'little sister' provides fertile ground for exposition: is she the Church in her early years as referred to by the 'Synagogue' of Israel? If so, this is a pleasingly peaceful relationship. For Bede the Venerable (673–75), 'The Lord Himself speaks these words to the Synagogue as she wonders at the faith and acceptance of the Church of the Gentiles.' The idea is that Christ confers authority on the Church – *my sister, my bride* (see 4:9 and 5:1) – and he wants Israel to know this 'so that the synagogue herself may recall that she too has been made the sister of her creator by grace, and may rejoice more and more in what He has added to her in the gift of a sister's society'.[275] Bede boldly interprets Paul to the Romans: 'that he might be the firstborn among many brothers and sisters' (Romans 8:29).

My vineyard is my very own

Solomon had a vineyard in Baal Hamon; he let out his vineyard to tenants. Each was to bring for its fruit a thousand shekels of silver. But my own vineyard is mine to give; the thousand shekels are for you, Solomon, and two hundred are for those who tend its fruit (vv. 11–12) The Bride is here contrasting her own life with that of Solomon, leading commentators to conclude that the love song is indeed one between a shepherd girl and her lover, as she scorns the wealth of the king for her true love. Or it may be that it is the man speaking in a kind of 'boasting song'[276]: I am scorning the wealth of Solomon for the glories of *my own vineyard*.

Solomon's vineyard is let out, looked after by and its yield shared with others. The contrast with the Bride's vineyard is that *my own vineyard is mine to give*. It may not compare in size or yield to the other but it is hers and hers alone. This is a similar idea to those of the sealed fountain, the enclosed garden, the walled city. The Song began with the sentence: They *made me take care of the vineyards – my own vineyard I had to neglect* (1:6). Here, it seems, things have come full circle and the Bride is caring completely for her 'vineyard', fully confident concerning its fruit. It is quite a contrast with the start of her journey.

In the divine romance, this verse gives rise to the reflection: having travelled through this Song, will we be shown to have taken care of our own vineyard? I take 'vineyard' in this sense to mean our love relationship and intimacy with God. Mixing our metaphors somewhat, will we be of those who have the oil of the Holy Spirit in our lamps and keep them burning in the darkness? Will we bear fruit in season? Will we behave like sons and daughters – heirs, rather than slaves? Will we 'come back to our first love', so that our own life is aromatic and bears the fragrance of Christ all over it? Will we daily enjoy him and say, 'Let him kiss me with the kisses of his word?' In a sense the whole of this book is intended to help us reflect on and say yes to this, and the spiritual exercises have been designed to strengthen us in the application of this choice.

Your voice, let me hear it

You who dwell in the gardens with friends in attendance, let me hear your voice (v. 13)

Of all the themes evoked in the poem concerning the holy longing and the bridal romance, it is fascinating to me that in its final moment, the Song comes back to say: *let me hear your voice*. Early in the Song, the Bridegroom was tenderly coaxing the Bride, saying: *My dove in the clefts of the rock . . . let me hear your voice.* Now it is the Bridegroom asking to hear her voice in the presence of others – before the watching world.

The appeal is widened, and I believe this is another call for the Church today, perhaps especially in the West, to shake off her silence and speak. Too often we go the other way – we are ever more silent, when there is all the more need to speak. Martin Luther King said: 'Our lives begin to end the day we become silent about the things that matter.'[277]

When John the Baptist emerged in the desert as a forerunner, to prepare for the coming into view of Christ, he replied to the question 'Who are you?' by saying, 'I am the voice of one calling in the desert, Make straight the way for the Lord' (John 1:23).

I believe the Church has taken on his mantle and is emerging from the desert as the voice crying in the wilderness, preparing people for the second coming of Christ. She must therefore find her voice.

But what can help us in this endeavour to discover our true voice? In meditating on the example of leaders in the Bible as they 'find their voice', I believe that an initial difficulty is in fact quite common. Stammering is frequently mentioned as the people of God find their voice: the prophet Jeremiah heard the word of the Lord saying, 'Before I formed you in the womb I knew you, before you were born I set you apart; I appointed you as a prophet to the nations.' Yet he still stammered and said, '"Alas, Sovereign LORD . . . I do not know how to speak; I am too young."' In the prophet's subsequent epiphany, the Lord encouraged him to find his voice, even reaching down to touch and transform his speaking: 'Then the LORD reached out his hand and touched my mouth and said to me, "I have put my words in your mouth. See, today I appoint you over nations and kingdoms"' (Jeremiah 1:5–6, 9–10).

Moses and others such as Esther go through a similar coaching and coaxing, from God and Mordecai respectively, to find their God-given voice. So it may well help for us to hear this word in Song of Songs 8, which says to the Bride again and now in public: *let me hear your voice*. We must, it seems, learn to speak. This can begin in the desert, in the place of prayer, in the place of intimacy. As we hear of and encounter the intimate embrace of the lover of our soul, we find we have something to speak about: we have a testimony. If we have no encounter, we have no testimony. If we try to speak without an encounter, we will end up mimicking the voice of others, or saying what we think people want to hear. Or we will simply be a clanging gong or crashing cymbal without love, as Paul says. But where there is encounter, where there is testimony: anything is possible.

So, paradoxically, speaking begins with listening. This is certainly something of a lost art today. The words of German martyr Dietrich Bonheoffer speak of this need. In his book on community, *Life Together*, he wrote:

> Many people are looking for an ear that will listen to them. They will not find it among Christians because these Christians are talking when they should be listening. But he who can no longer listen to his brother will soon be listening no longer to God either; he will be doing nothing but prattle in the presence of God too. This is the beginning of the death of the spiritual life, and in the end there is nothing left but spiritual chatter and clerical condescension arrayed in pious words. One who cannot listen long and patiently will presently be talking beside the point and be no longer really speaking to others, albeit he be not conscious of it. Anyone who thinks his time is too valuable to be spent keeping quiet

will eventually have no time for God and his brother, but only himself and his own follies.[278]

God will speak in the silence, if we will listen. Moses experienced this when he set up the 'Tent of Meeting'. We read of this: 'When Moses entered the Tent of Meeting to speak with the LORD, he heard the voice speaking to him from between the two cherubim above the atonement cover on the ark of the Testimony. And he spoke with him' (Numbers 7:89). If this kind of encounter is on offer, maybe we would all do well to have some such meeting place in our homes – or at least create one in our hearts.

Sometimes it is in creation that his voice is heard. Psalm 26 is rich for its description of this: 'The voice of the LORD strikes with flashes of lightning. The voice of the LORD shakes the desert . . . and strips the forests bare. And in his temple all cry, "Glory!"' (Psalm 29:7ff).

The absolute importance of listening to the voice of God before speaking is emphasised in Psalm 95:7–8: 'Today, if only you would hear his voice, "Do not harden your hearts . . ."' This is taken up by the writer to the Hebrews as a reason for the people of God not entering their 'rest'. Listening to his voice will result in the divine romance blossoming within us, which in turn will give us back our voice.

What are the areas in which we need a voice? It may begin with simply telling our story to others: in talking with others about how we met and found Christ, and how marvellous he is. The Bride is asked: *How is your beloved better than others . . .* And she replies that he is *outstanding among ten thousand* (5:9–10).

It may continue in public. Our voice is to be heard in preaching without fear: 'How, then, can they call on the one they have not believed in? And how can they believe in the one of whom they have not heard? And how can they hear without someone preaching to them? And how can anyone preach unless they are sent? As it is written: "How beautiful are the feet of those who bring good news!"' (Romans 10:14–15).

There is romance here as we read of the beauty in the feet of those who will take this news; in Proverbs 1:20, we read that wisdom 'raises her voice in the public square'. It is indeed time to speak up. One of my recurrent prayers is that people who have a voice that is authentic and godly will be raised up for the media platforms and talk shows of the world. There is a need for what I would call 'prophetic sound bites': wise answers to taunting questions, similar to those of Christ when faced with all kinds of 'foxes' and traps trying to catch him out. He knew how to speak in a way that silenced his accusers and made ordinary people listen to him gladly. Again, listening first is the key to having something to say and knowing how to say it.

Jesus himself says that our voice is to be heard before kings: 'you will be brought before governors and kings as witnesses to them and to the Gentiles. But when they arrest you, do not worry about what to say or how to say it. At that time you will be given what to say, for it will not be you speaking, but the Spirit of your Father speaking through you' (Matthew 10:18–20).

Jesus also speaks of the voice that will be heard ever more widely: 'You will be my witnesses in Jerusalem and . . . to the ends of the earth' (Acts 1:8). And Paul in Romans continues from saying 'How beautiful are the feet of those who bring good news!' to this same theme: 'Their voice has gone out into all the earth, their words to the ends of the world' (Romans 10:14, 16).

We have been considering this inviting word at the end of the Song: *You who dwell in the gardens with friends in attendance, let me hear your voice.* We have noted the different places in which the Bride's voice may be heard. We come now, though, to the enigmatic, mysterious and touching last line of the Song.

Come away, my beloved, and be like a gazelle or like a young stag on the spice-laden mountains (8:14)

In the thirteenth century, John of Ford (relying on the Septuagint translation 'Flee away') interprets this as calling the Bridegroom home to heaven after the work of atonement: 'Flee therefore, Make a dash for the things of heaven. Return again to your own place, which is the bosom of your omnipotent father. Deliver to your eternal father the product of your obedience. Show him the victorious banners of your passion. Bring the glory of your cross to heaven itself. Let your life-giving blood, as it cries out for your Church, strike the heart of your father. Let those mountains of spices wonder at you when you are lifted high above the top of the mountains.'[279]

However, Spurgeon and many others give a different interpretation, namely that this refers to the call to Christ to come back at the end of the age: 'Maranatha'. So it is that finally, the voice of the friends of the Bridegroom and the Bride will go into heaven as at the end of time. It will be a voice calling out for the Return of Christ: 'Maranatha'. 'The Spirit and the Bride say, "Come." And let the one who hears say, "Come!" . . . He who testifies to these things says, "Yes, I am coming soon." Amen. Come, Lord Jesus' (Revelation 22:17, 20).

We will devote our concluding chapter to this.

Spiritual Exercises for finding your voice

Go through the whole Song, saying out loud the passages addressed by the Bride to the Bridegroom as an intention to the beloved.

Memorise Chapter 2:8–17 and speak it as a conversation to the beloved.

Write a letter to the lover of your soul expressing your heart and your affection, then read it out as a prayer.

Spend time in Recollection, Quiet, and Union and Communion.

'The Song of Songs describes the love of Jesus Christ to his people, and it ends with an intense desire on the part of the Church that the Lord Jesus should come back to her . . . Is it not somewhat singular that as the last verse of this book of love has this note in it, so the last chapter of the Revelation, the last verses of the whole book of God which I may call the Book of Love have that thought in them? . . . "Even so, come, Lord Jesus."'
C. H. Spurgeon[280]

'Now you are no longer caught
in the obsession with darkness
and a desire for higher love-making
sweeps you upward . . .
And so long as you haven't experienced
this: to die and to grow,
you are only a troubled guest
on this dark earth.'
Von Goethe, '*Selige Sehnsucht*' 'The Holy Longing'[281]

'There is a German word, *Sehnsucht,* which has no English equivalent: it means "the longing for something". It has Romantic and mystical connotations; C. S. Lewis defined it as the "inconsolable longing" in the human heart.'
Julian Barnes, *Levels of Life*[282]

CHAPTER EIGHTEEN

The Final Cry of the Song of Songs

Come away, my beloved, and be like a gazelle or like a young stag on the spice-laden mountains.

Song of Songs 8:14

We have travelled through all eight chapters of the Song and come to the end. This last word is enigmatic for the love song of the human heart. It can be translated variously – *Make haste, my beloved, and be like a young stag* (ESV and KJV) or *Run to me, dear lover* (*The Message*). The NIV translates it: *Come away, my beloved*. It can suggest that the lover has gone away and that the Bride is requesting his return. This suggestion implies that at the end of the Song there is separation. As incomplete as this may appear, it is sadly true even of authentic human love. Human beings know no absolute fulfilment, no definitive togetherness, and are inevitably destined for parting in the end. 'Regardless of the quality or frequency of the lovemaking, there is always a measure of yearning present.'[283]

But in terms of the Bride of Christ in the divine romance, these lines take on a rich tone of meaning; for they speak of the longing and the yearning in the Bride for the return of Christ.

If this is its meaning, it is the perfect end to a perfect song. The spice-laden mountains then become the place where the fragrant offering of Christ was made on Mount Calvary to heal the rotting sin of the whole world. The Song the beloved sings is like that of a barren woman who now has hope. Her song tenderly trusts that the 'young stag' or 'gazelle' has enough power and strength and swiftness to leap over the hills of difficulty, over the mountains of opposition to 'come away' and be on earth all that he is heaven. We have seen that this is Spurgeon's view: 'The Song of Songs describes the love of Jesus Christ to his people, and it ends with an intense desire on the part of the Church that the Lord Jesus should come back to her . . . Is it not somewhat singular that as the last verse of this book of love has this note in it, so the last chapter of the Revelation, the last verses of the whole book of God which I may call the Book of Love have that thought in them? . . . "Even so, come, Lord Jesus."'[284]

Eugene Peterson also identifies this last cry of the Song with prayer for the return of Christ. He says: '"Make haste my beloved" is the equivalent to the New Testament church's cry: "*Maranatha*" (1 Cor 16:22) . . . The language of prayer is always in some degree urgent.'[285]

The Challenge of the Return of Christ

This year I have been trying to pray: 'Maranatha. Even so, come, Lord Jesus', the prayer of the early Church. It is a challenging prayer, because I think for many of us we are not quite sure if we want him to come back just yet.

I recently sat with dear friends at a wedding reception discussing this. I was saying that I felt a healthy Church would be one in which we longed with all our hearts for Christ's soon coming. My wife said: 'But don't you want to see your grandchildren grow up?' And another friend said to her husband: 'Don't you want to see your boys get married?' To which he replied: 'No – it's miserable and dangerous here

– let the Lord return soon.' It was a classic male–female split perhaps, but the conversation revealed the complex implications of the return of Christ.

In fact we were living out one of the classic tensions of the Christian life. We groan and struggle in this valley of tears; we long to 'be clothed instead with our heavenly dwelling . . . For while we are in this tent, we groan and are burdened, because we do not wish to be unclothed but to be clothed instead with our heavenly dwelling, so that what is mortal may be swallowed up by life' (2 Corinthians 5:2, 4–5). And yet at the same time we cling to life. We want to see our children's children grow up. At times we so love what God is doing we can't imagine it coming to an end. At other times of grief or yearning, we long for his return.

I think it is a tremendous challenge today actually to desire and ask for the Lord Jesus' return, and yet I believe it is something that the lovesick Church will express and something, I trust, that we will see more and more.

I remember recently talking to one of my young grandsons about the future and I gently said about the sad stories of chaos on earth that we were watching on the news and discussing: 'It will get worse; that is if Jesus does not return before that.'

'What – you mean, Jesus is coming back?' he asked.

I said: 'Yes, and it will be the end of things as we know them.' His reaction surprised me: it was to start crying. He cried inconsolably.

'Why are you crying, my darling?'

'Because the world is going to end.'

It took a little child to remind me how desperate and disturbing the return of the Lord Jesus will be.

Of course I then spent as much time as we had trying to

calm him, discussing and answering his questions, talking about the absolute goodness of God, so that my grandson could go to sleep in peace.

According to Revelation 21 and 22, heaven and earth will finally be united. As N. T. Wright says, 'Eventually heaven and earth will be impregnated with each other . . . God's heaven, God's life, God's dimension impregnating, charging the present world, eventually producing new or renewed heavens and new or renewed earth integrated with each other.' This is quite hard to explain to a nine-year-old, but it is N. T. Wright's understanding of the New Heavens and the New Earth, and I think he is right.[286] I tried to give my grandson the joyful hope of the return to earth of Christ, making all things new. But I reflected: maybe this is why the Church by and large does not, will not, pray for, prepare for or look for the Lord's return. It is just too challenging.

It was not ever thus. One nineteenth-century pietist pastor, Johann Christoph Blumhardt, kept a new carriage in his parish grounds, to be used for the first time by the Lord Jesus when he comes, 'then I will drive him in it'. How certain the waiting Blumhardt was about the coming of Christ; how he planned his life to be ready for that moment! His mind was fixed on how he would fare at the moment when he stood before the Lord Jesus. Such certainty is strange to us today. Dietrich Bonhoeffer, who tells the story, comments: 'The faith of Blumhardt is great. But it is too small for the second coming of Christ. For when this happens the whole creation will be shaken and changed. Creation reaches out before him. The sea roars and tosses in anguish and joy . . .'[287]

It is challenging, even to the point of the seas roaring in anguish. Yet, despite this massive, mourning-causing upheaval, we do long for his return, 'his glorious appearing'

(Titus 2:13; KJV) – because of all the sadness in the world and the ache and longing for home. I certainly do. We want him to come back because he is the Beauty and the Hope – the Desire of the nations. His return will make the world cry, but even so it will be an end to sorrow and sadness. As usual, C. S. Lewis helps us when he has Mr Beaver say of Aslan:

> Wrong shall be right, when he comes in sight
> At the sound of his roar, sorrows will be no more
> When he bares his teeth, winter meets its death
> When he shakes his mane, we shall have spring again.[288]

The fact is, every Christian can and should pray with longing and affection for the imminent return of Christ. As I say, I believe we can anticipate this. Incidentally, it seems to be the case that nearly all revivals documented in the history of the Church have been marked by an anticipation and longing for the return of Christ. As we have said, the Song of Songs speaks to us in the language of revival.

We can say with the Song: *Make haste, my beloved, and be like a gazelle or a young stag on the mountains of spices* (8:14; ESV). We can call him 'my beloved'; that is already a comfort. He is good and altogether lovely and he loves us. Our response is to call out to him to return, because we love him and we trust him. We call to him because his return will bring love to earth. His return will bring an end to suffering, an end to tears, and an end to evil. It will mean a great harvest, countless conversions, the salvation of a full number, the salvation of Israel, the resurrection from the dead and the time of *seeing* his glorious appearing. This is why we can and must cry, at the end of the Song, and at the end of our own song: 'Maranatha – Make haste, my beloved.' And we do.

We have reached the end of the journey. We have been swept upward by what Goethe calls 'the Holy Longing' (*Selige Sehnsucht*). The great German poet expresses the same longing for 'Home' that was explored in the first chapter of this book. He says that without this desire sweeping us upward, without a longing for 'higher lovemaking', we are 'only a troubled guest on the dark earth'. I believe he is right. Perhaps if we experience and embrace this holy longing we can enjoy being a guest here more fully. This has been one of the messages of this book. In a section of his book *Sacred Fire*, headed 'Inchoate Nostalgia . . . to "Come home" to Roots, to Moral Companionship, to a Soul Mate, to Quiet, to Solitude', Ronald Rolheiser writes of this, talking about different stages of life from adolescence through young adulthood into middle and old age: 'In the end whether we know it or not all these struggles are about one thing: finding our way back home again.'[289]

The Song of Songs has led us through this holy longing by means of many earthy scenes. From the urgent *Let him kiss me* of the first verses, we have seen the maturing of the Bride. The one who originally said: *Do not look on me* is now free to be her beautiful self. She has been through the winter and come into springtime and fragrance and the budding of virtues. She has experienced the night and kept searching for her lover without getting bitter or losing heart. She has found him and loved him to the limit. When attacked and beaten she has continued to proclaim: *My beloved is outstanding among ten thousand!* She has come out of the desert leaning on the beloved. They make a glorious team. She knows the romance of going to the fields with her beloved. The fire of love within her has not been extinguished by the many waters she has travelled through. She has her lover's seal on her heart and on her arm.

And now here she is longing – yearning for his return over the spice-laden mountains. She calls out to him to come back to her.

May we too learn to love. May we be in love with the beloved. May we in this generation find our voice to express this love and to speak about him. May we let our voice be heard in the earth as we speak about him. May it also ring out in heaven as we sing and call out: 'Make haste, my beloved. Maranatha. Even so, come, Lord Jesus.'

APPENDIX I

The Lord's Prayer

Praying the Lord's Prayer
The Lord's Prayer is a model for the Church at prayer and for disciplined personal prayer. This appendix is intended as a practical aid to help you pray longer and more fruitfully.

Our Father in heaven
Begin with intimate worship and thanking God for his Fatherhood . . . for free access to the throne of grace . . . and receive healing in his intimate embrace.

Hallowed be your name
Whether it is the Old Testament names of God – YHWH Shamah, YHWH Raphé, YHWH Tsidkenou, YHWH Jireh – or the New Testament names of Jesus – Good Shepherd, Light of the World, Bread of Life, Resurrection and Life, Baptiser in the Holy Spirit and with fire – it is good to continue worship and meditate with a daily hallowing of the name of God. To declare out loud these facts about God's character is deeply faith-building and edifying.

Names of God from the Old Testament

YHWH Hesed	Loving God	Exodus 34:6
YHWH Tsebaaoth	The Lord of hosts	1 Samuel 17:45
YHWH Elyon	God Most High	Psalm 7:18
YHWH Jireh	God my Provider	Genesis 22:14
YHWH Roï	The Lord my Shepherd	Psalm 23:1
YHWH Nissi	The Lord my banner	Exodus 17:15
YHWH Shalom	The Lord my peace	Judges 6:24
YHWH Shammah	The Lord who is there	Ezekiel 48:35
YHWH Tsidkenou	The Lord our Righteousness	Jeremiah 23:6
YHWH Mekadesh	The Lord who sanctifies	Leviticus 20:8
YHWH Raphé	The Lord who heals	Exodus 15:26
Elohim	God in Three Persons	Genesis 1:1
El-Elohé Israël	The Lord God of Israel	Genesis 33:20
Adonaï	My Lord	Genesis 15:2
El Shaddaï	All-powerful Lord	Genesis 17:1
El Olam	Eternal Lord	Genesis 21:33
El Gibbor	Strong God (Champion)	Isaiah 9:5
El Elyon	Most High God	Genesis 14:18

Names of Christ from Isaiah 9:6

Wonderful Counsellor
Mighty God
Everlasting Father
Prince of Peace

The seven 'I Am' statements of Christ from John's Gospel

I am the Bread of Life (6:35, 51)

I am the Light of the World (8:12)
I am the Door (10:7, 9)
I am the Good Shepherd (10:11, 14)
I am the Resurrection and the Life (11:25)
I am the True Vine (15:1, 5)
I am the Way, the Truth and the Life (14:6)

Your kingdom come, your will be done, on earth as it is in heaven
Ask now for the leading of the Holy Spirit, for his direction with regard to what aspect of his kingdom to pray for. This could include healings and deliverance that are sought for, church planting, guidance about growth of the Church, missionary activity and praying for the nations, being a house of prayer for all nations, the conversion of the lost, and the coming rule of God (his kingdom) into different parts of society.

Give us today our daily bread
John Wimber said, 'Give us tomorrow's bread today.' We can pray that the provision of the kingdom flows into our lives today: money needed for projects or survival, jobs for the unemployed, spiritual food for us and for our children.

And forgive us our sins as we forgive those who sin against us
'If I had cherished sin in my heart, the Lord would not have listened' (Psalm 66:18). Confession of sin must begin at a personal level. Take time to ask the Holy Spirit to reveal what does not please him in your life and confess it. More and more churches are being taken into corporate confession on behalf of the Church, community or nation. Study Nehemiah 1 for this practice and several other passages (Nehemiah 9, Ezra 9, Daniel 9).

Often reconciliation between churches is on the Holy Spirit's agenda, with the need in the praying church to give time for interceding for the growth of other churches – that they may be blessed even more than your own.

And lead us not into temptation but deliver us from the evil one
Strong spiritual warfare against the forces of darkness is something more and more churches are being led to do. Be careful not to pray above your authority: to do so can be either meaningless or dangerous. Know that pulling down strongholds is as much to do with preaching the gospel as with prayer warfare. But there is a need to take authority, to 'bind the strong man' or the territorial spirit that may influence a situation that is blocked. A praying church needs to grow in authority and discernment in this area.

For thine is the kingdom, the power and the glory,
For ever and ever, Amen.
Be sure to end a time of private or corporate prayer with praise and worship, which can put things back into a right perspective and brings the reward of a sacrifice of praise to the Lamb who was slain for us.

Selected Musical Settings of the Song of Songs

Classical

Bantock, Sir Granville (1922), *The Song of Songs*, Orchestral Piece/Opera

Ceballos, Rodrigo de (1525–91), *Hortus Conclusus*

Gombert, Nicolas (1490–1556), *Tota Pulchra Es, Quam Pulchra Es*

Guerrero, Francisco (1528–99), *Ego Flos Campi, Surge, Propera Amica Mea, Trahe Me Post Te*

Lassus, Orlande de (1562), *Sacrae Cantiones: Veni, dilecte mi and Veni in hortum meum*

Marais, Marin (1656–1728), *Passacaille*

Palestrina, Giovanni Pierluigi da (1584), *Canticum Canticorum: Song of Solomon*

Papa, Jacob Clemens non (16th century), *Ego Dormio, Ego Flos Campi*

Penderecki, Krzysztof (1973), *Canticum Canticorum Salomonis*, Schott Music

Tomkins, Thomas (1668), *My Beloved Spake*

Victoria, Tomás Luis de (1561), *Nigra Sum Sed Formosa, Vadam et Circuibo, Vidi Speciosam*

Vivanco, Sebastian de (1551–1622), *Veni Dilecte Mi*

Walton, Sir William (1938), *Set Me as a Seal*

Williams, Mark (2014), *My Beloved's Voice*, directed by Mark Williams, Choir of Jesus College Cambridge, Sigma Records,

2014, which contains the following: 'Sicut lilium' by Antoine Brumel (c.1460–1515); 'As the apple tree' by Robert Walker (b.1946); 'My beloved spake' by Patrick Hadley (1899–1973); 'Ubi caritas' by Maurice Duruflé (1902–86); 'Rise up my love' by Howard Skempton (b.1947); 'How fair is thy love' by Howard Skempton; 'My beloved is gone down' by Howard Skempton; 'How fair and how pleasant' by Howard Skempton; 'Set me as a seal' by Nico Muhly (b.1981); 'Ego flos campi' by Clemens non Papa (c.1510–c.1556); 'Aubade from Pieces de Fantasie' by Louis Vierne (1870–1937); 'Rise up my love' by Healey Willan (1880–1968); 'I beheld her beautiful as a dove' by Healey Willan; 'Nigra sum' by Pablo Casals (c.1479–1528); 'Anima sum' by Martin de Rivafrecha (d.1528); 'How fair is thy face' by Edvard Greig (1843–1907); 'I sat down under his shadow' by Edward Bairstow (1874–1946); 'Set me as a seal' by Gerald Finzi (1901–56); 'Blessed be the God & Father' by Samuel Sebastian Wesley (1810–76).

Contemporary worship

Edwards, Misty (2003) *Eternity*; (2005) *Always on His Mind*; (2007) *Fling Wide*; (2009) *Relentless*, Forerunner Music

Prosch, Kevin (1991), 'His Banner over Me', from the album *Even So, Come*, Mercy/Vineyard Publications

Richards, Noel and Tricia (1995), 'You are My Passion', from the album *The Best of Noel Richards*, Thankyou Music

Salyn, Dean (2015), 'He is Yahweh', from the album *The Way (The Way – Volume 1)* Mercy/Vineyard Publishing

Smith, Martin (2013), 'Song of Solomon', from the album *God's Great Dancefloor*, Step 02, Integrity Music

Thurlow, Jon (2010), 'Fragrance', from the album *Strong Love*, Audiobook Publishing

Bibliography

Selected commentaries on the Song of Songs

Bergant, Dianne, *Song of Songs: The Love Poetry of Scripture* (New City Press, New York, 1998)

Bernard of Clairvaux, *The Works of Bernard of Clairvaux: Song of Songs*, trans. Kilian Walsh (Liturgical Press, Minnesota, 1971)

Bickle, Mike, *Song of Songs: The Ravished Heart of God, Part 1: The Bride's Inheritance in Jesus* and *Part 2: Jesus' Inheritance in the Bride* (Friends of the Bridegroom, Kansas City, 1999)

Durham, James, *An Exposition of The Song of Solomon* (The Banner of Truth, Edinburgh, 1840)

Gledhill, Tom, *The Message of the Song of Songs: The Lyrics of Love* (InterVarsity Press, Leicester, 1994)

Hudson Taylor, J., *Union and Communion* (Lutterworth Press, London, 1914)

Longman III, Tremper, *Song of Songs* (Wm. B. Eerdmans Publishing, Cambridge, 2001)

Nee, Watchman, *The Song of Songs: Unveiling the Mystery of Passionate Mystery with Christ* (CLC Publications, 2006)

Pennington, M. Basil, *The Song of Songs: A Spiritual Commentary* (Skylight Paths Publishing, Woodstock, 2004)

Pope, Marvin H., *Song of Songs: A New Translation with*

Introduction and Commentary by Marvin H. Pope (Doubleday, New York, 1977)

Seddon, Philip, *Redeeming Eros: Reading the Song of Songs* (Grove Books Ltd, Cambridge, 2010)

Simpson, A. B., *Loving as Jesus Loves: A Devotional Study of the Song of Songs* (Christian Publications, Pennsylvania, 1996)

Spurgeon, C. H., *The Most Holy Place: Sermons on the Song of Solomon* (Christian Focus Publications, Ross-shire, 1996)

Tang, Susan, *Demands of Love: Song of Solomon – a Devotional Study* (Stations of Life, Sabah, East Malaysia, 1997)

Wilken, Robert Louis, *The Song of Songs: Interpreted by Early Christians and Medieval Commentators*, translated and edited by Richard A. Norris Jr, 2nd edition (Wm. B. Eerdmans Publishing, Cambridge, 2003)

Wurmbrand, Richard *The Sweetest Song* (Marshall, Morgan & Scott, 1988)

Selected books on the Divine Romance

Bell, Rob, *Sex God: Exploring the Endless Connections between Sexuality and Spirituality* (Zondervan, Grand Rapids, 2007)

Bickle, Mike, *The Pleasures of Loving God* (Charisma House, Florida, 2000)

Clement, Oliver, *The Roots of Christian Mysticism* (first published in English by New City, London, 1993)

Cleverly, Charlie, *Epiphanies of the Ordinary: Encounters that Change Lives* (Hodder & Stoughton, London, 2012)

Cleverly, Charlie, *The Discipline of Intimacy* (Kingsway Publications, East Sussex, 2002)

Hopkins, Gerard Manley, *Poems and Prose* (Penguin Group, London, 1953)

Jeanrond, Werner G., *A Theology of Love* (T & T Clarke International, London, 2010)

John of the Cross, *Selected Writings by Saint John of the Cross*, trans. and ed. Kieran Kavanaugh (Paulist Press, New Jersey, 1987)

Keller, Timothy, *Prayer: Experiencing Awe and Intimacy with God* (Hodder & Stoughton, London, 2014)

Keller, Timothy, *The Meaning of Marriage: Facing the Complexities of Commitment with the Wisdom of God* (Hodder & Stoughton, London, 2011)

Lane, Belden C., *Ravished by Beauty: The Surprising Legacy of Reformed Spirituality* (Oxford University Press, Oxford, 2011)

Lewis, C. S., *A Preface to Paradise Lost* (Oxford University Press, London, 1942)

Lewis, C. S., *The Business of Heaven: Daily Readings*, ed. Walter Hooper (Fount Paperbacks, 1984)

Lewis, C. S., *The Lion, The Witch and The Wardrobe* (HarperCollins, London, 1980)

Loyola, Saint Ignatius of, *The Spiritual Exercises of Saint Ignatius of Loyola*, trans. Michael Ivens (Gracewing, Hertfordshire, and Inigo Enterprises, Surrey, 2004)

Mason, Mike, *The Mystery of Marriage: Meditations on the Miracle* (Multnomah Books, Colorado, 1985)

Nouwen, Henri J. M., *The Way of the Heart*, 2nd edition (Daybreak, London, 1981)

Nouwen, Henri J. M., *In the Name of Jesus: Reflections on Christian Leadership* (The Crossroad Publishing Company, New York, 1989)

Peterson, Eugene H., *Eat This Book: The Art of Spiritual Reading* (Hodder & Stoughton, London, 2006)

Peterson, Eugene H., *Five Smooth Stones for Pastoral Work*, Eerdmans Publishing, 1992)

Rolheiser, Roland, *The Holy Longing: The Search for Christian Spirituality* (Doubleday, New York, 1999)

Rutherford, Samuel, *Letters of Samuel Rutherford*, ed. Revd Andrew A. Bonar, DD (Oliphant Anderson and Ferrier, Edinburgh and London, 1891)

Turner, Denys, *Eros and Allegory: Medieval Exegesis of the Song of Songs* (Cistercian Publications, 1942)

Notes

1 Psalm 42:1.
2 C. S. Lewis 'The Weight of Glory' in *Essay Collection* (HarperCollins, 2002), p. 96.
3 Thus Olivier Clément in his definitive 1980s anthology *The Roots of Christian Mysticism* – translated from the French title *Sources* (New City, 1993), p. 15.
4 *The Holy Longing* is the title of Ronald Rolheiser's 1999 book on 'The Search for a Christian Spirituality' (Doubleday).
5 Michael Mayne, former Dean of Westminster Abbey, in *The Sunrise of Wonder* (Darton, Longman and Todd, 2008, p. 29), quoting George Steiner in *Real Presences* (Faber, 1989).
6 Johann Wolfgang von Goethe, 'The Holy Longing', trans. Robert Bly, in Bly: *A Poetry Anthology* (Harper, 1993), p. 382. Ronald Rolheiser takes this poem's title and makes it the title of his book *The Holy Longing*.
7 Throughout the *Confessions*, Augustine offers an auto-biographical analysis of his own self-estrangement – in which his will is divided, torn in many directions. He describes his process of conversion or transformation, in which the dividedness of the soul is finally overcome. And it is just as prevalent in secular thought: although the idea of alienation was not fully developed until the

modern period, in the *Republic*, Plato considers the human being as only achieving happiness through a rightly ordered soul.

8 Julian Barnes: BBC Lent talks. In the semi-autobiographical *Nothing To Be Frightened Of* (Jonathan Cape, 2008), this author of some of the great twenty-first-century fiction tells how he used to be an atheist, but is now an agnostic.

9 *Notes from the Underground* (1864).

10 Fyodor Dostoyevsky, *The Idiot*.

11 Douglas Coupland, *Life after God* (Simon & Schuster, 1994), p. 359.

12 Ibid.

13 Jawlensky took his painting cues from the Christian artists Van Gogh and Matisse. His final works before his death in 1941 were basically meditations – small dully glowing abstract heads of Christ. Matisse's final great masterpiece was the chapel he designed at Venice.

14 'Mythic' not in the sense that it is a myth that never happened, but in the sense that the story actually happened in space and time but now also stands as a powerful description of alienation today.

15 Psalm 95:5.

16 Mother Teresa's Nobel Prize speech, 11 December 1979.

17 Rob Bell, *Sex God* (Zondervan, 2007), p. 45.

18 Donne was a metaphysical poet, a term coined by the poet and critic Samuel Johnson to describe a loose group of English lyric poets of the seventeenth century, whose work was characterised by speculation about the themes of love and Christianity.

19 Hosea 2:14, 16, 20, 23.

20 We might include also the *Wisdom of Solomon* and *Sirach* from the Apocrypha.

21 Bernard began to produce these in 1135, and died with his series, at eighty-six sermons, incomplete.

22 Karl Barth, *Church Dogmatics*, Vol. 3, Part 1 (T&T Clark, 1986), p. 313. (Quoted, among others, by Eugene Peterson, *Five Smooth Stones for Pastoral Work*, p. 36.)

23 Eugene H. Peterson, *Five Smooth Stones* (Wm. B. Eerdmans Publishing, 1992), p. 57.

24 *Spiritual Exercises of St Ignatius of Loyola* (Gracewing edition, 2004), p. 1.

25 For a detailed description of *Lectio Divina*, see Chapter 8.

26 Philip Seddon, *Redeeming Eros: Reading the Song of Songs* (Grove Books, 2010), p. 3.

27 Eugene H. Peterson, *Five Smooth Stones*, p. 42.

28 Ronald Rolheiser, *Sacred Fire* (Image, 2014), p. 31.

29 Sermon, 'A bundle of myrrh', 1864, op. cit., p. 112.

30 Erich, Auerbach. *Mimesis: The Representation of Reality in Western Literature* (1936). Fiftieth anniversary edition, trans. Willard Trask (Princeton University Press, 2003).

31 The body of exegesis along with homiletic stories as taught by Jewish rabbinic sages of the post-Temple era. The purpose of Midrash was to resolve problems in the interpretation of difficult passages of the text of the Hebrew Bible.

32 In *The Church's Bible: The Song of Songs Interpreted by Early Christian Commentators*, ed. Richard A. Norris Jr (Eerdmans, 2003), p. 8.

33 Denys Turner, *Eros and Allegory* (Cistercian Publications, 1995), p. 151.

34 Ibid., p. 87.

35 See Dianne Bergant's otherwise excellent *Song of Songs:*

The Love Poetry of Scripture (New City Press, 1998) and Tom Gledhill, *The Message of the Song of Songs* (The Bible Speaks Today series, IVP, 1994) for examples of this school.

36 Christopher West, *At the Heart of the Gospel* (Image, 2012), p. 132.

37 C. S. Lewis, *The Voyage of the Dawn Treader* (Geoffrey Bles, 1952), p. 177.

38 Peterson, *Five Smooth Stones*, p. 39.

39 Tremper Longman III, New International Commentary, *Song of Songs* (Eerdmans, 2003).

40 Seddon, *Redeeming Eros*, p. 3.

41 C. S. Lewis, *The Four Loves* (William Collins, 2012).

42 In *The Church's Bible*, op. cit., p. xi.

43 Mike Bickle, *The Pleasures of Loving God* (Charisma House, 2000), p. 94.

44 J. Hudson Taylor, *Union and Communion* (China Inland Mission, 1914), p. 1.

45 Eugene Peterson, *Eat this Book: A Conversation in the Art of Spiritual Reading* (Hodder, 2006).

46 Marvin H. Pope, *The Song of Songs* (Anchor Bible: Yale University Press, 1994).

47 *Works of Bernard de Clairvaux*, Vol. 2 (Cistercian Publications, 1976), p. 6, Sermon on the Song of Songs, section 5.

48 Herman Hesse, from *Narcisuss and Goldmund* (Fischer Verlag, 1930; this translation: Noonday Press, 1988).

49 Agnes de Mille, choreographer and novelist (1905–1993, niece of Cecil B. DeMille), is known for her work on *Rodgers & Hammerstein: The Sound of American Music* (1985), *Oklahoma!* (1955) and *Carousel* (1956).

50 Agnes de Mille; Alfred Lord Tennyson, 'Fatima', 1832.

51 Herman Hesse, from *Narcissus and Goldmund* (Fischer Verlag, 1930; this translation: Noonday Press, 1988).

52 Bergant, *Song of Songs*, p. 21.

53 Emil Ludwig, *Of Life and Love*, (Kessinger Publishing, 2005), p. 29 (Über das Glück und die Liebe, 1940).

54 Mike Bickle, *Song of Songs: The Ravished Heart of God* (Friends of the Bridegroom, 1999), Vol. 1.

55 In *The Church's Bible*, ed Richard A. Norris Jr, op. cit., p. 21.

56 'Here is Love', words: William Rees (1802–83), music: Robert Lowry (1876).

57 See Bernard of Clairvaux, *On the Song of Songs*, Vol. 2 (Cistercian Publications, 1976), pp. 5, 8 and 10.

58 James Durham, *Song of Songs* (The Banner of Truth Trust, 1982), p. 74.

59 M. Basil Pennington, *The Song of Songs* (Skylight Paths, 2004), p. 15.

60 Bernard of Clairvaux, *The Church's Bible*, ed. Richard A. Norris Jr, p. 23.

61 Spurgeon, *The Most Holy Place* (Sermons on the Song of Songs) (Christian Focus edition, 1996), p. 70.

62 Timothy Keller, *Prayer* (Hodder & Stoughton, 2014), p. 16.

63 Henri Nouwen, *In the Name of Jesus* (Crossroad, 1989), p. 43.

64 In Belden Lane, *Ravished by Beauty: The Surprising Legacy of Reformed Spirituality* (Oxford, 2011), p. 106.

65 Article in *Encyclopaedia Britannica*.

66 Lane, *Ravished by Beauty*, p. 107.

67 See *Spiritual Exercises*, para. 23, 'Principle and Foundation', p. 11.

68 2 Corinthians 2:14–15.

69 Origen and Bernard of Clairvaux, in *The Church's Bible*, ed. Richard A. Norris Jr, pp. 39–41.

70 Isaiah 5:7.

71 Revelation 2:3–4.

72 W. H. Auden, 'September 1 1939', *Another Time* (Random House, 1940).

73 In *Tutu: The Authorised Portrait* (Macmillan, 2011).

74 Friedrich Nietzsche, *Thus Spoke Zarathustra*. Whether he meant this ironically or in earnest, it seems to me certainly to approach a deep truth.

75 W. H. Auden 'September 1 1939'.

76 A. Cadman, 'His name is as ointment poured forth', © Kingsway Publications Ltd.

77 Gregory the Great, *The Church's Bible*, ed. Richard A. Norris Jr, p. 33.

78 Fernand Dumont, French-Canadian poet and theologian: *La Région du cœur* ([*trois récits*], Éditions du Groupe surréaliste en Hainaut, 1939).

79 See Ruth 3:3.

80 Kate Lord Brown, *The Perfume Garden* and see, of course, Proust, *À la recherche du temps perdu*, where the smell and taste of a madeleine cake unlock a whole world of memories for the author.

81 In Norris, op. cit., p. 73.

82 Spurgeon, op. cit., pp. 114–15.

83 This is a word repeated often through the OT to describe the nature of God. Moses asked: 'Show me your glory.' The great revelation he was granted of the 'name' of God is that God is 'Loving God', 'God of loving-kindness: Jehovah Hesed': 'The LORD, the LORD, the compassionate and gracious God, slow to anger, abounding in love and faithfulness, maintaining

love [*hesed*] to thousands, and forgiving wickedness, rebellion and sin' (Exodus 34:5).

84 C. S. Lewis, 'The Weight of Glory', op. cit.

85 Ignatius of Loyola, *Spiritual Exercises*, p. 21.

86 Ibid., p. 11. This is the famous 'principle and foundation' of the exercises of Ignatius.

87 M. Basil Pennington, *The Song of Songs*, p. 30.

88 See Bergant, *Song of Songs*, p. 36.

89 John Stott, *Issues Facing Christians Today* (Zondervan, 4th edn, 2006).

90 Watchman Nee, *Song of Songs: Unveiling the Mystery of Passionate Intimacy with Christ* (Christian Literature Crusade, 1965), p. 24.

91 Spurgeon, *The Most Holy Place*, p. 146.

92 Pennington, *The Song of Songs*, p. 30.

93 Such is the case for the British movement 'New Wine', which gathers upwards of twenty thousand people each year for its annual tented festivals, and see Pierre Cranga's book *La maison du vin nouveau*, written following the renewals of 1994 in France and the 'Toronto Blessing'.

94 Alan de Lille in Turner, *Eros and Allegory*, p. 88. Alan goes on with an application more for his context than ours: 'And just as a person who lives in a cell, as does a solitary hermit, is withdrawn from the clamour of the times, so is a person in heaven withdrawn from the clamour of the world.'

95 Pennington, *The Song of Songs*, p. 30.

96 *Her Uncommon Discoveries of the Divine Perfections and Glory; and of the Excellency of Christ* by Sarah Pierrepont Edwards, 1710–58, from Sereno Dwight, *The Works of President Edwards: With a Memoir of His Life*, Vol. I

(New York: G. & C. & H. Carvill, 1830), pp. 171–90 (Chapter XIV).

97 In C. and M. Peckham, *Sounds from Heaven: Revival on the Island of Lewis* (Focus Publications, 2001).

98 In Matthew O'Donovan, sleeve notes to 'Song of Songs' sung by 'Stile Antico' (Harmonia Mundi).

99 See Ronald Rolheiser, *The Holy Longing* (Doubleday, 1999), pp. 204ff. and Henri Nouwen, 'From Loneliness to Solitude', in *Reaching Out: The Three Movements of the Spiritual Life* (Doubleday, 1986). For Rolheiser, the starting point for any theology is God's statement that 'it is not good to be alone', and that marriage and sexual union are what God intended as the norm. But I would add that living as part of real community is a gift and provision in this movement from loneliness to solitude.

100 'It is called Recollection because the soul collects together all the faculties and enters within itself to be with God.' From Saint Teresa of Avila, *The Way of Perfection* (Cosimo Inc., 2007), p. 160.

101 Psalm 46:1, 4, 8, 10: 'God is our refuge and strength . . . Therefore we will not fear . . . There is a river whose streams make glad the city of God . . . Come and see what the LORD has done . . . "Be still, and know that I am God."'

102 In Richard Foster, *Prayer* (Hodder & Stoughton, 1992), p. 172.

103 J. Hudson Taylor, *Union and Communion*.

104 In Foster, *Prayer*, p. 168.

105 Originally produced in a tract in November 1907 then published in *Confidence* magazine, October 1908, pp. 11, 15–16. Later published in *Redemption Tidings*, 14 February 1947, p. 4.

106 Gregory of Nyssa, in Clément, *The Roots of Christian Mysticism*, p. 152.

107 Durham, *Song of Songs*, p. 133.

108 From the album *God's Great Dancefloor* (Integrity Music, 2013).

109 Durham, *Song of Songs*, p. 133.

110 Foster, *Prayer*, p. 169.

111 *Bible in One Year* commentary.

112 Quoted by Gledhill, *The Message of the Song of Songs*, p. 135.

113 Durham, *Song of Songs*, p. 135.

114 C. S. Lewis, *The Lion, the Witch and the Wardrobe* (Geoffrey Bles, 1950).

115 Origen, 'Homilies on the Song of Songs' in Clément, *The Roots of Christian Mysticism*.

116 Wm Paul Young, *The Shack* (Hodder Windblown, 2008).

117 'Everything will be okay in the end. If it's not okay, it's not the end' is a quote attributed to John Lennon.

118 In *The Church's Bible*, ed. Richard A. Norris Jr, p. 122.

119 Interview with *The Daily Telegraph*, 12 July 2013.

120 Stacy Horn, article in *Time*, 13 August 2013.

121 Michael Mayne, *The Sunrise of Wonder*, p. 76.

122 Ann Angel, *Janis Joplin: Rise up Singing* (Harry Abrams, 2010).

123 Gerard Manley Hopkins, 'Spring', in *Poetry and Prose* (Penguin edition, 1953), p. 26.

124 Joyce Meyer, *Conflict Free Living* (Charisma House, 2012).

125 Norris, op. cit., p. 128.

126 Augustine is referring to the story of Samson burning the corn of the Philistines (Judges 15), ibid., p. 129.

127 Ignatius of Loyola, *Spiritual Exercises*, p. 22.

128 In *The Church's Bible*, ed. Richard A. Norris Jr, p. 139.

129 Bernard of Clairvaux. Sermon 75 on the Song of Songs.

130 Ibid.

131 C. S. Lewis, *The Screwtape Letters* (Geoffrey Bles, 1942).

132 *Sonnenfinsternis* (Darkness at Noon) is a novel by Arthur Koestler, first published in 1940.

133 Bernard of Clairvaux, op. cit.

134 Gregory of Elvira (fourth century), *The Church's Bible*, ed. Richard A. Norris Jr, p. 137.

135 Bernard of Clairvaux, Sermon 75 on the Song of Songs, 'On seeking Him with the whole heart'.

136 Spurgeon, *The Most Holy Place*, pp. 254ff.

137 Durham, *Song of Songs*, p. 170.

138 *Soul Cry*, Edwards, Misty, Campbell, Cassie © 2009 Forerunner Music (Adm Song Solutions www.songsolutions.org) All rights reserved. Used by permission.

139 Durham, *Song of Songs*, p. 176.

140 Nicky and Sila Lee's 'Marriage Preparation Course' and Care for the Family's 'Marriage by Design' are recommended.

141 Thomas Brooks, *The Unsearchable Riches of Christ* (Google Books: Complete Works of Thomas Brooks), p. 263.

142 Spurgeon, op. cit., pp. 267ff.

143 In Wikipedia's excellent article on *Lectio Divina*.

144 Matthew Henry, *Commentary on the Whole Bible*.

145 Ibid.

146 Charlie Cleverly, *Epiphanies of the Ordinary* (Hodder & Stoughton, 2012).

147 See also 2 Chronicles 26:14 for an OT preview: Uzziah's courageous arming of his troops.

148 Martyn Lloyd-Jones' Introduction to *The Christian Warfare*, Commentary on the Book of Ephesians, Ch. 6 (Banner of Truth).

149 Daniel T. Rodgers, *Age of Fracture* (Belknap Press, 2011). In the last quarter of the twentieth century, the ideas that most Americans lived by started to fragment. See also the album *Age of Fracture* by the London band, Cymbals.

150 Alan Jones, *Reimagining Christianity: Reconnect Your Spirit Without Disconnecting Your Mind* (John Wiley & Sons, 2004).

151 Thomas Merton, *Thoughts in Solitude*, 19th edn (Farrar, Straus Giroux, 1999).

152 Tim Dearborn is Associate Director of Faith and Development for World Vision International.

153 E. M. Bounds, *E. M. Bounds on Prayer* (Whittaker House, 1997), p. 468.

154 Jeanne Gnyon, *Experiencing the Depths of Jesus Christ* (formerly entitled *Short and very easy methods of prayer*) (Sowers of Seed Inc., 1975).

155 Bickle, *Song of Songs: The Ravished Heart of God*, Vol. 1, Session 11.

156 Gregory the Great, *Commentary on the Song of Songs*, in Turner, *Eros and Allegory*, p. 222.

157 Bickle, *Song of Songs*, from whose work these equivalences come.

158 In *The Church's Bible*, ed. Richard A. Norris Jr, p. 161.

159 Ibid., p. 157.

160 See Colossians 4:6, James 3:9–10, Ephesians 4:29.

161 Durham, *Song of Songs*, p. 212.

162 In *The Church's Bible*, ed. Richard A. Norris Jr, p. 166.

163 Bickle, *Song of Songs*, Volume 2, Session 11. I am

indebted to him for many insights, including also the paradigm of a God with strong feelings affected by the glance of the Bride.

164 Hudson Taylor, *Union and Communion*, first printed in 'China's Millions', published in book form by CIM, 1914 p. 42.

165 Nee, *Song of Songs*, p. 10.

166 Ibid., 120.

167 Durham, *Song of Songs*, p. 222.

168 *Union and Communion*, p. 42.

169 There is an eighth-century BC example of this in the Ashmolean museum in Oxford – a necklace belonging to Esarhaddon's wife.

170 Spurgeon, *The Most Holy Place*.

171 See Charlie Cleverly, *The Passion that Shapes Nations* (Cook, 2005) for more on martyrs.

172 *The Spiritual Exercises of St Ignatius of Loyola*, pp. 42ff (trans. Elder Mullan, 1914) (Public Domain at sacred-texts.com).

173 Spurgeon, *The Most Holy Place*, p. 311.

174 In Nicky Gumbel, *Bible in One Year*. Nicky Gumbel's daily commentary is read online by tens of thousands worldwide, helping to stem the tide of the modern Church's biblical illiteracy. I believe it may be as significant a contribution to the health of the Church as the development of the Alpha course, his life's work.

175 Bergant, *Song of Songs*, p. 84.

176 Spurgeon, *The Most Holy Place*, p. 311.

177 Lane, *Ravished by Beauty* (Oxford University Press USA, 2011).

178 *Letters of Samuel Rutherford*, ed. Andrew Bonar (Edinburgh, 1894), p. 410.

179 *Letters of Samuel Rutherford*, p. 30.

180 Hudson Taylor, *Union and Communion*, p. 46.

181 Malcolm Muggeridge, sermon *Living Water*, delivered at Queen's Church, Aberdeen, May 26th 1968.

182 See Simon Ponsonby, *God Inside Out* (Kingsway, 2007), Ch. 13, for a full discussion of the differences and similarities between Catholic, Pentecostal and Protestant positions on the baptism in the Holy Spirit, together with Simon's position: 'a three stage initiation with emphasis more on process than event, releasing the effects of the received Spirit' (p. 248).

183 Quoted in Lloyd-Jones, *Joy Unspeakable* (Shaw (Harold) Publishers, 1985).

184 Gordon Fee, *God's Empowering Presence*, reprint edition (Baker Academic, 2009), pp. 8–9.

185 Origen, 'Sermon on the Song of Songs', 1.7, in Clément, *The Roots of Christian Mysticism*, p. 189.

186 Bergant, *Song of Songs*, p. 92.

187 Marvin Pope and numerous commentators speak of the 'well known use of "feet" as a euphemism for genitals'. In Pope, *The Song of Songs*, p. 515.

188 Longman III, *Song of Songs*, p. 166.

189 Ibid., 174.

190 Gregory of Nyssa in Clément, *The Roots of Christian Mysticism*, p. 173.

191 St John of the Cross, 'The Dark Night', from *The Collected Works of St John of the Cross*, trans. Kieran Kavanaugh and Otilio Rodriguez (ICS Publications, 1991).

192 St John of the Cross, 'Prologue to The Ascent of Mount Carmel', in *Selected Writings* (Paulist Press, 1987), p. 59.

193 Richard St Victor (d.1173), in 'Song of Songs', *The Church's Bible*, p. 212.

194 John of Ford (d.1214), in 'Song of Songs', *The Church's Bible*, p. 217.

195 Psalm 23:2.

196 Apponius (c. seventh century), in 'Song of Songs', *The Church's Bible*, p. 218.

197 Mark 10:21.

198 The great Scottish divine John Owen thought the Song of Songs 'totally sublime, spiritual, mystical' and strongly commended Durham's commentary as 'an assistance and help to what he is reaching out for'; Foreword to Durham, *Song of Songs*, p. 22; quotation from p. 305.

199 See John 17, Romans 8.

200 This phrase and others are from Bickle, *Song of Songs*, p. 31.

201 Bernard Ramm in *Questions of Life*, p. 35.

202 Durham, op. cit., p. 310.

203 Hesse, *Narcissus and Goldmund*.

204 Richard Sibbes, *The Bruised Reed* (1631) (The Banner of Truth Trust, 1999).

205 Samuel Rutherford, *Letters* (Portage Publications, 2007) (available to download from http://www.portagepub. com/products/caa/sr-letters.html).

206 Henry Finck, *Romantic Love and Personal Beauty* (1887). Finck, a nineteenth-century music critic, may hereby have inspired a famous Mae West line: 'A man's kiss is his signature.'

207 St John of the Cross, 'The Dark Night', p. 192.

208 Bergant, *Song of Songs*, p. 115.

209 See Gledhill, *The Message of the Song of Songs*, p. 185.

210 1 Kings 4:32.

211 See 1 Kings 11.

212 Pope, *The Song of Songs*, p. 557.

213 This is the view of Mike Bickle, from whom I take this interpretation, following several of the Church Fathers; Bickle, *Song of Songs*, Vol. 2, Session 16.

214 Bickle, *Song of Songs*, Vol. 2, Session 16.

215 *Spiritual Exercises*, p. 43.

216 I am indebted to Mike Bickle for this insight. His view also is that 'this describes the pre-eminence of the Bride above angels. The Bible clearly describes the angelic hosts as inferior in glory to His Bride (1 Cor. 6:2–3; Heb. 1:14)'. Ibid.

217 A. W. Tozer, *That Incredible Christian* (Authentic, 2009) p. 157.

218 In *The Church's Bible*, ed. Richard A. Norris Jr, p. 236.

219 Lewis, *The Screwtape Letters*.

220 Fernand Dumont, *Région du cœur et autres textes* (Es Hainault, Mons, 1939).

221 Bergant, *Song of Songs*, p. 116; Longman III, *Song of Songs*, p. 185.

222 Henry, *Commentary on the Whole Bible*.

223 Matthew Henry is most remembered today for his *Commentary on the Whole Bible*. J. I. Packer comments: 'Simple and practical in style while thoroughly scholarly and well-informed for substance, the Commentary remains an all-time classic, standing head and shoulders above any other popular exposition produced either before or since.'

224 Spurgeon, *The Most Holy Place*, pp. 520ff.

225 Ibid.,

226 Ibid., p. 522.

227 See Pope, *The Song of Songs*, p. 603.

228 John Bunyan and Richard Sibbes are referenced in Spurgeon's sermon 'Inward Conflicts', and Spurgeon

himself was prone to depression and struggle. We read in the notes to his sermon on this theme: 'Mr. Spurgeon has been laid aside by sickness for two Sabbaths, but is now recovering and hopes to be again in the pulpit next Lord's-day. He earnestly begs the prayers of loving friends that his frequent infirmities may be sanctified to the glory of God and the profit of the church; and then, if it were the Lord's will, eventually removed.'

229 Henri Nouwen, 'Making All Things New', in *Seeds of Hope* (Darton, Longman and Todd, 1989), p. 14.

230 Mike Mason, *The Mystery of Marriage* (SPCK, 1997), p. 18.

231 In Peterson, op. cit., p. 56.

232 Justin (second-century apologist and convert from Stoicism, died around 165), in Clément, *The Roots of Christian Mysticism*, p. 83.

233 Bergant, *Song of Songs*, p. 127.

234 West, *At the Heart of the Gospel*, p. 18.

235 Mason, *The Mystery of Marriage*.

236 Cheryl Exum, *Song of Songs: A Commentary* (The Old Testament Library: WJK Books, 2005).

237 *The Church's Bible*, ed. Richard A. Norris Jr, p. 255.

238 Ibid., p. 258.

239 See Bickle, op. cit., Ch. 17.

240 Gregory of Nyssa, *Homilies on the 'Song of Songs'*, in Clément, *The Roots of Christian Mysticism*, p. 245.

241 Thus C. D. Ginsburg's plea: 'We earnestly request those who maintain the allegorical interpretation of the Song to reflect whether this verse, and indeed the whole of this address, can be put into the mouth of Christ as speaking to the Church. Would not our minds recoil with horror were we to hear a Christian using it publicly,

or even privately, to illustrate the love of Christ for his Church?' (C. D. Ginsburg, *The Song of Songs*, 1857, in Pope, *The Song of Songs*, p. 634.)

242 *The Church's Bible*, ed. Richard A. Norris Jr, p. 262. See also Augustine: 'The heavenly Bridegroom left the heavenly chambers with the presage of the nuptials before him. He came to the marriage bed of the cross, a bed not of pleasure but of pain, united himself with the woman, and consummated the union forever . . .', in West, *At the Heart of the Gospel*, p. 123.

243 Ignatius of Loyola, *Spiritual Exercises*, p. 70.

244 George Whitefield, describing the eighteenth-century revival in England (in *Journals of George Whitefield*).

245 Apponius was a fifth-century Italian monk whose commentary on the Song is quoted by both Gregory the Great (d.604) and the Venerable Bede (d.735). In *The Church's Bible*, ed. Richard A. Norris Jr, p. 269.

246 Website of People's Church, Toronto.

247 On occasion people have come in off the streets asking if there was a spare table. For those looking to present such a course, I recommend '*The Marriage Course*' by Nicky and Sila Lee – www.relationshipcentral.org.

248 James 1:27.

249 Hudson Taylor, *Union and Communion*, p. 67.

250 Durham, *Song of Songs*, p. 391.

251 In *The Church's Bible*, ed. Richard A. Norris Jr, p. 269.

252 Spurgeon, *The Most Holy Place*, p. 544.

253 During this time I was pastor of l'Eglise Réformée de Paris-Belleville in the French Reformed Church in inner-city Paris's 20th arrondissement.

254 Murray Stein, *Jung on Christianity* (Princeton University Press, new edn, 2012).

255 Charlie Cleverly, *Discipline of Intimacy* (Kingsway, 2002), p. 8.

256 Ibid., p. 269.

257 Seddon, *Redeeming Eros*, p. 13.

258 Julian Barnes, *Levels of Life* (Vintage Books, 2014), p. 67. Barnes is speaking of the death of his wife, Pat Kavanagh.

259 Dietrich Bonhoeffer, *Letters and Papers from Prison* (SCM, 2001 edition).

260 Julian of Norwich, *Revelations of Divine Love* (Methuen, 1901), p. 31.

261 In *The Church's Bible*, ed. Richard A. Norris Jr, p. 275.

262 Seddon, *Redeeming Eros*, p. 13.

263 Thérèse de Lisieux, *Autobiography* (Doubleday, 1957), p. 62.

264 Pennington, *The Song of Songs*, p. 126.

265 It is an interesting fact of the ebb and flow of God's dealings with his people that in the sadness of Isaiah 6:1, 'In the year that King Uzziah died', with all the disappointment concerning what might have been for that reign, Isaiah nevertheless at this point of death of dreams 'saw the Lord . . .'.

266 See Bickle, *Song of Songs*, Vol. 2, to whom I am indebted for the list of things for which we need to 'lean' in this section.

267 Ecclesiastes 12:12: 'Of making many books there is no end'.

268 Peterson, *Five Smooth Stonesop*, cit. p. 45.

269 Bergant, *Song of Songs*, p. 144.

270 Tozer, *Keys to the Deeper Life*.

271 William Congreve. The entire quote reads: 'Heaven has no rage like love to hatred turned, / Nor hell a fury like

a woman scorned', spoken by Perez in Act 3, Scene 2, *The Mourning Bride* (1697).

272 A popular saying that has been printed on many posters and credited to Martin Luther King Jr (1929–68). Source unknown.

273 Steve Jobs, Stanford University commencement speech, 2005.

274 Thus Bergant (*Song of Songs*, p. 147): 'Believing that the Song really ended with the preceding poem in praise of love, many commentators consider the rest of the chapter to consist merely in miscellaneous appendices.'

275 In *The Church's Bible*, ed. Richard A. Norris Jr, p. 289.

276 This is Bergant's view: *Song of Songs*, p. 150.

277 See footnote at start of chapter.

278 Dietrich Bonhoeffer, *Life Together* (SCM, 1972), p. 75.

279 John of Ford (c.1200), in *The Church's Bible*, ed. Richard A. Norris Jr, p. 297.

280 Spurgeon, *The Most Holy Place*, p. 598.

281 Von Goethe, 'The Holy Longing'. Ronald Rolheiser takes this poem's title and makes it the title of his book, *The Holy Longing*.

282 Barnes, *Levels of Life*, p. 112.

283 Bergant, *Song of Songs*, p. 152.

284 Spurgeon, *The Most Holy Place*, p. 598.

285 Peterson, *Five Smooth Stones*, p. 70.

286 N. T. Wright, *New Heavens, New Earth: The Biblical Picture of Christian Hope* (Grove Books, 1999).

287 *'I stand at the door': Advent Sermons of Dietrich Bonhoeffer*, ed. E. H. Robertson (Eagle, 2003), p. 100.

288 C. S. Lewis, *The Lion, The Witch, and the Wardrobe* (HaperCollins, 2009).

289 Rolheiser, *Sacred Fire*, p. 39.

Acknowledgements

Thanks go to Ian Metcalfe and the excellent team at Hodder for believing in this project and bringing it to birth.

I am grateful to the beloved members of St Aldates Church Oxford and many at the New Wine summer conferences in the UK who have listened to me preaching on the Song of Songs at different times over the past ten years, and always with attention. I am grateful to these saints who have welcomed and embraced in their lives the passionate love for God that is to be found in the Song.

I am grateful to the St Aldates pastoral team who have encouraged me in this, and particularly to Simon Ponsonby, friend and now colleague for the past 13 years in Oxford, who has always encouraged me to press through to publication, linking times of revival to an understanding of the Song.

I am grateful to those who have read and commented on the manuscript giving at times crucial advice, particularly my colleagues Kate Seagrave and Mark Brickman, and Church members Jo and Vince Vitale of RZIM who kindly combed through the manuscript giving encouragement and helpful advice, as did Kosta Milkov from Macedonia who encouraged my love for the Church fathers.

I thank God for other friends who wrote commendations: Mark and Karen Bailey of New Wine; Phil Potter, head of Fresh Expressions for the C of E; Nicholas King, my kind

Jesuit spiritual director and neighbour for many years; Eddie Lyle of Open Doors; Eliot Tepper of Betel Madrid, who loves God and rescues drug addicts and their families; and Heidi Baker, outstanding missionary to the poor in Mozambique and lover of Jesus. These are an eclectic bunch. I thank you for your generous endorsements but especially for your friendship.

I thank God for Pete Greig and for his brilliant foreword and immediate understanding of the heart of this book and my previous book, *Epiphanies*. Pete has led the church in England back to prayer and brought hope to a generation.

I am grateful to my assistant Lydia Smith who has corrected different versions of this manuscript, given wisdom, printed hard copies, chased up copyright permissions, and a hundred other tasks. Thank you for your servant-hearted brilliance.

Finally, I thank with all my heart my wife Anita, who had the vision for me to write a book treating at last the double interpretation of the Song – both divine romance and romance between a man and a woman – and for this to be developed in each chapter. It is to you, the beloved wife of my youth and still now, to whom I dedicate this book.